OMAHA

The Omaha Experience

By Eileen Wirth

Photography by Drickey/Malone Studio

Greater Omaha Chamber of Commerce

Published by
LONGSTREET PRESS
Atlanta, Georgia

Published by
LONGSTREET PRESS, INC.
a subsidiary of Cox Newspapers
a subsidiary of Cox Enterprises, Inc.
2140 Newmarket Parkway
Suite 118
Marietta, Georgia 30067

Printed in the United States of America

1st printing, 1996
Library of Congress
Catalog Number: 96-76-032

ISBN: 1-56352-292-6

DIRECTOR, ENTERPRISE DIVISION
Nancy Bauer

MANAGING EDITOR
Erica Fox

ART DIRECTION AND PRODUCTION
Audrey Graham

CONTENTS

◆ FOREWORD   vi

◆ INTRODUCTION   1

    A BRIDGE BETWEEN EAST AND WEST   4
    A BLEND OF SOPHISTICATION AND CONVENIENCE   7
    A TASTEFUL MIX OF INGREDIENTS   8

◆ BUSINESS IN OMAHA: INNOVATIVE AND INTERNATIONAL   18

    ENTREPRENEURSHIP   22
    OMAHA: THE TELECOMMUNICATIONS CAPITAL OF THE NATION   27
    INTERNATIONAL BUSINESS: OMAHA'S OUTREACH TO THE WORLD   29
    OMAHA BUSINESS: AN OVERVIEW   34

◆ HEALTH AND INSURANCE: HIGH-TECH AND HIGH-TOUCH   46

    INSURANCE: A NATIONAL POWERHOUSE   50
    HEALTH CARE: RESEARCH AND TREATMENT   53
    WELLNESS: AN OMAHA HALLMARK   57

◆ GOVERNMENT AND SERVICES: SOPHISTICATED AND SUCCESSFUL   66

    TRANSPORTATION: THE LIFEBLOOD OF OMAHA   70
    UTILITIES: IT'S ALL PUBLIC POWER   73
    LOCAL GOVERNMENT: DOING THE ESSENTIALS WELL   74
    OMAHA: HOME OF U.S. STRATEGIC COMMAND   79

◆ CULTURE AND RECREATION: DIVERSE AND DISTINCTIVE   90

    CULTURAL OFFERINGS: FROM THE AVANT-GARDE TO THE TRADITIONAL   94
    SPORTS AND OUTDOOR RECREATION: AAA FUN   97
    RETAIL: IT'S FUN TO SHOP AND EAT IN OMAHA   102
    SOMETHING TO SUIT EVERY TASTE   105

◆ THE OMAHA LIFESTYLE: COMPASSIONATE AND COMMITTED   118

    HOUSING AND NEIGHBORHOODS: SOMETHING FOR EVERYONE   122
    EDUCATION: NO SUCH THING AS A BAD SCHOOL   128
    RELIGION AND PHILANTHROPY: SERVING OTHERS AND THE COMMUNITY   131
    OMAHA: A CITY OF SURPRISES   134

◆ ENTERPRISE   152

◆ ACKNOWLEDGMENTS   260

◆ INDEX   261

FOREWORD

ocated in the center of the nation's heartland, Omaha is a Norman Rockwell kind of community, with involved citizens, a strong work ethic, high productivity, and an excellent educational system. We raise our children with the idea that they are important and that they can make a difference in this world. They grow up believing in their ability to succeed and lead efforts that will make a difference in the lives of others.

Omaha is a center for telecommunications, transportation, insurance, and food processing and was the first city to be completely wired with fiber-optic access to business loops. There are over 660,000 people in the metro area and over one million within a 50-mile radius of downtown. The nation's 48th-largest city and 60th-largest metro area, Omaha is located in the geographic center of the United States and has seen steady upward growth over the past five decades. At the intersection of Interstates 80 and 29, Omaha is on the great Missouri River, which forms the border of Iowa and Nebraska.

Nebraska ranks among the nation's top states in public investment in both its infrastructure and education. We build for the future. Eppley Airfield's $100 million expansion added a new terminal and enhanced both operations and general aviation facilities. Omaha is served by all major national air carriers and is a mini-hub for Midwest Express Airlines. It is the home of the Union Pacific Railroad. A major redesign and reconstruction of the metro area's interstate system is nearing completion.

Omaha consistently ranks as one of the U.S. cities with the lowest environmental stress rating. The survey rated air quality, water quality and availability, sewage, toxic releases, and population changes for cities over 100,000 people.

Omaha was selected as a model of business/education partnerships to kick off America 2000. Nebraska students consistently rank in the top five states for ACT and SAT scores, and the average math proficiency of public school eighth-graders has been fourth best in the nation.

Omaha is the headquarters for four Fortune 500 companies: ConAgra, Peter Kiewit Sons, Berkshire Hathaway, and Mutual of Omaha. Over 30 insurance companies, two dozen direct-response/telemarketing centers, and several other national and international firms have their headquarters in Omaha. It is also the headquarters of the new U.S. Strategic Command.

A cultural center of the Great Plains, Omaha has 24 live theaters; a professional symphony orchestra, opera company, and ballet troupe; a children's theater; a children's museum; and a youth orchestra. Joslyn Art Museum just completed a $45 million expansion. The Henry Doorly Zoo has an international reputation for its breeding programs, and its outstanding "no-bars" facility boasts one of the world's largest indoor jungles, cat complexes, and aviaries. Omaha is also home to the NCAA College World Series, Omaha Royals AAA baseball, the Racers (Continental Professional Basketball Association), and the Lancers (U.S. Hockey League).

Yet Omaha has a small-town feel when it comes to getting things done. Business and community leaders tell us that what makes Omaha unique is its responsiveness to individuals and to companies. It doesn't erect barriers, it eliminates them. People know their city, state, and U.S. elected representatives and can talk to them easily. With all of this, Omaha enjoys a cost of living as much as 10 percent lower than the national average.

Take a moment to let us share our *Omaha Experience* with you. This book was produced by Omaha writers and photographers and highlights some of our great success stories. Add up the advantages and you will discover the secret shared by Omahans: on a day-to-day basis, you can have a better overall quality of life in Omaha.

GREATER OMAHA CHAMBER OF COMMERCE

"I'm a very lucky guy. I have a great job, and one of the luxuries of my job is that I can live and work wherever I want. I choose to live in Omaha because I like it here. I enjoy the people as well as the city. I've lived in Washington, D.C., and New York, but, in my view, Omaha is a much better place to call home. It is better for my family and for me. Omaha has everything you would expect in a much larger city. It is a regional center for the arts. It is home of the College World Series. In fact, there is something for everyone in Omaha in terms of sports, entertainment, and things to do. One of the best things about Omaha is the first-class educational system. My kids have gotten a great education in Omaha's public schools. The parochial schools are first class, too. Everyone has to decide where they want to spend the rest of their lives, and for me, no question about it, it's Omaha."

WARREN BUFFETT,
CHAIRMAN, BERKSHIRE HATHAWAY

rom transcontinental railroads to "roads" of fiber-optics. From visionary pioneers conquering the West to entrepreneurs conquering new worlds of research, science, and technology. From the world's largest stockyards to laboratories developing food products for Healthy Choice. From telephones to telecommunications.

Omaha.

It's a city of surprises, even to those who think they know it well—a city that combines the best in sophisticated industry and technology with the openness and warmth of the heartland to provide residents with an extraordinarily high quality of life.

It's a quality of life enhanced significantly by several of the city's unique attributes. Omaha is a city where people and businesses can succeed because of the pro-business climate, the outstanding infrastructure, and the productive, well-educated workforce. It's a supportive community, where people care about the welfare of their neighbors and their city. It's a dynamic community, where entrepreneurship thrives. Omahans combine the best of their midwestern heritage, especially its emphasis on personal accomplishment and responsibility, with an openness to change, especially in business and technology.

The 300-foot-tall fountain in Heartland of America Park is a popular evening gathering spot in downtown Omaha.

O*maha's history is interwoven with that of the*
Union Pacific Railroad, headquartered in the city.

A Bridge between East and West

The history of Omaha starts with its picturesque setting on the timbered bluffs of the Missouri River. From these bluffs, explorers Meriwether Lewis and William Clark first glimpsed the potential of the vast new lands that Thomas Jefferson had acquired.

Omaha was founded in 1854 by settlers from Council Bluffs, Iowa, just across the Missouri. Settlement of the lands west of the Missouri had been delayed for years by a federal law that prohibited settlement, with the aim of containing the slavery controversy to the lands east of the Missouri. As soon as the ban on settlement ended, Council Bluffs residents crossed the river to establish the new community.

It didn't seem very promising at first. The village, whose mud streets clung to the banks of the river, was just one of several struggling Nebraska towns that dreamed of becoming the dominant city in the territory. For a time, it appeared that other communities might win the contest.

At the height of the Civil War, however, President Abraham Lincoln made a decision that guaranteed Omaha's future growth. He selected the Omaha-Council Bluffs area as the eastern terminus of the great transcontinental railroad designed to link the "Union" to the "Pacific." Although ground for the Union Pacific was broken in 1863, serious construction did not begin until after the war, in 1867, when General Grenville Dodge of Council Bluffs was named chief engineer.

Slowly but surely, Omaha became a city and a regional commercial center—the largest city between Chicago and Denver. The railroad brought jobs and people and attracted other businesses, such as South Omaha's great packinghouses. Immigrants poured into Omaha from every corner of Europe. They brought with them their foods, religions, and cultures. Even before the turn of the century, Omaha included a fascinating mix of people.

With its strategic location on the Missouri River, Omaha became what it has remained—a bridge city between East and West. Both Omaha's mind-set and its economy are defined in large measure by this fact. Omahans have always looked to both East and West, belonging wholly to neither, preserving strong ties to both. Wing tips and cowboy boots; classical music and country and western; French cuisine and steakhouses; an urban lifestyle and rural roots—seeming opposites, they co-exist comfortably in Omaha.

And always there's the river—ever old, ever new. In the 1990s, the accent is definitely on "new," as the city continues to expand its magnificent riverfront development area. What seemed an impossible dream in the early 1970s has become a reality as Omahans have rebuilt the riverfront area into the showplace of a modern city. Beginning with the construction of the Eugene Leahy Mall and its extensions east to the river, downtown Omaha has taken on an exciting new look, especially since the construction of ConAgra's magnificent headquarters campus and adjacent Heartland Park. Union Pacific's renovation of its historic freight house into the Harriman Dispatch Center and several other projects in the riverfront area create a new image for a progressive city.

Condos and apartments in converted warehouses, new stores, and renovated office buildings are attracting thousands of residents to Omaha's urban core. An arts and entertainment scene, which includes art galleries, experimental theater, fine restaurants, and live music, gives today's Omaha a new sophistication. From its spectacular and constantly expanding riverfront area, Omaha reaches to the future.

Hilly terrain and mature trees line the tees, greens, and fairways of Happy Hollow Country Club, in the heart of Omaha.

B*lessed with more than
five decades of continuous
economic growth, Omaha
is less susceptible to the
booms and busts that occur
in other areas.*

In Omaha, you can leave your office on a summer evening and be home in time for a round of golf before sunset. You may even have the luxury of playing on a course designed by a member of the Professional Golf Association tour. The Omaha lifestyle combines the sophistication of a large city with the comfort and convenience of a smaller community. However, in both its economic opportunities and its cultural and recreational amenities, Omaha is unmistakably metropolitan.

Omaha's outstanding lifestyle starts with its healthy economy. Omahans live well because the local economy is robust and has been for several generations. Living costs are below average. Luxuries like weekend trips or dining out are more affordable in Omaha because housing and utilities cost less than in other American cities.

Omaha is known as a recession-proof city, because its economy is so diverse. Although the city is recognized as the nation's telecommunications capital, the local economy also includes insurance, transportation, food processing, health care, education, and many other industries.

What the packinghouses were to turn-of-the-century Omaha, the information industry is today. Some 50,000 residents are employed in a wide range of high-tech jobs at 800 small and large telecommunications companies. Chances are that whether you're purchasing an item with your credit card, making a hotel reservation, or experimenting with a new voice-messaging system, you're intersecting with the hub of the Information Superhighway: Omaha.

Agriculture, the traditional base of the local economy, now means agribusiness, food-product development, marketing, and international trade. If you're making "healthier choices" in how you eat or trying an intriguing new food, it's likely an Omaha food scientist was involved in developing the product or that it was test-marketed in Omaha. The insurance, construction, banking, and health care industries also are high-tech.

Omaha is hospitable to new businesses. Its start-ups have experienced rapid growth. And many of its largest employers are homegrown companies, including the city's three Fortune 500 firms.

Omaha is also hospitable to patients from around the world, many of whom seek out local doctors because of their expertise in organ transplants. Doctors at the city's two medical colleges are also doing pioneering genetic research, finding ways to alleviate the bone disease osteoporosis and other ailments. They are even advising the U.S. Olympic Committee on sports nutrition.

But no matter how high-tech its economy becomes, Omaha also remains proudly traditional in many ways. The *Chronicle of Philanthropy* ranks Omaha among the 10 most generous American cities. An old-fashioned sense of service is pervasive. You don't have to live in Omaha long to meet people like the grade school principal who called at night to make sure that the special transportation arrangements she made for a child worked out or the elderly woman who checks to see if it is okay for her neighbor's toddler to ride her tricycle all the way down the block.

Omaha.

It's a blend of so many ingredients—a marriage of high-tech and high-touch. When you live in Omaha, you can count on both.

A Tasteful Mix of Ingredients

If you like your living bland, stay away from Omaha. Diversity is a keynote to life in this city. Long before the term "multicultural" became part of the nation's lingo, Omahans were living with people of all backgrounds—and enjoying doing so.

Omahans are open to tasting the new whether it means exploring avant-garde art at the Bemis Center for the Contemporary Arts in downtown or sampling an unfamiliar cuisine at one of the city's half dozen Thai restaurants. From art openings to softball, you'll find something to suit you year-round in Omaha.

During the summer you might want to join the casually dressed throngs sitting on the ground (like the original Elizabethan audiences) at the annual free Shakespeare on the Green festival at Elmwood Park or listen to street-corner musicians offering everything from Beethoven to blues in the Old Market as a horse-drawn carriage and bicycles built for four compete with autos for space on the city's original brick streets.

If sports are more to your liking, you can attend the NCAA College World Series at Rosenblatt Stadium—Omaha's premier sporting event for nearly 50 years—or an Omaha Royals AAA baseball game. Summer also is the time for outdoor sports at the many convenient city and state parks and for ethnic festivals. Festivals continue into fall, culminating in the River City Roundup parade through downtown. Fall also brings road and bicycle races, including the Omaha Riverfront Marathon, one of the nation's most popular events for those attempting to qualify for the famous Boston Marathon.

As winter approaches, you might be able to be part of a black-tie gathering at the Orpheum Theater for the opening performance of Opera Omaha. You'll find many ways to celebrate the holiday season, including taking in Dickens at the Old Market or enjoying one of many special concerts, such as Mannheim Steamroller's annual performances at the Orpheum. The group, which holds the national record for sales of its Christmas albums, is headquartered in Omaha. Outdoor enthusiasts can cross-country ski in parks or ice skate on lagoons. For downhill skiers, the resorts of Colorado are an easy day's drive.

Year-round, you can visit a jungle or the depths of an ocean at the city's world-class zoo, escape to nature at Fontenelle Forest, or spend a fascinating afternoon at an art or historical museum. There's lots to choose from, especially if you're willing to volunteer any of your time. You'll almost be assaulted with opportunities to volunteer for worthy causes of all descriptions. Your biggest problem may be deciding how to fit everything into your over-booked calendar. Whatever you decide to do, you'll probably have fun.

Throw a party and Omahans will come. Call it St. Patrick's Day, Cinco de Mayo, Native Omaha Homecoming Week, the Ak-Sar-Ben Coronation, or the Santa Lucia Festival. Hire a band. Serve your best food—lots of it. Share what's best in your heritage and enjoy the offerings of others. If you don't understand it, don't knock it. Don't spectate, participate.

That's the spirit of life in Omaha.

Artists are attracted to Omaha by the big sky and the quality of the light, while residents appreciate being able to get away from it all within a 20-minute drive of wherever they work.

Gamble Hill Hounds, one of two registered fox hunts in Omaha, welcomes new members for fast-paced rides in beautiful wooded hills, while Fontenelle Forest Nature Center attracts hikers to its natural forests just 10 minutes from downtown.

Designed by Thomas Kimball,
St. Cecilia's Roman Catholic
Cathedral is a gathering place
for Omahans of all faiths who
attend its year-round community
art and musical events.

E*lmwood Park, which surrounds the campus of the University of
Nebraska at Omaha, is a tranquil spot to picnic or cross-country ski.*

*O*nce occupied by fruit and vegetable stalls, the Old Market is now one of America's finest restored commercial areas. Alive with activity day and night, it attracts residents and visitors looking for one-of-a-kind options in shopping, dining, and entertainment.

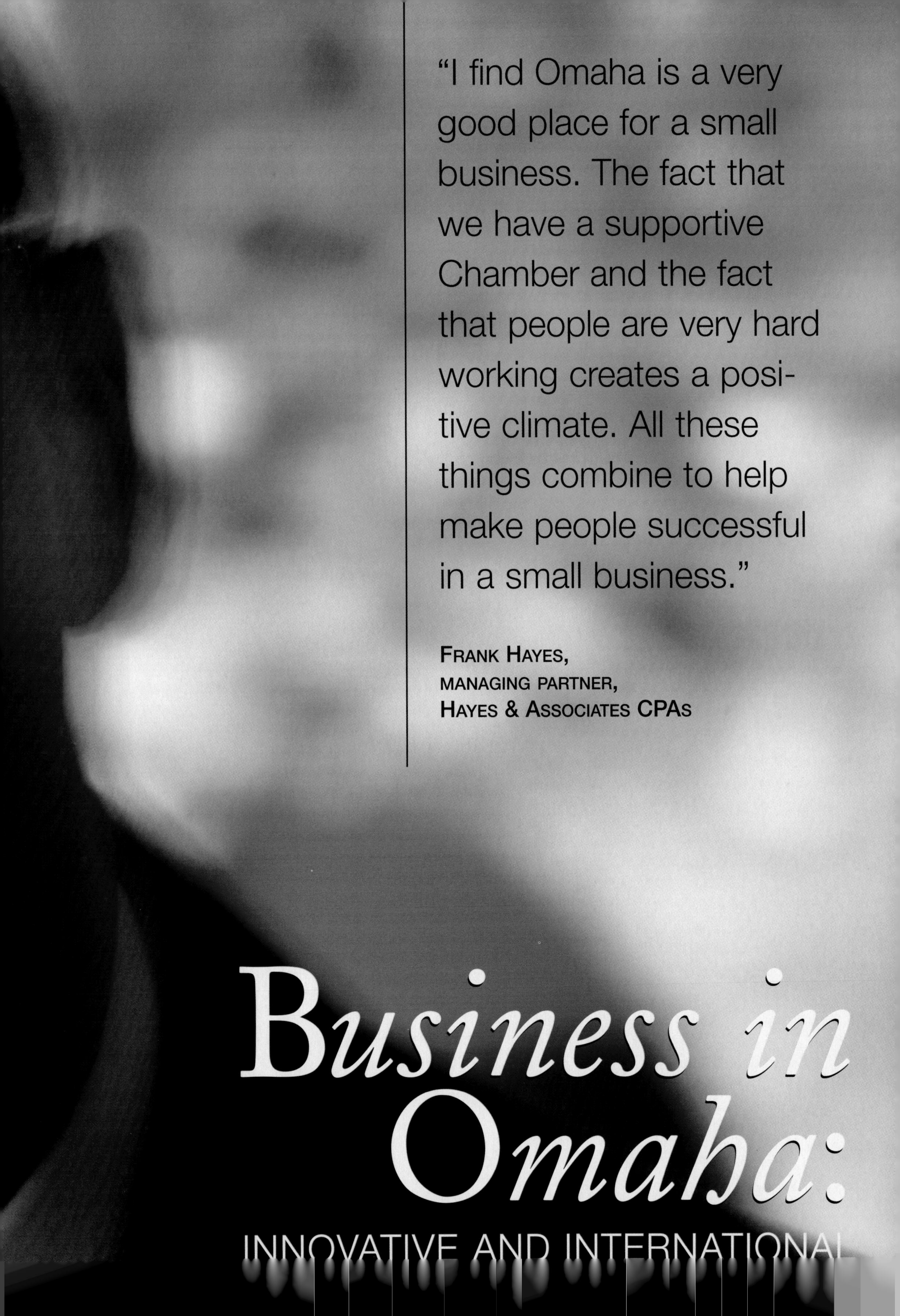

"I find Omaha is a very good place for a small business. The fact that we have a supportive Chamber and the fact that people are very hard working creates a positive climate. All these things combine to help make people successful in a small business."

FRANK HAYES,
MANAGING PARTNER,
HAYES & ASSOCIATES CPAs

Business in Omaha:
INNOVATIVE AND INTERNATIONAL

*J*ust west of downtown Omaha sits a medium-rise white stone office complex. Motorists passing by on Farnam Street probably pay more attention to the colorful logo of a nearby television station than to this understated fixture of Omaha's business life. The complex wouldn't draw much attention in most other cities, either.

But it does get lots of attention in some places—on Wall Street, for instance; at Capital Cities-ABC, the Coca-Cola Company, and American Express; in state road departments around the country; even in the Pentagon and among the leaders of the nation's press. To these people, what happens at Kiewit Plaza is interesting—very interesting indeed. Decisions made here routinely are written about in stories that appear on the front pages of the *Wall Street Journal* and the *New York Times*.

Kiewit Plaza is the headquarters of both the nation's wealthiest man, Warren Buffett, and his Fortune 500 company, Berkshire Hathaway. It's also the headquarters of Peter Kiewit Sons, the nation's largest private construction business. In this modest office building, decisions are made that affect the nation's economy and help shape the nation's and the world's infrastructures.

How did so much wealth, power, and talent end up in a medium-sized city like Omaha—let alone in one midtown office building? It's a question that has intrigued many, including a writer for *Forbes* magazine, who once asked, "What's in the Omaha water that the place breeds business geniuses like Warren Buffett and [Kiewit's chairman] Walter Scott?"

The answer is complex, but it goes a long way toward explaining why Omaha's diverse economic base has grown steadily for the past 50 years and why Omaha is home to numerous world-class companies in a variety of fields. Omahans often call their community the nation's best kept secret, but one extremely important group of people knows what a great place it is in which to live and do business—Omaha residents.

Motivated by such features of the city as its quality of life, the education available for their children, and the city's supportive business climate, Omahans with good ideas for new businesses tend to start them at home—and then to stay home when their businesses grow to become world-class enterprises. Warren Buffett and Walter Scott are just two of the homegrown business stars who could go anywhere but choose to live and work in Omaha.

*D*ecisions of global significance are made daily at a growing number of Omaha companies. Shown here is the headquarters of Peter Kiewit Sons, the nation's largest road builder and a leader in fiber-optic telecommunications and computer outsourcing. The offices of Berkshire Hathaway, owned by Warren Buffett, are in the same building.

S*trong public-private partnerships have helped revitalize Omaha's central city
for businesses and for people by supporting new office development, the restoration
of historic buildings, and the creation of inviting public places.*

ENTREPRENEURSHIP

Omaha has a strong entrepreneurial bent. According to *Entrepreneur* magazine, Omaha is one of the nation's "20 Best Places to Start a Business." Between 1982 and 1993, the number of business establishments in the Omaha area grew nearly 35 percent to more than 17,000. Homegrown enterprises range from major insurance companies, such as Mutual of Omaha, to newer firms like Oriental Trading Company, whose rapidly growing mail-order novelty business has drawn admiring attention in *Forbes* and other national publications. According to business leaders, Omaha's strong sense of community helps young businesses get started.

"You don't just come into this city, if you will, and kind of flounder around," notes one such leader. "To me, that's positive. There apparently is some kind of structure here that allows me to form alliances with others and get things done, not only for the betterment of the community but for the betterment of my company."

Because Omaha has the talent base that start-up businesses need, people with good ideas readily find associates to help them turn their dreams into reality. Omaha's educational system is recognized as one of the best in the nation, and its workforce is extremely productive.

About 85 percent of the population has at least a high school education, 10 percent higher than the national average. The ratio of production/dollar of wages in Omaha is an astonishing 40 percent higher than the national average ($14 versus $10.50).

Ernest Goss, holder of the Jack MacAllister Chair of Free Enterprise at Creighton University, attributes Omaha's entrepreneurial character to its "human capital."

"Omaha has many individuals capable of engaging in entrepreneurship," he says. "In the Midwest and West, you find a lot of people with more desire to be in charge of their own destinies. People who are independent are more likely to be interested in founding their own companies."

"Independent" certainly describes Omaha's many fascinating entrepreneurs. They range from a tiny 100-year-old woman who escaped from Russia as a teenager and went on to become a tremendously successful retailer to a distinguished banking executive who helped start the nation's credit card business. They work in construction, manufacturing, family retail businesses, and numerous other fields. They are men and women united by their dreams—and they help make Omaha a dynamic place in which to do business. Here are a few of their stories.

Few local entrepreneurs have directly touched more Omahans where they live—literally—than Rose Blumkin, the tiny centenarian who founded Nebraska Furniture Mart, the nation's largest furniture store in one location. The image of Mrs. B., as she is known, riding on a golf cart around the Furniture Mart's carpet department offering instant bargains to lucky consumers will be part of Omaha's business lore for generations. Dazzled newlyweds who have had such experiences as they bought furniture for their first homes never forget the encounters.

As a young woman in 1917, Mrs. B. tricked a border guard to escape the pogroms of her native Russia. She made her way via Asia to Omaha, where she settled, married, and raised a family. During the Depression, she opened a small pawn shop, which grew into a modest furniture store. At one time when she was near bankruptcy, she decided to take a massive risk. She borrowed money to purchase stock for a mammoth sale and advertised it heavily. Her gamble paid off. She earned enough to pay her creditors and to expand the enterprise.

Today's Furniture Mart is a huge complex of showrooms and warehouses crammed with furniture, appliances, electronic merchandise, and carpeting. It sprawls for several square blocks on 72nd Street. Customers from hundreds of miles away flock to this home furnishings mecca when they're making major purchases. Omaha natives sometimes come home to shop for furniture, then have their purchases delivered to distant states.

Mrs. B. attributes her success to her motto: "Sell cheap, tell the truth, don't cheat, and don't take kickbacks. That's the worst." She also credits her customers, whom she calls "the world's best," with helping her build her business.

Even after she sold the Furniture Mart to Warren Buffett, Mrs. B. continued to roam the aisles of the carpet department in her golf cart, and members of her family manage the enterprise to this day. Buffett makes no secret of his enormous admiration for Mrs. B., which he demonstrated most concretely when he purchased the Furniture Mart from her without an audit.

"We gave Mrs. B. a check for $55 million, and she gave us her word," Buffett says. "That made it an even exchange. I would rather have her word than that of the Big Eight auditors. It's like dealing with the Bank of England."

Mrs. B. is far from the only Omaha entrepreneur who has turned a small family business into a national leader in its field. Another member of the Omaha Business Hall of Fame, Allan Lozier, built his father's small store-shelving manufacturing firm into Lozier Corporation, the nation's largest supplier of retail store fixtures and accessories.

The firm, which began with 25 people and Omaha manufacturing facilities totaling 20,000 square feet in 1956, is almost a classic example of the way many Omaha business stars have started small and expanded nationally. By the mid-1990s, Lozier had grown to more than 2.4 million square feet of manufacturing space in seven cities and employed about 2,500 people. The firm's standards in design, quality, and service revolutionized the fixtures industry.

Lozier, who stands well over six feet tall, had originally planned to be a scientist and in his teens was critically wounded when a homemade rocket with which he was experimenting misfired. He abandoned thoughts of a scientific career and went into his father's business, becoming president at age 26. He designed the original fixtures line and established a business philosophy based on selling better products at a lower cost.

He says that the keys to his business success are related to science: "Curiosity, impatience, a thirst for knowledge. Even as a businessman, I thirst to know what's going on. I always want to know more than anybody else. It's a strong part of my personality, that and my impatience. I like to know why we're doing something and that it's been thought out. Casual

Because Omaha has the the talent base that start-up businesses need, people with good ideas readily find associates to help them turn their dreams into reality.

Homegrown businesses of every size instill in Omahans—young and old—a strong belief that they, too, can realize their dreams of success.

activity taking place with no focus, that just drives me nuts, because I see the world as a big fabric, everything sort of joined together. You touch something here, and it sends little shock waves everyplace."

Sometimes entrepreneurship in Omaha runs in families. For example, the Kavich family has owned All Makes Office Equipment Company for four generations. The firm, which furnishes and equips the majority of Omaha's offices, exemplifies the Omaha emphasis on customer service, the loyalty that Omaha entrepreneurs have to their city, and the way local businesses help each other as they simultaneously grow.

"We have actually seen one account grow from two people to a Fortune 500 company with 25,000 employees in branches all over the country," says Larry Kavich, All Makes president and CEO. "When Omaha customers branch out in the world, they often take the All Makes team with them." All Makes serves accounts across the country and in Europe, South America, and Canada. However, All Makes is firmly committed to its base in Omaha.

"If I could lift up my business and relocate it anywhere in the country or in the world, I wouldn't move it an inch," says Kavich. "We're in a pocket of controlled growth. This isn't like a gold rush, but every year the city stretches farther and farther."

Kavich attributes his firm's success to its emphasis on traditional Midwestern values, such as family and service.

"I grew up around the dining room table talking about the values we held for the business—treating customers right and delivering what we say we'll deliver. We've stayed centered on that philosophy—considering every customer vital to our business—and that's what drives our success."

Newer entrepreneurs include people like Robert Campos, a Mexican-American who developed a highly successful construction business and encouraged his sons to begin their own businesses while they were still in high school. His firm, which he started with $500, has advanced to being the general contractor for multimillion-dollar projects locally and nationally. Some 90 percent of its customers do repeat business with the firm, which occupies a prominent location in a South Omaha industrial area. The Campos Construction Company has helped renovate such national landmarks as the homes of Presidents Harry S Truman in Independence, Missouri; Herbert Hoover in West Branch, Iowa; and Abraham Lincoln in Springfield, Illinois. It also constructed the Gerald R. Ford Conservation Center in Omaha.

Campos is fond of a quote from Truman that typifies the independence Goss says successful entrepreneurs exhibit: "As Americans, we believe that every man should be free to live this life as he wishes. He should be limited only by his responsibility to his fellow countrymen. If this freedom is to be more than a dream, each man must be guaranteed equality of opportunity. The only limit to an American's achievement should be his ability, his industry, and his character."

Minority entrepreneurs like Campos and an immigrant Omahan who invented an entire new high-tech industry demonstrate how few limits there are on Omaha dreamers. Vinod Gupta, a native of India who graduated from the University of Nebraska at Lincoln,

created the nation's list industry after his employer asked him to buy a list of potential customers and Gupta found that none existed. It occurred to Gupta that other businesses must have similar needs, so he ordered phone books from around the country and began a new list-making business, working from his basement. Today, American Business Information is the nation's leading supplier of computerized lists and has branched into additional business information services.

Not all of Omaha's entrepreneurs started life as outsiders. Buffett, for example, is the son of a congressman. Entrepreneur John Lauritzen is a member of the family that has run First National Bank since pioneer days. Heading First National wasn't enough for Lauritzen, however, who simultaneously ran his own chain of rural banks and helped invent the bank credit card.

"I started our card in 1953 and called it First Charge. In 1968, Bank of America wanted to franchise its credit card, known as BankAmericard, so they contacted the leading people in the business, of which we were one. . . . We felt we should join with other banks to broaden the scope of First Charge," he says.

Some of Omaha's newer enterprises, such as Tenaska, illustrate the way individuals displaced by corporate upheavals have turned to entrepreneurship because they refused to leave Omaha, and, in the process, they have turned adversity into success. Tenaska develops, owns, and operates electric-generating and cogeneration plants throughout the U.S. and in several foreign countries. President Howard Hawks and its other founders were with Enron when it moved its headquarters from Omaha to Houston. They decided they could do what they knew well in a place where they wanted to be—Omaha.

The point these stories illustrate is that Omaha's business community is characterized by companies with "made-in-Omaha" labels. Among other major examples of this phenomenon are ConAgra and Ag Processing, both of which are Fortune 500 companies; international architecture and engineering firms Leo A Daly, HDR, and Dana Larson Roubal and Associates; Valmont Industries, the world's largest irrigation company; First Data Resources, the nation's leading processor of credit card transactions; Applied Communications, a world leader in automated banking technology; Prairie Systems, a rapidly growing firm working in voice mail and other automated office technologies; Godfather's Pizza, one of the nation's largest pizza franchisers; and such insurance giants as Mutual of Omaha, Woodmen of the World Life Insurance Society, Physicians Mutual, and Guarantee Life Insurance Company.

It's fascinating to speculate on what currently unknown Omahans are dreaming about and what will come of those dreams. Based on the city's history, many are working in basements and garages, installing a couple of extra phones, faxes, and computers, pioneering who knows what. As they drive around their city, they see numerous examples of businesses that 10 or 50 years ago were where they are today.

Will any of these dreamers be the next Warren Buffett or Mrs. B.? In Omaha, you never know. You just never know.

Omaha: The Telecommunications Capital of the Nation

Many of Omaha's most successful new entrepreneurs are in the telecommunications industry, turning the city into the generally recognized telecommunications capital of the nation. The city has between 800 and 1,000 information-related companies, and more are starting all the time. Some 50,000 Omahans are employed in various fields directly related to information technology or telecommunications, 10,000 of them developing hardware and software or working as programmers and systems analysts.

Steve Idelman, chairman of ITI Marketing, one of Omaha's largest telemarketing groups, told the *New York Times Magazine* some of the reasons Omaha has enjoyed such success in the field: "One: The Strategic Air Command (SAC) over in Offutt Air Force Base; they built one of the first fiber-optics networks in the U.S. Two: Northwestern Bell. It took that huge phone capacity and in the '60s and '70s lured hotel reservation and bank card centers to Omaha. Three: Guys like me working out of our basements with three phones somewhere; we discovered in the '80s that Omaha real estate, Omaha living costs, Omaha wages were way low, the workforce here was pretty well educated and best of all, Omaha is right in the middle of the country . . . easy access to both coasts, all four time zones. Four, Five, Six, Seven, Eight, Nine: The phone company would install a new 800 line here in one day. One day! And the legislature is pro-business. Ten: Soon I'm looking for a bigger house."

As Idelman indicates, Omaha got a head start in developing a modern telecommunications industry because in 1948 the Air Force selected Offutt Air Force Base as the headquarters of SAC. To support SAC's mission of leading U.S. military operations in the event of a nuclear war, a massive and extremely complex telecommunications infrastructure with vast overcapacity was installed. It was available for civilian use starting in the 1980s.

Omaha's workforce was well prepared for the telecommunications revolution because the city had been a telecommunications center for generations. For many years, Northwestern Bell was one of the city's largest employers. Since the 1950s, another of Omaha's largest payrolls has come from a Western Electric/AT&T plant that produced telecommunications equipment. Thousands of Omahans have backgrounds and skills in telecommunications. These well-educated, hard-working people help make the city a magnet for current and future telecommunications businesses.

In the past decade, Omaha's outstanding infrastructure has continually improved with the addition of some of the world's most sophisticated technology. It is the first metropolitan area to have total ISDN coverage—an all-digital communications system that moves voice, data, facsimile, telemetry, image, video, and signaling information at many times the speed of older analog systems.

Major communications companies select Omaha for pioneering applications of communications technology and continually enhance the city's infrastructure and its reputation. For example, Omaha is the flagship city for both U S West's integrated digital services network, which was specifically designed for small businesses, and for its PC/Phone Service. MCI selected Omaha as the site of its $100 million, 180,000-square-foot high-tech data center, which helps support the firm's $20 billion investment in the Information Superhighway. Cox Communications, through its partnership with Sprint and cable firms, is making Omaha one of the first places in the nation to offer competitive local phone service, an experiment the national media are watching closely.

There is a favorable business climate in Omaha in terms of regulations and tax rates. Nebraska is friendly to businesses, both those here and those it's trying to attract."

—ERNEST GOSS,
JACK MACALLISTER
CHAIR OF FREE
ENTERPRISE,
CREIGHTON UNIVERSITY

In addition to the city's infrastructure, Omaha's telecommunications industry greatly benefits from the state's pro-business, anti-regulatory climate. Nebraska passed the nation's first state law deregulating telecommunications, and it offers incentives for companies to move into or expand in Nebraska.

Goss notes the benefits of this pro-business climate. "There is a favorable business climate in Omaha in terms of regulations and tax rates," he says. "Nebraska is friendly to businesses, both those here and those it's trying to attract."

The Greater Omaha Chamber of Commerce and educational institutions work to promote the growth of the telecommunications industry through the Applied Information Management Institute (AIM). Bob Sweeney, director of AIM, believes that the future holds "enormous opportunities" for Omaha's information industry.

"Omaha has shown an ability to spawn and grow information companies," he says. "Most of the high-tech industry that is here was started here and grew up here. We've got successful companies and entrepreneurs. We have our midwestern value system and work ethic. The emerging world is creating enormous opportunities for places like Omaha."

Of the several world-class information companies in Omaha, First Data Resources began in typical Omaha fashion with a few entrepreneurs working out of a office at 72nd and Pacific Streets, where they spent so much time that they even slept over on occasion. Eventually, they built a company that enjoys worldwide eminence and employs about 7,000 Omahans. Applied Communication's software is used in more than 1,000 electronic commerce and payment systems in more than 60 countries on six continents. In Russia, England, Australia, and many other nations, businesses and their customers are using telecommunications technology made in Omaha to do business the modern way.

Omaha's most visible information-based businesses—those that provide toll-free long-distance services—also have a worldwide thrust. Omaha is the recognized 1-800 capital of the world and home to more than two dozen telemarketing firms, as well as the capital of the nation's hotel-booking business. More than 30 million calls a year come into the Hyatt, Marriott, Radisson, Omni, and Westin hotel reservation centers in Omaha. Telemarketing has become an extremely sophisticated business in which firms such as ITI, West Telemarketing, and SITEL Corporation develop sales and marketing campaigns for Fortune 500 companies.

Omaha is proud of its eminence in telecommunications and is determined to preserve it. Initiatives from local educational institutions will help. Creighton University's new information technology program, which offers classes at various sites, was designed specifically to respond to the needs of the business community.

The University of Nebraska at Omaha is establishing a College of Information Science and Technology and the Omaha Institute of Science and Technology. Both will enhance engineering education in Omaha by expanding graduate and undergraduate offerings in computer information technology to support the city's information industry.

Increasing numbers of Omahans realize that the information industry has become as central to the city's economic well-being as meatpacking was for generations. Employment growth in information companies is expected to set the pace for the city's economy during the next decade. The city that loves winners of all types is determined to stay number one in telecommunications.

INTERNATIONAL BUSINESS: OMAHA'S OUTREACH TO THE WORLD

It's hardly surprising that a city with Omaha's entrepreneurial spirit, in which information/telecommunications is a central industry, is dramatically expanding its outreach to global markets. The miracles of the information revolution have erased many of the barriers of miles and oceans for both corporate giants and home-based entrepreneurs.

"I don't think it matters where you are," says Mogens Bay, president and CEO of Valmont Industries, the global leader in producing irrigation equipment. "It's a mind-set more than physical location. You can reach anyplace instantly by fax."

Throughout Omaha, globalization is a growing theme. Evidence is everywhere. At ConAgra headquarters in Omaha's riverfront development area, the flags of more than 25 nations fly proudly alongside the Stars and Stripes. They symbolize the food giant's $24 billion global operations, which were launched in 1965 with a joint venture in Spain. Today, ConAgra is Australia's largest manufacturer of processed beef and one of the largest processors of potatoes in the Netherlands. In Mexico, ConAgra has large investments in pork and poultry production. In Austria, it produces malt barley for export to China and throughout Europe for Carlsberg Beer. ConAgra even reintroduced popcorn into Russia.

But it's not just Fortune 500 companies like ConAgra that have learned to market their products globally. Large numbers of small Omaha companies, many started since 1980, are finding international customers.

"You have to become aware of the market outside the United States," says Dick Beard of Beard Enterprises. "You either export or die."

A sampling of small businesses indicates that an amazing variety of local products are being marketed internationally. American Laboratories turns meat byproducts into more than 230 commodities ranging from chewing gum to health foods, and Raven Biological Laboratories produces a chemical test to determine if medical and dental equipment has been sterilized—a growing concern worldwide because of the threat of AIDS. Forty percent of Raven's products are sold in Austria, Australia, Italy, Germany, France, Belgium, and Switzerland.

Throughout the world, Omaha firms are making an impact. A new $100 million office tower in downtown Hong Kong was designed by Leo A Daly, for example, as well as a new airport terminal in the Philippines and two new $50 million office towers in the United Arab Emirates. Daly, which is headquartered in Omaha and was founded by the late Leo A. Daly (one of Omaha's legendary entrepreneurs), established its first overseas office in 1967, in Hong Kong. Since then, Daly has opened offices in Tokyo, Madrid, and Berlin. It has become one of Asia's leading architectural firms.

Omaha was one of the first cities to provide citywide access to fiber-optic technology. Its companies manage worldwide operations, knowing they have the telecommunications capacity and reliability they need.

In the heart of America's richest agricultural region, Omaha is a food-processing center for several international companies.

Union Pacific has long had marketing offices in several Pacific Rim locations and is a major rail link between the U.S. and Mexico. Coal and grain shipped on Union Pacific to West Coast ports help fuel and feed people in Japan and other Asian countries. Omaha-based California Energy is helping the people of the Philippines and Indonesia meet their energy needs by tapping their geothermal resources. Valmont's irrigation systems and other products are used worldwide. Valmont's newest international venture is a factory in China.

Omaha businesses entering global markets find excellent support at home. Several major banks provide international banking services, and major accounting firms are available for international work. A number of law firms have extensive experience in global protection of intellectual property and international financial matters. Several consultants offer advice on how to get started in international trade. Whether a firm needs translation services or transportation, it can meet its needs in Omaha.

Local universities are also active in international business. University of Nebraska at Omaha staff members are advising some of the new eastern European democracies on how to create a capitalist economy. The University of Nebraska at Omaha has about 400 international students from about two dozen countries. Many come to study English as a second language and remain to complete undergraduate or graduate degrees. An Omahan visiting Indonesia was delighted to meet a former student whose car still proudly carried a UNO bumper sticker.

Global trade isn't a one-way street. Some Omaha businesses have grown rapidly by importing products. Oriental Trading Company, for example, has grown from a small supplier of novelties for carnivals into one of the world's largest distributors and direct marketers of value-priced toys, novelties, and giftware, most of which are produced overseas. It proudly proclaims that its business is fun, and it has shown how much money can be made from products such as inflatable guitars, hamburger yo-yos, feather boas, and chattering teeth. The rapidly expanding firm occupies a massive site in a West Omaha industrial park and employs several thousand people in Omaha and nearby communities.

Shopping in Omaha has also taken on an increasingly international accent. Whether you're looking for a funky batik skirt and blouse and silver bracelets from India or bamboo furniture from the Philippines, you can find what you want in Omaha. The Old Market is especially noted for its interesting boutiques with an international accent. Gourmet cooks can find the supplies they need at Omaha's Asian grocery stores and even in supermarkets—a change from 20 years ago.

"I used to go grocery shopping whenever we went to New York or Chicago," says Ron Psota, a former Peace Corps volunteer in India who specializes in home-cooked Indian delicacies. He recalled filling his suitcases with exotic spices and specialized varieties of rice. No more. "I can get everything I need in Omaha."

*L*andmark Center, on Omaha's Leahy Mall, houses U S West's Communications Data Center and downtown businesses.

MOGENS C. BAY

Valmont's president and CEO, Mogens C. Bay, grew up in Denmark and has lived in some of the world's most cosmopolitan cities, including Hong Kong and Madrid, but he says that "it would be tough to leave Omaha." Bay, who heads a business with seven international manufacturing locations, says that, unlike other cities where newcomers can feel like outsiders, Omaha "embraces people coming in from different places." ◆ "Omaha is not too big, and it's not too small," he says. "It's big enough to have the opera, the symphony, the ballet, Joslyn Art Museum, and the Henry Doorly Zoo. You can do a lot." ◆ Bay says doing business internationally today is a matter of "mind-set, not location," because of instant international communications and the ability to travel to any part of the globe in 24 to 36 hours. The notion that a business needs to be located in New York or Chicago to engage

in international trade has become outmoded by such advances, he says. Any business that wishes to pursue world markets, regardless of where it is located, can do so. ◆ Bay joined Valmont in 1979 and was initially headquartered in the firm's Hong Kong office. Before that, he had worked for the East Asiatic Company in China and at one time was the only Western businessman allowed to live in Beijing. Before becoming Valmont's president and CEO in 1993, he served as president and general manager of the International Division and later the Irrigation Division. ◆ Valmont, he notes, has been selling its irrigation systems, lighting, utility, and traffic structures, and other products internationally for the past 20 years. ◆ "More and more, whatever business you are in, you operate in a world market. Your competitor might be a company from France working here in the United States, or it might be an American company competing with you in France. You have to look at the world market as your marketplace and be active wherever it makes economic sense. ◆ "Our strategy is to leverage the market positions we have developed in the United States everywhere around the world where it makes economic sense," he says. "As a result, we often pick up technology or processes that we can successfully transfer back here. We are not intimidated by different cultures, and I have always been impressed by how well our people from here operate around the world. Sometimes people overmystify international business. The fact of the matter is, if you apply good judgment and logic, you'll do just fine." ◆ This trend toward internationalization will only strengthen as young people who have grown up with global communications and travel enter business. Bay notes that his daughter, for example, graduated from an Omaha high school and is attending the Chinese University in Hong Kong. ◆ "Most of our daughter's friends are very comfortable traveling," he says. "They're very relaxed about circling the world. They have a global mind-set. They are global citizens."

Omaha Business: An Overview

Ironically, one of Omaha's greatest business strengths—its diverse economy—has sometimes made the city difficult to categorize or explain to outsiders. The city's economy can't be summed up with a catch phrase like "Motor City" or "Steel Town," although this may change as Omaha increasingly becomes known as the capital of the telecommunications industry.

Omaha is many things. It's a city that consistently enjoys one of the nation's lowest unemployment rates and is always eager to grow. It's a city where the cost of living, especially for housing, utilities, and taxes, is low enough that the good life is about 10 to 15 percent more affordable than in the United States as a whole. Omahans can earn somewhat lower wages than average and still go skiing in Colorado or buy a car for their teenager.

Employers benefit greatly from a midwestern work ethic that translates into about $2,000 higher productivity per worker per year. They can count on employees to suggest ways their companies can save money or work more efficiently. There's a pride in workmanship and a cooperative spirit between labor and management. Strikes are rare. Nebraska is a right-to-work state, and union and nonunion members work cordially on the same jobs. Litigation is less common than nationally, and the courts are not noted for making

massive damage awards.

Jeff Poley is one entrepreneur who appreciates the strong midwestern work ethic. Poley ran a home renovation business in Maryland before returning to his native Nebraska.

'We've got workers who are so intelligent and well educated," he says. "I'm just amazed at the difference this makes." He cited the skill with which one contractor adapted Poley's design for a basement renovation and the artistic touches the contractor added on his own initiative.

Omaha understands that creating a climate in which businesses can succeed is critical to its future. This is evident in everything from Chamber of Commerce workshops and institutes to help small businesses get started to an Omaha public schools project in which the curriculum is designed so students graduate with the skills businesses need. Businesses, in turn, support the schools. All Omaha public schools have "Adopt-a-School" partners, and each high school has several. Business leaders gain stature by contributing to their community. The late James Paxson, who spearheaded the development of the Gerald Ford Birthsite, summed up the community ethos: "It's not what you take out," he said. "It's what you give back that counts."

Omaha is willing to invest heavily in creating a better community, whether that means adding capacity for growth at the airport or supplying the infrastructure for new business parks. Fiscally, the city is soundly conservative, as its rare AAA municipal credit rating demonstrates. It expects the highest quality. Nothing else will do.

Outsiders are sometimes baffled by Omahans' almost fanatical loyalty to their city. Gov. Ben Nelson summed up this devotion when he said that outsiders are sometimes reluctant to come to Omaha because they know nothing about it but that "once they come, they never want to leave."

Regency and One Pacific Place offer high-style living, office space, and shopping in a suburban setting.

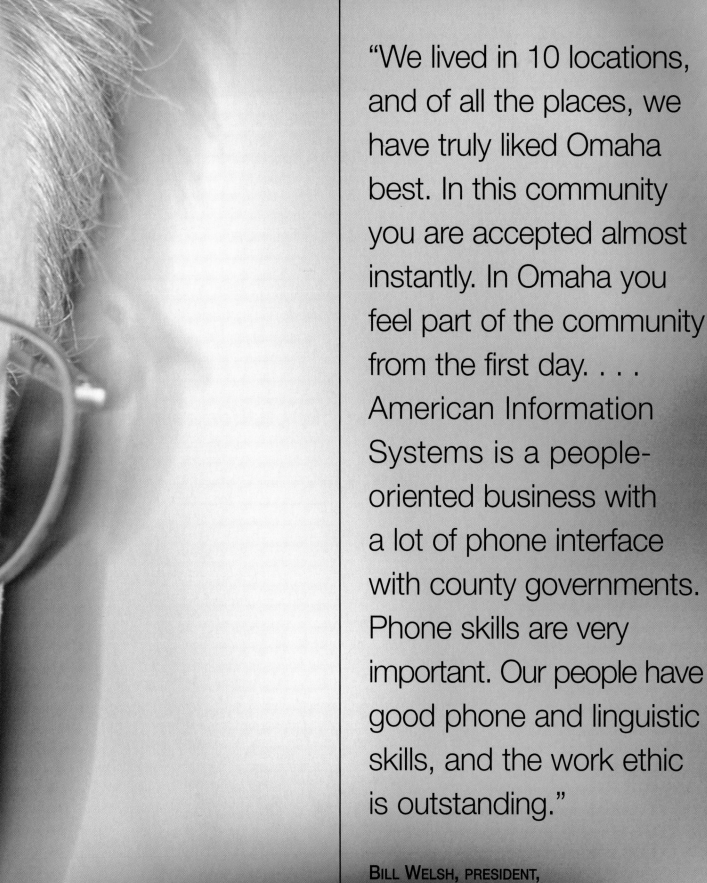

"We lived in 10 locations, and of all the places, we have truly liked Omaha best. In this community you are accepted almost instantly. In Omaha you feel part of the community from the first day. . . . American Information Systems is a people-oriented business with a lot of phone interface with county governments. Phone skills are very important. Our people have good phone and linguistic skills, and the work ethic is outstanding."

BILL WELSH, PRESIDENT, AMERICAN INFORMATION SYSTEMS

From Union Pacific's Harriman Center, in a renovated building with a long history, railroad personnel keep their eyes on 172 giant panoramic computer screens as they monitor a nationwide railroad network composed of 22,800 miles of track and up to 2,000 trains. Another beautifully restored building in downtown Omaha is now the Westin Aquila Hotel, noted for its elegant suites.

A new department store anchors Westroads, one of the nation's largest indoor shopping malls. Below, the headquarters of the Nogg Paper Company anchors Riverfront Industrial Park, near Eppley Airfield.

*B*usinesses in Omaha
boast that they are more
productive working short-
staffed than fully staffed
ones are anywhere else.

ConAgra's $24 billion operations span the food chain and the globe. Above is CEO Phil Fletcher at the Omaha headquarters.

A *national center of*
telecommunications and
information technology,
Omaha is growing out
as well as up. More than
a million people now
live within 50 miles of
downtown.

"This is a service-oriented business. It's high-touch. Our associates deal with sensitive problems that are of enormous impor- tance to people. One of the real advantages of being in Omaha is the consistent high quality of employees, who are very service-oriented and have a strong work ethic."

ROBERT D. BATES, PRESIDENT AND CEO,
GUARANTEE LIFE INSURANCE COMPANY

Health and Insurance:
HIGH-TECH AND HIGH-TOUCH

*A*t major airports around the world, harried travelers find friends from Omaha—Mutual of Omaha, that is. The booths marked with Mutual's distinctive Indian-head logo offer reassurance to passengers worried about many potential ills. If there's been a major airline crash recently, flight insurance becomes very popular. Other people want to protect themselves against lost luggage or canceled trips. Still more take advantage of conveniences such as Mutual's foreign currency exchange or its comfortable lounges for conducting business. Mutual is one of the nation's largest providers of traveler's insurance.

Mutual is one of those companies every city wishes it had. Not only does its local workforce of more than 4,000 people make Mutual one of the largest private employers in Omaha, but its name makes it one of Omaha's best ambassadors. If you're not stopping at the Mutual counter en route to boarding a plane, you might be watching Mutual's *Wild Kingdom* on your local PBS affiliate, sharing the wonders of sharks or Bengal tigers with your children.

Yet another example of a local company that has achieved world stature, Mutual was founded in 1909 by Dr. C. C. Criss as the Mutual Benefit Health and Accident Association. By 1939, despite the Great Depression, it had more than 600 employees. Under the late V. J. Skutt's leadership during the 1950s and 1960s, the company grew from a regional insurer to become an international financial services organization and the nation's leading accident insurance company.

St. Joseph's Center for Mental Health (above) and the Creighton Center for Metabolic Imaging are among only a few facilities in the world that are using a Positron Emission Tomography (PET) scanner in clinical settings.

Insurance: A National Powerhouse

Mutual is just one reason Omaha has become one of the nation's leading centers of the insurance industry. Since the 1960s, Omaha has rivaled such traditional powers as Hartford and Boston in protecting the nation's lives, health, and property. By the mid-1990s, Omaha was headquarters to more than 20 insurance companies employing about 12,000 people. Several of the city's best-known landmarks, including the Woodmen of the World Tower, the tallest building in downtown Omaha, and Mutual's Dome, a spectacular underground meeting area, are connected with the industry.

Many of today's prominent firms followed the pattern of other Omaha entrepreneurial businesses: an Omahan with a good idea started small and built a major company. Encouraged by Nebraska's favorable insurance laws and pro-business state regulatory agencies, Omaha insurance companies chose to grow where they began—at home. In this way, the city and state fostered the development of a homegrown major industry.

Like all service industries, insurance firms benefit from Omaha's well-educated, hard-working employees, who take their commitment to serving beneficiaries seriously. Because many insurance firms rely heavily on having outstanding phone service, Omaha's telecommunications infrastructure is also a major asset.

Omaha's historic connection with insurance dates to the fraternal benefit societies founded to help immigrants cope with life in the new world and especially on the frontier prairies. Some of these organizations were originally burial societies for immigrants from particular countries. Gradually, they branched out to protecting people in the event of numerous other potential disasters.

Omaha's first insurance company, the Western Exchange Fire and Marine Insurance Company, was chartered by the Territorial Legislature in 1855 and was actually in the banking business. The oldest of today's major insurance companies, Woodmen of the World is an example of a fraternal benefit society that succeeded beyond the wildest dreams of its founders.

Woodmen began in 1890 and issued its first policy from the home of one of the directors. That policy provided for a $3,000 death benefit and a $100 monument benefit. Today, with 856,000 members and nearly $29 billion in life insurance, Woodmen is one of the nation's largest fraternal benefit companies. Still taking the "fraternal" aspect of its operation seriously, it sponsors camps and numerous other services that make its beneficiaries far more than just customers of excellent insurance products.

Another Omaha insurance pioneer, Physicians Mutual, was founded by a medical equipment salesman who noticed that doctors often lacked insurance to cover the costs of accidents.

He began his direct-mail business in his garage, selling to doctors and their families. Today, Physicians Mutual is the nation's 10th-largest individual accident and health insurance provider. Physicians Mutual and Physicians Life have paid more than $3 billion in claims since their founding.

Like all industries in Omaha and elsewhere, insurance is changing. Guarantee Life, for example, which had ranked among the 50 largest mutual life insurance firms in the country, is converting to a stock life insurance company.

Some Omaha insurance companies are closely connected with the economy of rural America. Acceptance, for example, is the nation's third-largest crop insurer, protecting the livelihoods of 150,000 farmers nationwide. While corn is the largest crop covered, Acceptance insures numerous other commodities, including spearmint, cranberries, rice, squash, and canola.

Many insurance companies have expanded their services into a broad range of financial planning and management activities, as demonstrated by Mutual's affiliation with Kirkpatrick Pettis, a top regional securities brokerage and investment firm. Increasingly, insurance companies are playing a central role in private efforts to contain the nation's health care costs. Whatever the changes, however, Omaha expects to remain a major center of a vital service industry.

Omaha is the nation's smallest city with two medical colleges: the University of Nebraska Medical Center and Creighton University.

When Robert Redford's son needed a liver transplant, he came to the University of Nebraska Medical Center (UNMC) for the surgery, partly because of the reputation of Dr. Byers Shaw, chief of solid-organ transplantation. A Redford family spokesman described the UNMC program as "world class." Dr. Shaw was "definitely one of the top liver transplant surgeons," she said, noting that "excellence extends throughout the program."

While Omahans who accidentally encountered Robert Redford during his son's Omaha hospital stay couldn't help being a little starstruck, Omahans are accustomed to reading of transplant patients from distant corners of the nation and the world finding the care they need at UNMC. The seemingly unlikely people who have come to Omaha include a physician-researcher from New York who reviewed all his options for liver transplant surgery and chose UNMC.

Some of the stories are especially heartwarming, such as the Irish infant with a rare bone marrow disease whose life was saved in Omaha. The girl's mother recalls the kindness and professionalism of the hospital staff and the generosity of Omaha's people, who contributed both financial assistance and friendship.

"We have a warm spot in our hearts for Omaha," says the mother.

Omaha's prominence as a center for transplants will only grow with UNMC's development of a $42 million center for transplantation, scheduled for completion before the year 2000. Omaha expects to become an even more important national center for medical research and treatment. UNMC's physicians currently represent 1 percent of all the U.S. doctors listed in a directory of the "Best Doctors in America."

Omaha is the nation's smallest city with two medical colleges: UNMC and Creighton University. Both also operate pharmacy, nursing, and allied health programs. Increasingly, in recent years, the colleges have cooperated in meeting public needs with joint programs in fields such as psychiatry and pediatrics.

Omaha's rich offerings in medical education also include outstanding nursing and allied health programs, provided by Clarkson College and the Methodist Health System. A student interested in any medical-related career, including a business degree to prepare for a position in health care administration, offered by Clarkson, can find a suitable program in Omaha.

Both UNMC and Creighton have developed nationally recognized specialties in research. A leader in transplants of all sorts, UNMC is among the five most active liver and pancreas transplant centers in the nation and is also renowned for its bone marrow and small bowel transplants.

UNMC also is home to the Eppley Institute for Research in Cancer and Allied Diseases. The American Cancer Society has chosen the Eppley Institute as one of only 14 centers to be devoted to the study of the causes and prevention of cancer.

U.S. News & World Report ranks UNMC 14th among all medical colleges in America, and according to *Healthcare Infomatics* magazine, the center is one of the nation's 10 most computer-advanced clinical laboratories.

DR. CAROL ASCHENBRENER

When Dr. Carol Aschenbrener talks about the University of Nebraska Medical Center, she repeats the words "leadership" and "future" frequently. ◆ As chancellor, her goals include making UNMC the leading academic health care institution in the Heartland. She wants the institution to be "at the forefront of designing the educational and clinical programs of the future." ◆ Dr. Aschenbrener also is concerned with developing leadership at all levels of the medical center. She and several colleagues have begun a leadership institute to train faculty and staff in leadership skills and ultimately to "build a critical mass of leaders." ◆ Such leadership is becoming more and more necessary as organizations have fewer "positional titles" and people have to assume more responsibility, she says. ◆ Health care is changing, and UNMC's corporate culture must be flexible, creative, innovative, and continuously open to new ways of delivering education and services to patients, she adds. ◆ "In many different places in the medical center, people are taking the initiative to challenge old ways of doing things," she says. ◆ A native of Dubuque, Iowa, Dr. Aschenbrener is a neuropathologist who became chancellor of the medical center in 1992–making her the first woman in the nation to head a public academic medical center. ◆ Before that, she had spent years as a professor, researcher, and administrator at the University of Iowa Medical College. ◆ Dr. Aschenbrener says she accepted the position at UNMC because she was "excited by the potential I saw here. There were many really good people poised for a big leap forward in quality. The decision to come here has proven to be one of the best in my life. The medical center has made tremendous progress in the last 15 years in terms of the development of its educational and research and patient care programs. It is of a manageable size." ◆ Dr. Aschenbrener says she expects to see UNMC "adding to its strengths" and international reputation in transplantation, cancer research, and primary care. Transplant patients already have come to UNMC from 42 states and 16 foreign countries. ◆ She also wants the institution to develop its strengths in the application of information technology to primary health care across Nebraska–a major need in more sparsely populated areas of the state. ◆ Dr. Aschenbrener has been "really pleased with the strong support" she has received from all over Omaha, and she enjoys living in the city. ◆ "When I moved to Omaha, I expected that I would have a period of feeling sort of like I didn't fit in or that this wasn't really home for me because I'd been in Iowa City for 23 years. Within a week I felt right at home. People have been extraordinarily warm and welcoming. Over the years I lived in Iowa, I often came to Omaha for cultural activities," she adds. "It has a wonderful reputation for theater, for example, so I knew something of the city, but it's been wonderful to explore all the attractions it has—the Henry Doorly Zoo, the Royals, Fontenelle Forest–as well as the many cultural attractions."

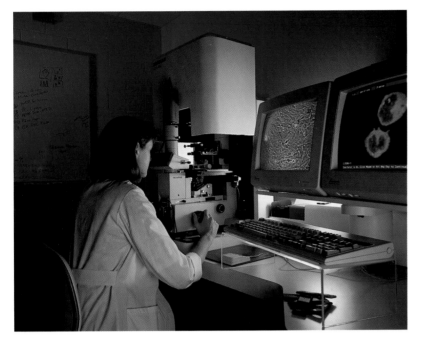

Creighton, one of only five Catholic medical schools in the United States, has developed a national reputation in several medical specialties. A Jesuit university, it has developed particular expertise in medical ethics. Its Center for Health Policy and Ethics is devoted to studying the challenges of medical ethics in a rapidly changing health care environment. The center, which is directed by Dr. Ruth Purtilo, sponsors an annual Institute on Ethics and Health Care. Dr. Purtilo is the author of several major books on medical ethics and served on Hillary Rodham Clinton's health care reform task force.

Creighton University researchers are studying health care problems that affect millions. For example, for 25 years they have been conducting a study of osteoporosis, and they have been among the leaders in encouraging women to take calcium supplements to prevent the disease. And research in the use of lasers, being conducted in the Creighton University Dental College, may eventually take some of the trauma out of a visit to the dentist. Dr. Richard Blankenau, who conducts this pioneering work, cites the example of a seven-year-old girl from Iowa who came to his clinic for gum surgery. In contrast with earlier surgery, which had left her nauseous, the laser treatment was almost pain-free.

"Her mother told me that on the way home, they stopped for lunch and the little girl wanted pizza," Dr. Blankenau says.

The health problems of children arouse special attention in Omaha. Childrens Hospital is nationally recognized for many services, including its large Poison Control Center. Other specialized health services for children include the Center for Human Nutrition, one of the nation's leading pediatric nutrition programs, and the Boys Town National Research Hospital (BTNRH), which the National Institutes of Health designated as its first National Research and Training Center for Childhood Deafness.

Omaha has long been noted as a regional health care center. About 29,000 people (more than 7 percent of the workforce) are employed in health care. Omaha's reputation in this area is boosted by the excellence of its 15 hospitals. Many of these health care organizations, including Methodist Health System, St. Joseph Regional Health Center, and Alegent Health, provide outpatient services throughout Omaha and have satellite clinics, extending their services beyond the metropolitan area.

In Omaha, as elsewhere, health care institutions are realigning, entering into agreements to provide managed care, and forming new networks. Increasing emphasis is being placed on promoting wellness. Like insurance, health care in Omaha will change greatly by the year 2000, but the city will remain a regional center of medical research and treatment. Excellence in these fields will continue to contribute to the high quality of life in the city.

WELLNESS: AN OMAHA HALLMARK

Nebraskans take pride in being hardy people who live longer than the national average. That's true in Omaha as well as in the rest of Nebraska. The National Institutes of Health ranks Omaha as one of the 10 healthiest places to live in America. But Omahans are taking no chances. They work aggressively to promote wellness, and several Omahans or Omaha firms have gained national prominence for their efforts.

The Wellness Councils of America (WELCOA) were founded in Omaha to promote physical fitness programs in the workplace. William M. Kizer, who was then CEO of Central States Health and Life Company, conceived the idea, contending that the answer to America's rising health care costs was the reduction of employee illnesses brought on by unhealthy lifestyles. In support of Kizer's claim, companies that have instituted wellness programs report dramatic decreases in medical costs and absenteeism.

Several major Omaha firms have on-site fitness centers, including Mutual of Omaha and Union Pacific Railroad. Many other firms subsidize employees' memberships in health clubs or the YMCA or sponsor smoking cessation classes. Growing numbers of workplaces and buildings are smoke-free. And the annual Corporate Cup Race through downtown Omaha draws thousands of runners and walkers each fall.

St. Joseph Regional Health Center provides care for trauma patients, some of whom are airlifted to the hospital.

Recognizing that alcoholism, mental health problems, and family concerns can result in loss of productivity, numerous Omaha employers offer confidential employee assistance programs. Union Pacific was one of the nation's pioneers in the field.

A few Omahans have made healthy living a personal crusade, notably businessman Phil Sokolof, who launched a personal national campaign, complete with full-page ads in major newspapers, aimed at persuading fast-food chains to lower the cholesterol in their products. Sokolof has also been credited with creating the demand for the federal nutrition labeling rules, which give consumers easily understood information about fat, calories, and sodium in packaged food products.

One of the nation's favorite healthy choices has an invented-in-Omaha label. ConAgra's Healthy Choice packaged meals were among the first prepared foods to cater to Americans' desire for tasty, low-fat/low-sodium convenience foods. Mike Harper, CEO of ConAgra at the time, directed ConAgra's food researchers to develop the products after he suffered a heart attack.

Nebraskans boast of their state's "good life." Efforts that help Omahans live longer, healthier lives contribute greatly to both the area's productivity and the quality of life Omahans enjoy.

"I've had the pleasure of serving as a professor of medical ethics at both Creighton and the University of Nebraska Medical Center. During that time, I've taught hundreds of students in the health professions. I've been impressed with the values they bring to their professions. I have been even more impressed with the commitment of Creighton and the University of Nebraska Medical Center to nurturing their compassion and competence."

DR. RUTH PURTILO,
DIRECTOR, CREIGHTON UNIVERSITY CENTER FOR
HEALTH POLICY AND ETHICS

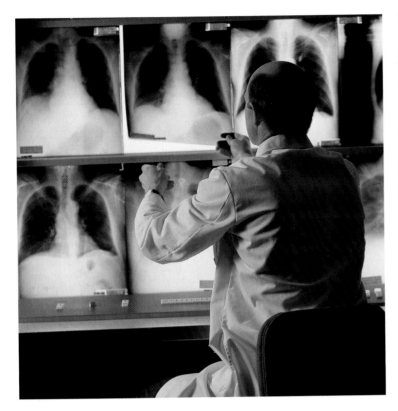

Patients from around the world come to the University of Nebraska Medical Center for organ and bone marrow transplants.

Both Creighton University Medical School and the University of Nebraska Medical Center are known for focusing on the whole person in health care education, research, and treatment.

S*t. Joseph Hospital is one of several medical facilities that provide services at both the hospital and throughout Omaha in satellite clinics.*

One of five Catholic medical schools in the country, Creighton offers fully accredited programs in medicine, nursing, dentistry, pharmacy, and allied health fields. Creighton University Dental College, shown here, is a national leader in both education and research.

Ranked among the top
20 comprehensive medical
schools in the U.S., UNMC
is renowned for its excellence in research, clinical
care, and education. Its
teaching initiatives serve as
models at other institutions.

64

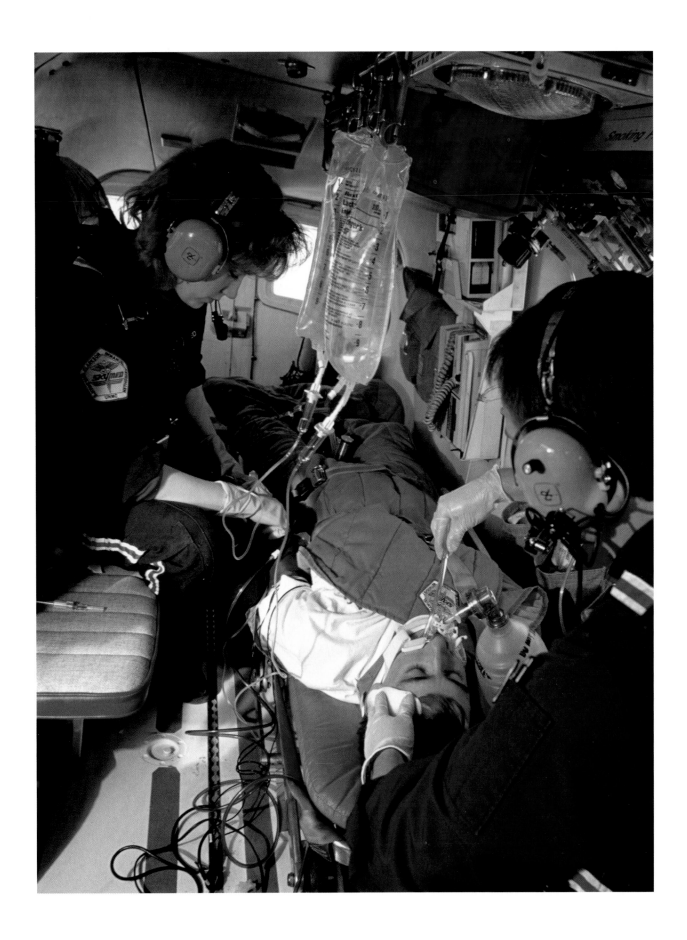

"This is a great city to do business in. In my years of experience, each administration has made an honest attempt to work with business. We have a AAA credit rating, and overall the mayors and city councils I've worked with during the past 50 years have been very honorable people."

MARY GALLIGAN CORNETT, CITY CLERK

Government and Services:

SOPHISTICATED AND SUCCESSFUL

When nostalgia buffs ask railroaders to describe their industry's golden era, they usually expect the answer to be the era of the Streamliner passenger trains or steam locomotives. They're astonished when railroaders tell them that the golden age of railroading is now—and nowhere is that more evident than in Omaha.

In Omaha's spectacular renovated riverfront area sits a historically significant building that is the highest of high-tech: Union Pacific's Harriman Dispatch Center. This $50 million center is a monument to both Union Pacific's history and its future.

Located in the completely renovated freight house where E. H. Harriman purchased a bankrupt Union Pacific (UP) at auction more than a century ago, the center houses some of the nation's most sophisticated transportation technology. Every mile of track on UP's 22,800-mile system, in addition to every switch and every signal light, are displayed on 172 giant screens that stretch the length of two football fields.

From the center, dispatchers control rail traffic a thousand miles away, giving crews instructions and clearances and alerting them to any problems. Dispatchers in Omaha have even stopped runaway trains in California and averted a head-on collision.

Great-Great-Grandpa who came to Omaha from Ireland with his pick and shovel to help build Union Pacific would be thrilled by today's railroad system.

Refreshingly lacking in corruption in its government, Omaha maintains a AAA bond rating. The strong spirit of cooperation between its public and private sectors helps make it one of the "20 Best Places to Start a Business," according to Entrepreneur magazine.

TRANSPORTATION: THE LIFEBLOOD OF OMAHA

As the Harriman Dispatch Center demonstrates, Omaha has a sophisticated transportation infrastructure. Since pioneer days, transportation has been the lifeblood of Omaha. The central location of the city both enables it to reach out to all parts of the nation and almost requires that it do so. From Omaha, it's easy to reach regional and national markets quickly and efficiently by air, land, rail, and water.

Omaha's first lifeline was the Missouri River, then a treacherous trek north from St. Louis by steamboat. Many boats sank en route, but enough made it to sustain Omaha's initial growth, at least until the construction of Union Pacific in the late 1860s.

Omaha is served by 16 major national and international air freight express and cargo companies.

Today, Omaha has many additional transportation lifelines, including two intersecting interstate highways and a rapidly growing airport with excess capacity. Today, a channelized Missouri River and modern dock facilities make the river an important asset both as a means of transportation and a place for recreation.

The expansion of Omaha's Eppley Airfield is typical of the way Omaha invests in its infrastructure. When it became apparent that Omaha needed a bigger airport, the Airport Authority built for the future. Since completion of a $70 million expansion program in 1989, Eppley has continually increased the number of passengers served—more than 3 million a year by the mid-1990s. The expansion of the airport and the steady increase in passenger traffic have helped Omaha attract nonstop flights to about 20 major cities, including Los Angeles, Newark, New Jersey, and Washington, D.C. More carriers than ever serve Omaha, and they're adding flights to handle the increased demand. Today, you can leave Omaha on a business trip in the morning and fly home the same night without stop-overs in Chicago or Denver. Eppley is a convenient five minutes from downtown Omaha and half an hour from suburban business locations.

Such convenience increases productivity, says Robert Bates, CEO of Guarantee Life Insurance Company. Workers with mid-morning flights routinely stop at the office first.

Eppley also is an important air freight center. It is served by all major national and international air freight and express mail companies, which process more than 130 million pounds of cargo a year in Omaha. If your package has to be on one of the coasts in the morning, Omaha's efficient air transportation system will ensure delivery.

In contrast with cities where simply getting to work in the morning is an ordeal, part of the high quality of life that Omahans enjoy is the ease of getting around in their city. A typical commute time is 18 minutes one way. Local radio stations carry no eye-in-the-sky traffic reports after 5:45 P.M. because rush hour is over.

Time saved on commuting is important in both human and economic terms. Most Omahans arrive at their offices at 8 A.M. and work until 5 P.M., not the legendary 9 to 5 they hear about elsewhere. If workers have small children, they can deliver them to baby-sitters at 7:30 A.M. and still be on time for work. They can pick them up before 6 P.M., giving families "quality time" together.

To many Omahans, commuting is synonymous with local interstate travel, but the city's excellent interstate connections also are important to businesses. Omaha is located at the intersection of Interstate Highways 80 and 29, giving it easy access to both east-west and north-south markets.

In addition to the interstates, four U.S. and eight state highways converge in Omaha. This is important to manufacturing businesses like Modern Equipment Company that depend on motor transportation to bring in supplies and ship finished products out. CEO Richard Johnson cites Omaha's outstanding interstate access as a major asset in the operation of his equipment manu-facturing business.

Omaha's strategic highway location has resulted in the growth of a major local trucking industry; more than 100 motor carriers serve the city. It's easy to ship goods from Omaha to almost any-where in the continental U.S.—a day by truck from Omaha to Chicago and just three days to Los Angeles and New York.

Omaha also is home to sophisticated intermodal transportation facilities. Rail shipments can reach Chicago and Denver in one day, Los Angeles in two days, and New York in three days. Omaha's

central location complements its well-developed infrastructure in attracting businesses that market their products throughout the United States.

Omaha's first "highway"—the Missouri River—is still a major commercial asset. Shippers find it an economical route for sending bulk commodities to national and inter-national markets. Omaha's five barge lines carry grain, fertilizers, molasses, salt, cement, animal foods, chemicals, iron, steel, and newsprint to markets along the Missouri and Mississippi Rivers and to the mouths of the Illinois, Ohio, Tennessee, and Arkansas Rivers.

While Omahans regard their central location as a great benefit, it means they will always place a high premium on maintaining an efficient transportation system. Transportation is still the lifeblood of the city.

Just five minutes from downtown Omaha, Eppley Airfield, with non-stop service to both coasts and most major U.S. cities, is one of the top 10 fastest-growing airports in the United States.

Outstanding utility service is as important to business as excellent transportation, and Omaha offers ample power at lower than average rates. To a certain extent, Omahans can thank Nebraska's legendary Sen. George Norris for their excellent service. Norris, who sponsored the Tennessee Valley Authority in the 1930s, was the father of public power nationally. As a result of his legacy, Nebraska is the nation's only completely electric public power state. Utilities in Omaha are mostly nonprofit and customer-owned, although privately owned Peoples Natural Gas provides some suburban gas service. Electric rates are as much as 21 percent below the national average, while natural gas rates are 18 percent below the national average.

The Omaha Public Power District (OPPD), which serves 5,000 square miles in eastern Nebraska, also is noted for its dependability. It has an average system reliability of more than 99 percent. In addition to its baseload generating capacity of 1.9 million kilowatts, it has a reserve generating capacity of over 20 percent. "Brownouts" are a problem with which Omahans are familiar only because they have read about them elsewhere.

OPPD is especially proud of the high quality and dedication of its employees, who exhibit an extraordinary midwestern work ethic. When a major storm disrupts service, OPPD crews are on the job around the clock, if necessary, in the worst weather, making repairs.

Like OPPD, Omaha's major gas and water supplier, the Metropolitan Utilities District (MUD), is nonprofit and governed by a publicly elected board. As noted, gas rates are notably lower than the national average, and service is excellent.

Industries that require an ample supply of water also recognize Omaha's great advantages. The city's water supply, which comes from the Missouri River and Platte River valley wells, is limited only by the water purification system's mechanical capabilities. That's no problem, either. MUD's two water treatment plants have a capacity more than two and a half times as large as the average daily consumption of about 90 million gallons, and it plans to treat an additional 70 million gallons per day by the year 2000.

Omaha is proud of the way its modern infrastructure meets today's environmental standards. The water quality meets or exceeds all current and proposed federal standards, and the city's sewage treatment plants have won awards from the Environmental Protection Agency. The sewage treatment plants have the capacity to handle more than twice their current daily load of 82 million gallons.

Like its transportation infrastructure, Omaha's utilities are a major civic asset. The vital skeleton of the city can support future growth.

Local Government: Doing the Essentials Well

A classic study of local government, Paul Peterson's *City Limits*, says that successful cities understand that their major mission is to support economic development. Elected officials can feud about "housekeeping" issues like whether to spend more on museums or golf courses and it doesn't matter much as long as they realize that they must support efforts to attract industry and keep the local economy healthy.

Peterson could well have been writing about Omaha. Regardless of who is mayor or who sits on the city council, Omaha's city government has always strongly supported economic development. The city works closely with the Greater Omaha Chamber of Commerce and local businesses to enhance the business climate.

Omaha's city government is well run. For generations, the city of Omaha has maintained an extremely rare AAA credit rating, and both city officials and citizens take seriously their obligation to invest in the infrastructure. Bond issues for street and sewer improvements pass almost automatically because old bonds are replaced by new ones without raising taxes.

Unlike cities that have been strangled by their suburban rings, Omaha has ample growing room because Nebraska's annexation law allows Omaha to annex anything within Douglas County. This means that affluent suburban industrial and residential areas are within the city limits and enhance Omaha's tax base and overall economic health.

Nebraska has strong populist roots, and city officials generally assume it is their duty to listen to the people. City officials are noted for their accessibility. They seek partnerships with private industry and organizations. Most city departments have citizens boards that donate countless hours to improving the parks and the public library, arbitrating zoning disputes, and performing other services.

Nebraska's open meetings law is one of the strictest in the nation, requiring that the public's business be done in public. Any citizen can get up at city council meetings and express an opinion on any proposal.

At the same time, Omaha's local politics are far from dull. Having attended to the major task that Peterson says is essential—supporting economic development—city officials often engage in freewheeling battles over city governance. Both the mayor and city council are elected on a nonpartisan basis, which tends to result in strong and colorful individuals winning office. Elected officials have to be self-starters merely to play the game.

Nebraska's general love of maverick politicians is apparent from Omaha's mayors. Beloved past mayors include A. V. Sorensen and Eugene A. Leahy. Sorensen was a dignified, influential, and civic-minded business leader before agreeing to run for mayor. His impact on the city went beyond an administration that was noted for its honesty and efficiency. He also founded the Boys Clubs of Omaha and obtained funding for them. The Sorensen Recreation Center and Library in Dundee is named in his honor.

Leahy, who succeeded Sorensen in 1969, could scarcely have been a more different type of person. An ebullient Irishman who seemingly never met a stranger, Leahy conceived the dream of the riverfront development. Planning for the massive enterprise began under his leadership, although critics considered the idea so visionary that development efforts were often viewed as almost a boondoggle.

Simultaneously, Leahy was becoming a legend of another sort—as the mayor who read the funnies on TV on Sunday mornings and who once appeared in public in a bunny suit. That was Mayor Leahy—a visionary with a sense of humor. The mall in downtown Omaha is named in his honor.

In addition to city government and Douglas County government, the metropolitan area includes smaller government subdivisions, most of which have officials elected on a nonpartisan basis. While Nebraska's love affair with nonpartisan direct democracy puts it a little out of step with the national norm, what else would you expect in a state that boasts the nation's only unicameral state legislature (elected on a nonpartisan basis, of course)?

In contrast with cities where simply getting to work in the morning is an ordeal, part of the high quality of life that Omahans enjoy is the ease of getting around in their city.

When Lormong Lo was 10, he went to school by day; at night, armed with a rifle, he guarded Hmong villages in his native Laos from Communist attack. At age 17, he escaped from the Communists, who had taken over Laos. A year later, he found himself in the Omaha suburb of Ralston speaking no English but determined to build a new life. ◆ Today, in his mid-30s, Lormong Lo is repaying the debt he feels to his adopted country and his adopted hometown by serving on the Omaha City Council. ◆ "I want to pay back the investment that America has made in me," says Lo, director of a national technical training and development organization serving Hmong-Americans. Lo says he feels his life shows that America still offers opportunities to those who are willing to overcome all obstacles to success. ◆ He vividly recalls his

youth in war-torn Laos, especially his escape from the country. The Hmong people were persecuted by the Communists because they had fought for the Americans. When the Communists took over the country in 1975, Lo knew staying meant either death or life in a reeducation camp. ◆ Lo used his student identification card to persuade guards at various checkpoints that he wanted to get to the capital of Vientiane to apply to study in the Soviet Union. When he reached the last checkpoint, he was in a taxi with two other Hmong. He heard the captain tell his soldiers, who had machine guns, to get those who appeared to be Hmong. As Lo prayed for escape, a bus pulled up and the captain redirected his unit to search the bus instead. ◆ In the capital, Lo located an agent who helped him cross the Mekong River into Thailand. After nine months in a refugee camp, he and several of his relatives were sponsored by Ralston's Messiah Lutheran Church and came to the Omaha area. ◆ Lo, who had completed three years of French-style secondary schooling, was determined to get an education. He graduated from Ralston High School in 1979 and from Creighton University in 1983. He also worked full or part time at fast-food establishments and grocery stores and as a hotel janitor. Married right out of high school, he and his wife, Nou, have five children. Lo remains grateful to the Omahans who helped him through the difficulties of resettlement. ◆ "Omaha is the place I grew up in America. It's my hometown. Wherever I go, I don't feel at home until I get to Omaha," he says. ◆ After graduating from Creighton, Lo worked with the local Lao-Hmong Association and later in community development and city planning. He also got involved in local politics, running unsuccessfully for the county board as a Republican. In 1994, the city council elected him to fill a vacancy in North Omaha's District 1. ◆ Lo says that on the council, he's concentrating on economic and neighborhood development programs that benefit his district. ◆ "I really enjoy my new hometown of Omaha," he says. "I enjoy its hospitality and support. I want to give back my services to the city of Omaha."

O*ffutt Air Force Base,*
one of Omaha's largest
employers, is the headquarters
of the U.S. Strategic
Command and the 55th
Wing of the U.S. Air Force.

OMAHA: HOME OF U.S. STRATEGIC COMMAND

The Omaha area is a regional center of federal offices and services and, most important, home of the U.S. Strategic Command, headquartered at Offutt Air Force Base, in Bellevue. For years, Offutt was the headquarters for the Strategic Air Command, the heart of the nation's nuclear defense against the Soviet Union. Omahans knew that the SAC commander slept with the famous "red telephone" (containing orders in the event of a possible atomic attack) by his bed and that a SAC Looking Glass aircraft was airborne 24 hours a day. They calmly accepted the fact that Offutt was a top target in case of nuclear war.

Throughout the 50 years of the Cold War, a sort of love affair developed between the city of Omaha and its military base. Omaha business leaders have always supported development projects at the base, and, in turn, the Air Force has been a good neighbor, participating actively in the life of the community and sponsoring major events such as an annual air show that attracts crowds of up to 100,000 people.

With the end of the Cold War, SAC was merged with another command, and Offutt became the headquarters of the U.S. Strategic Command, which is responsible for developing the nation's nuclear strategy. With approximately 11,000 military personnel and civilian employees, the base remains one of the metropolitan area's largest employers.

Omaha also is a major retirement center for Air Force personnel. Many military employees take their final tour of duty at Offutt so they can transition to civilian jobs in Omaha—a community they have come to love because of its quality of life and the excellence of the schools. SAC's presence in Omaha also was responsible for the installation of the city's extensive telecommunications infrastructure.

Offutt is the most significant federal entity in Omaha but hardly the only one. The U.S. Army Corps of Engineers has had a major presence in the city for many years, using it as a base for its extensive programs on the Missouri River. Omaha also is the regional headquarters of the National Park Service, a regional Immigration and Naturalization Service office, and an area office of the U.S. Department of Housing and Urban Development.

Omaha's healthy economy has an appropriate government sector and has benefited greatly from its Air Force partner in Bellevue.

"Omaha's central location is turning out to be a benefit because everyone is doing business everywhere. With direct flights to and from Omaha, this is a superb location in which to do business. Our utilities also are very strong because we are an all-public-power state. We have a strong power supply at below-average rates."

RICHARD JEFFRIES,
MEMBER, STATE AERONAUTICS BOARD,
AND FORMER MEMBER,
OMAHA PUBLIC POWER DISTRICT BOARD

Omaha's outstanding police and fire protection is a major reason the city ranks as one of the top five safest cities of its size and helps keep its fire insurance rates among the lowest in the nation.

Omaha's water supply is fed
by abundant ground and surface
resources. Capacity at the
Metropolitan Utilities District's
two water treatment plants is
projected to exceed 286 million
gallons per day by the year
2000. The water quality meets
or exceeds all current and
proposed federal standards.

Nebraska is the only all-public-power state in the U.S. Electric rates are as much as 15 percent lower than the national average.

L*ocated at the intersection of Interstates 80 and 29, Omaha has a highway infrastructure built to accommodate future growth. Rush hour is still just one hour.*

"In our first years, this was a hideaway. People didn't know we were even here. Now we're going from bankruptcy to expanding. We've had great word-of-mouth advertising."

IGNACIO CHAVEZ, CO-OWNER, EL ALAMO RESTAURANT

Culture and Recreation:
DIVERSE AND DISTINCTIVE

f rom the rugged hills of far north Omaha come the sounds Americans across the country listen to during the Christmas season: Mannheim Steamroller's Fresh Aire Christmas albums.

Since CBS News made the group's rendition of "Deck the Halls" its holiday theme in the late 1980s, Mannheim Steamroller's electronic renditions of classic carols have become increasingly popular. By 1995, the group's first two Christmas albums had sold more than five million copies each, making them the biggest-selling Christmas albums ever, while a new album released that year sold 3.1 million copies in the first four months.

But Christmas music isn't the only claim to fame for Chip Davis, owner and president of American Gramaphone Company, which produces Mannheim Steamroller's albums. After a fire devastated Yellowstone National Park, he raised funds through a series of concerts and a gold record album for its restoration. The $500,000 he donated made Davis the largest individual contributor to Yellowstone and the National Park Service.

In addition, years before creating Mannheim Steamroller's distinctive sound, which gives a rock-and-roll twist to classical music, Davis produced two gold country records, "Convoy" and "C. W. McCall," and was named country music "man of the year." All told, Davis has produced 11 gold records.

Davis, an Ohio native, came to Omaha in the 1970s to work on a production of the musical *Hair* and decided to stay. He teamed up with former Omahan Bill Fries in pro-

ducing the regionally famous Old Home Bread commercials, from which the character C. W. McCall emerged.

When interviewers on TV programs like *The Tonight Show* express surprise that Davis remains in Omaha, he tells them that Omaha is a great place to raise a family, the crime rate is low, and "You can see the sky and breathe fresh air." He constantly reminds audiences where he's from and promotes Omaha nationwide.

Chip Davis isn't alone in appreciating the quality of life in Omaha. The city has great appeal to people in all fields, who enjoy both its vibrant cultural offerings and its ample recreational facilities. The city has invested millions in its theaters, zoo, museums, and parks so that Omahans can enjoy stimulating, satisfying lives with their friends and families.

Omahans are fortunate to be able to attend symphony concerts, grand opera, ballet, or productions of Broadway plays at the magnificently restored Orpheum Theater (above). Joslyn Art Museum (facing page) has equally diverse offerings, from antiquities to modern works.

CULTURAL OFFERINGS:
FROM THE AVANT-GARDE TO THE TRADITIONAL

The New York newspaper the *Village Voice* once commented on Omaha's cultural offerings that "Omaha is a damned lucky town." Most Omahans would agree. The city has its own professional symphony, opera company, and ballet troupe, extensive theater and live music offerings, and varied visual arts attractions. Opera Omaha productions are reviewed in national newspapers. The Omaha Community Playhouse is the nation's largest community theater and is noted for the stars, such as Henry Fonda and Dorothy McGuire, who began their careers here.

Omahans with a passion for the visual arts can relax on Friday nights by making the rounds to openings at small galleries, where they can sip wine with the artists. Because they tend to be affluent, well educated, and well traveled, Omahans who patronize the fine arts demand excellence and variety in local cultural offerings.

The diversity apparent in the visual arts is epitomized by two Omaha institutions, one at the west end of downtown, the other at the east end. To the west stands Joslyn Art Museum, a striking marble structure that has become even more impressive since the addition of a $45 million pavilion designed by Sir Norman Foster and Partners of London in cooperation with HDR, Inc., of Omaha. The addition is a work of art in itself and enables the Joslyn to stage special exhibits without disturbing its permanent collection.

Thousands of people of all ages attend the free Nebraska Shakespeare Festival in Elmwood Park each summer.

The nation's only art museum with a Center for Western Studies, Joslyn is best known nationally for its western American collection, which features the world-renowned watercolors of Swiss artist Karl Bodmer. The works document his 1832–34 journey to the Missouri River frontier. The museum houses a rich assortment of Old Master, Italian Renaissance, and impressionist paintings, as well as a 20th-century collection featuring works by Henri Matisse, Jackson Pollock, George Segal, and others. It also has a collection of ancient Greek art.

But Joslyn is more than a visual arts museum. It was designed to be a community gathering place for the enjoyment of many fine arts. Its popular Sunday-morning "Bagels and Bach" series is a family affair that introduces children to the joys of classical music while they enjoy brunch. The Omaha Symphony's chamber orchestra also gives performances at Joslyn, and jazz musicians present summer outdoor concerts "on the green."

To the east, in the Old Market, stands a converted warehouse that symbolizes the dynamism of the visual arts in Omaha today. The nation's only urban artists' colony, the Bemis Center for the Contemporary Arts houses artists from all over the world, who competed for their coveted residencies in the Bemis's studios. During their stays in Omaha, the artists produce experimental works of painting and sculpture.

While visiting the Bemis, actress Jane Alexander, chair of the National Endowment for the Arts, commented that she hadn't "seen anything like it in the country, and I have been to over 100 communities.... It is a very special place in the United States of America today." Alexander's comments paid immediate dividends. A resident of another state who read the remarks made a major donation.

About 10 percent of the artists who come to the Bemis—and typically most know nothing about Omaha—settle in the city, building Omaha's reputation as a center for contemporary art and proving that artists do not have to locate on the East or West Coast.

Bringing talented people into the fabric of the Omaha community is a major unsung contribution of many of the city's arts organizations, says Sandy Matthews, a longtime volunteer with many groups. Artists of various types come to Omaha not because of its scenic beauty but because the community is open to innovative work. Young artists can find their voice—and audiences to appreciate it—here.

*T*he Bemis Center for the Contemporary Arts draws artists from around the world. Many, like Jun Kaneko, have made Omaha their home.

Omaha's theater community, for instance, is thriving. In addition to its outstanding Community Playhouse, Omaha is home to two progressive theaters, the Blue Barn and the Magic Theater.

The Blue Barn was started by four graduates from the State University of New York at Purchase who were looking for a place to stage experimental productions. One of the four, Kevin Lawlor, was a Minneapolis native who had spent his freshman year at Creighton University. He suggested Omaha. After outgrowing their first location at the Bemis Center, the group moved to its current space near the Old Market, where the company presents serious and sometimes radical works.

"The Blue Barn has done some pretty radical work and no one is up in arms," says Matthews, whose daughter, Amy, is affiliated with the company. "This is a very live-and-let-live community."

Another group that is doing exciting work is the Magic Theater, which tours both nationally and internationally with its avant-garde productions. Headed and founded by internationally known playwright Megan Terry, the theater often stages her dramas in unconventional settings, such as prisons. During the 1980 Winter Olympics, the Magic Theater was invited to entertain at Lake Placid.

The Omaha Community Playhouse includes not only gifted amateurs but a professional touring company, the Nebraska Theater Caravan. It is especially noted for its productions of an adaptation of Dickens's *Christmas Carol,* written by the Playhouse's director, Charles Jones. The Caravan has presented the play around the country.

The Playhouse received national attention when it was named the beneficiary of memorials for its most noted alumnus, Henry Fonda. These gifts helped the Playhouse construct the Fonda-McGuire stage, where experimental plays are performed.

The growing professionalism of Omaha's arts is evident in its concerts as well as its theater. The Omaha Symphony was originally a community orchestra that paid only its conductor. Today, there is a core group of 36 full-time professional musicians, giving the symphony regional stature. Many of these musicians have been attracted by the high quality of life in Omaha and have settled here. In addition to performing with the orchestra, they enhance arts education in local schools through numerous residencies and recitals.

Opera Omaha's productions have helped many Omahans become not only familiar with classical and contemporary operas but personally acquainted with performers who become international stars. Typically, the singers will spend a month or longer in Omaha preparing for a production. During this time, they live with local families and are hosted at social gatherings. The Matthews family, for example, has been friends with Sheri Greenawald for more than 20 years as a result of such an experience. When the Matthews's daughter, Amy, was attending high school in Washington, D.C., through an exchange program, Greenawald invited her to a performance at the Kennedy Center. Daughter Hope received a similar invitation during a trip to Naples, Italy.

Opera Omaha is nationally recognized for producing high-quality, innovative productions. It hosted the world premier of Sir Andrew Lloyd Webber's *Requiem Variations*, for example. And its annual Fall Festival draws national attention and reviewers by presenting world premiers of new works and rarely performed works of classical composers.

Omaha places great importance on introducing children to the arts. The Omaha Theater Company for Young People, the nation's fourth-largest professional children's theater, is headquartered in a magnificent former movie theater, now called the Rose. The theater was recently restored to its 1920s grandeur with the assistance of major donations from Rose Blumkin, founder of the Nebraska Furniture Mart, and Warren Buffett.

The Rose is the second of Omaha's great old movie theaters to showcase the live arts. The Orpheum Theater, which was restored a generation ago, is the home of the Omaha Symphony and Opera Omaha and presents concerts and plays by national touring companies. Stars such as folk singer Judy Collins have praised both the theater's beauty and its perfect acoustics.

Sports and Outdoor Recreation: AAA Fun

For many Omahans, the local sports highlight of the year occurs in June, when the NCAA College World Series comes to town. In college baseball, the rallying cry for half a century has been "On to Omaha." Each year, Omaha hosts about a quarter of a million people from all over the country, for whom the city throws quite a party. Filling Rosenblatt Stadium throughout the week-long tournament, crowds of local fans join fervent rooters who follow their teams to Omaha. National television gives broad exposure to both the games and their host city.

But the College World Series is just the start of what Omaha offers in sports and recreation. Omaha is a year-round sports community with something for nearly every taste, nearly every season.

Unquestionably, Omaha is in the high minor leagues of professional sports. It's no longer apologizing for that, as cities many times its size bid farewell to sports teams. That's not likely to happen in Omaha. When the AAA Omaha Royals were up for sale, Buffett, Kiewit's chairman, Walter Scott, and Union Pacific Railroad purchased the team to ensure that it would remain in the city. Omaha sports fans will attest that AAA baseball is very good. They simply see future superstars like George Brett a few seasons earlier than the rest of the country.

Basketball fans have plenty to cheer about, too. Omaha is home to the Continental Basketball Association's Omaha Racers, many of whom are heading to or coming from the NBA.

Omaha is a rabid hockey town. The U.S. Hockey League's Omaha Lancers is one of the nation's top youth professional teams and a former U.S. Hockey League play-off champion. Games at the Ak-Sar-Ben Coliseum are always sold out.

While Omaha is unlikely to ever have an NFL team, one of the nation's best college teams is just an hour away—the University of Nebraska Cornhuskers, national champions in 1994 and 1995. The Cornhuskers also enjoy another distinction that doesn't receive the attention it should. They have produced by far the most Academic All-Americans of any major football program.

For more than 30 years, the state of Nebraska has had a virulent case of Big Red Fever, which reaches epidemic proportions in Omaha. Omahans who can't get tickets to games in the stadium, which has been selling out for years, can follow the action on radio. Many local stores even broadcast the games.

Championship-caliber volleyball and gymnastics also draw fans to Lincoln. And the 1995 women's volleyball team, including two Omaha-area players, won the NCAA championship. Nebraska's men's gymnastics team also has won national championships. The stars who helped the University of Nebraska gain fame in the sport included Omaha native Jim Hartung, an Olympic gold medalist.

Omahans aren't content to just watch others play. The city offers a multitude of chances for everyone to keep fit and have fun. Omaha prides itself on being the nation's softball capital. Thousands of Omahans and their families spend countless summer evenings at the city's

many ball diamonds. Afterwards, they're likely to adjourn for pizza at one of many neighborhood sports restaurants, which attract people of all ages.

Sand volleyball has also grown increasingly popular, and more courts are opening all the time.

Omaha has a tradition of having strong organized sports programs for its young people, and they contribute to the city's excellent quality of life. Hall of Fame pitcher Bob Gibson, for example, credits his early development as an athlete to his participation in YMCA programs in North Omaha, where several other major league sports stars got their start.

No Omahan wants to live far from green space—and no one has to. Eventually, it will be possible to ride a bike on a continuous trail from northwest Omaha to Bellevue, at the south edge of the metropolitan area. In the meantime, Omahans with a hunger for the outdoors are easily satisfied by the city's extensive park system.

The city's original design called for a series of parks connected by boulevards. Today, the abundance of parks and trees soften the urban landscape and give Omaha an open, uncrowded feeling.

Many Omahans don't even need to go to a park to walk in a parklike setting—they live in one. Such areas can be found citywide. Most newer housing developments have trails that connect the green spaces to the next subdivision. And one upscale suburban development, Tomlinson Woods, is a former arboretum.

Such easy access to nature characterizes life in Omaha year-round. For example, cross-country skiers find Omaha a winter paradise. One lawyer routinely spends his noon hours on skis in a park just minutes from his office. Dodge Park, in far north Omaha, could be in a forest anywhere in the U.S.; it's within the city limits but provides a genuine escape to nature.

Other getaways are minutes from work or home, such as the ravine in centrally located Elmwood Park. Also in the metropolitan area are manmade lakes, which have increased the popularity of boating and other water sports.

Undoubtedly, Omaha's largest, most famous indoor-outdoor attraction is the Henry Doorly Zoo, which makes every list of the nation's top zoos and is especially known for its breeding program. No visit to Omaha is complete without a stop at its breathtaking indoor rain forest, exciting aquarium, and other exhibits, including one of the nation's largest collections of white tigers.

Other outdoor attractions are only half an hour's drive from Omaha, including several of Nebraska's largest and most popular state parks. Platte River and Mahoney State Parks both overlook the Platte River and offer extensive hiking, camping, horseback riding, and other recreational opportunities. The Henry Doorly Zoo is planning to build a North American wildlife area near Mahoney State Park, which will offer families a chance to take camera safaris. The SAC Museum also has plans for a major expansion near Mahoney, further enhancing this outstanding recreational facility.

Two Rivers State Recreation Area boasts unique lodging accommodations—10 Union Pacific cabooses converted to cabins. Another state-run park, the Louisville State Recreation Area, is a popular site for camping and water sports. Wildlife lovers especially treasure two of the Omaha area's finest attractions, Fontenelle Forest in Bellevue and the DeSoto National Wildlife Refuge in Iowa.

Omahans are people of the land. They find beauty in open skies, spectacular sunsets, the change of seasons, and the land itself. A typical Omahan craves escape to the outdoors, even in the heat of summer or the cold of winter.

Omahans' love of the land is apparent in many ways but especially in their strong urge to grow things and make their world green. Gardening is a common passion and yard care almost a religion.

Hall of Fame pitcher Bob Gibson credits his early development as an athlete to his participation in YMCA programs in North Omaha, where several other major league sports stars got their start.

DR. LEE SIMMONS

When the London Zoo wanted advice on how to build an aquarium, it called the Henry Doorly Zoo. That's just one example of the respect the zoo's director, Dr. Lee Simmons, receives from his peers. In the 25 years Simmons has been director, the zoo has added a jungle, the Kingdom of the Seas Aquarium, an outdoor aviary, and a cat complex housing white tigers, but that doesn't stop him from dreaming of ways to make the zoo even more spectacular. ◆ "We usually keep about 20 ideas on a pad at one time," says Simmons. "If we hang onto an idea, someone's eyes will light up." ◆ Simmons's confidence is well founded. The zoo, one of the five best in the nation, has spent $60 million to construct new attractions, including the Lied Jungle, which several national organizations have rated as the nation's top zoo exhibit; has a

membership of about 80,000, second only to the zoo in San Diego; and has the largest per capita attendance in the country. Total attendance can easily exceed 1.5 million people in years when a major new exhibit opens. The Henry Doorly Zoo also is recognized internationally for its successful breeding programs for big cats and other species. ◆ Simmons, a native of Tucson, Arizona, who received his veterinary degree from Oklahoma State University, recalls that when he came to Omaha as assistant zoo director in 1966, the zoo was just starting to take shape. But, unlike older zoos that had to adapt their antiquated facilities to display animals in more natural settings, the Doorly Zoo started more or less from scratch, opening one eagerly anticipated exhibit after another year after year. ◆ At the Doorly Zoo, the animals look like they're having almost as much fun as the people. Bears splash each other and visitors in the bear grotto, birds fly comfortably through the massive outdoor aviary, and big cats sun themselves in the grassy confines of the cat complex. ◆ The "Omaha Zoo Railroad," built and maintained with the help of Omaha's "other railroad"–Union Pacific–circles the grounds. ◆ Thanks to indoor exhibits like the Mutual of Omaha Educational Pavilion, the Lied Jungle, and the Kingdom of the Seas Aquarium, the zoo has become a year-round attraction. ◆ Simmons credits much of the zoo's growth to the fact that it is privately operated and to the generosity of Omaha's foundations and corporations. ◆ "This is a unique community," he says. "I don't know any other place where the community supports institutions that it believes in, like the zoo, to the same degree. There's just not any other place that compares with Omaha. We're able to do things here a lot faster and more efficiently and do a lot more with half the money it would take elsewhere." ◆ Simmons says the freedom Omaha offers him to exercise creative leadership has a great deal to do with why he has turned down offers to go elsewhere. ◆ "There would hardly be anyplace in the country where I could have the freedom of action to operate that I do here," he says. ◆ Simmons says he used to say that Henry Doorly Zoo was one of the nation's best kept secrets, but he can't say that anymore. Visitors from zoos all over the world have sought advice on how to build various types of exhibits, he says. ◆ What's in the future for the zoo 5 or 10 years from now? That depends, says Simmons, on whose eyes light up at one of the ideas on his pad!

RETAIL: IT'S FUN TO SHOP AND EAT IN OMAHA

When Berkshire Hathaway stockholders from all over the country come to Omaha for their annual meeting, many of them detour to Borsheim's Fine Jewelry and Gifts for a quick round of shopping. At the elegant store in the Regency shopping complex, they're sure to find a large selection of exquisite merchandise at prices far lower than they would pay for identical items in New York or Beverly Hills.

Omahans who read about the Beautiful People who have visited Borsheim's can't help being slightly amused. For years, they've counted on finding the perfect gift there, always at a discount. Older Omahans remember the crowded store downtown, which preceded today's elegant operation in the Regency complex.

Omaha's retail landscape is dotted with such locally run treasures, in addition to the standard quotient of chain stores and shopping malls. There's business enough for all of them. Omaha is the regional trade center for eastern Nebraska and western Iowa.

The five-county metropolitan area has a total population of over 665,000 people with a total effective buying income of $11 billion. Retail sales are more than $6.2 billion, the bulk of it in Douglas County. More than a million people live within a 50-minute drive of Omaha.

The Omaha market is large enough to ensure shoppers a choice of almost any type of merchandise. Although the major malls are concentrated in West Omaha, there are mini-downtowns scattered throughout the city, making shopping convenient for all residents.

Entrepreneurship is a hallmark of Omaha's retail community. In addition to such unique operations as Borsheim's and the Nebraska Furniture Mart, Omaha is the headquarters of two discount chains, 1/2 Price Stores and Pamida.

Another favorite pastime of Omahans is eating out, and with good reason: the city's restaurants offer numerous cuisines and choices in atmosphere. That wasn't always the case, though. Twenty years ago, people used to joke that Omaha was strictly a steak town with local tastes running to beef, beef, and more beef. The city is still best known for its numerous high-quality steakhouses, but Omahans' tastes in restaurants constantly grows more cosmopolitan. If you've got a craving for sushi, pad thai, or tandoori chicken, you can easily satisfy it in Omaha.

Omaha's variety in ethnic restaurants is apparent from the family-owned establishments from which to choose. The genuine flavor of Omaha today includes Czech dumplings and sauerkraut at the Bohemian Cafe, pasta at the Spaghetti Works, and stuffed grape leaves at the Greek Islands.

If a sweet tooth is your weakness, head straight to the Garden Cafe, which has restaurants scattered throughout Omaha. Founder Ron Popp raided his family's Iowa farm for the recipes for luscious pies, homemade cinnamon rolls, bread puddings, and other treats his customers swoon over.

The Garden Cafe isn't alone in giving Omahans a chance to indulge their taste for traditional midwestern cooking. Grandmother's restaurant is a similar establishment. One of its founders can't give it much attention these days, though. Sen. Bob Kerrey of Omaha is often occupied with other business.

Visitors to Omaha often are struck by another feature of local restaurants: the prices are lower than they are accustomed to for comparable quality. And service is usually prompt and friendly. Omaha's restaurant business is so competitive that owners know they must either please customers or fail. It's no wonder a dinner invitation in Omaha frequently means "Where would you like to go?" not "I'm cooking."

Omahans are people of the land. They find beauty in open skies, spectacular sunsets, the change of seasons, and the land itself.

Christmas at Union Station, held annually at the Western Heritage Museum, revives memories of train travel.

At first glance, a crowd of sweaty softball players relaxing over pizza and beer after a game may seem to have little in common with opera lovers stopping at the Old Market for a leisurely glass of wine and delicate pastries. But both groups exemplify the Omaha lifestyle. Whether your tastes run to the fine arts or down-home sports–or both–you'll find what you want here. The city is large and diverse enough to offer something for almost everyone and compatible people with whom to enjoy any pastime from sandlot volleyball to poetry reading. It's also small enough to make arts, sports, and recreational activities readily accessible and affordable.

It's easy to find out what's going on in Omaha and to get involved in whatever interests you. Your biggest problem won't be finding something to do but finding time to do all you want.

*J*oslyn Art Museum is a community gathering place for the enjoyment of both the visual and performing arts.

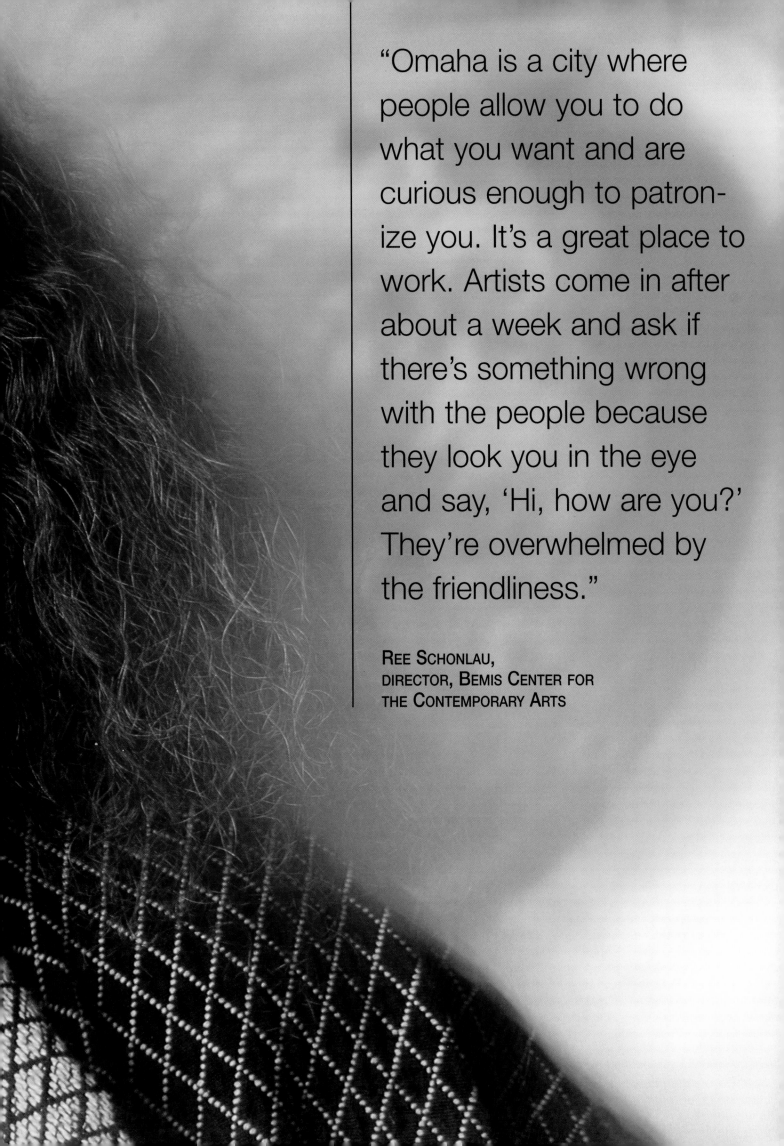

"Omaha is a city where people allow you to do what you want and are curious enough to patronize you. It's a great place to work. Artists come in after about a week and ask if there's something wrong with the people because they look you in the eye and say, 'Hi, how are you?' They're overwhelmed by the friendliness."

REE SCHONLAU,
DIRECTOR, BEMIS CENTER FOR
THE CONTEMPORARY ARTS

Omaha is unusual in its abundance of high-quality entertaining and educational attractions for children, including the city's world-class zoo and the Omaha Children's Museum.

Children are the focus at River City Roundup at the Central Park Mall. Among the attractions are stage coach rides, petting zoos, and canoe and riverboat rides—all for free. Below, Christmas shoppers are drawn to "Dickens in the Market" downtown.

*O*maha newcomers
are often surprised by the
abundance of mature trees
and lush green hills. March
through October is peak
season at the city's 45 public
and private golf courses.

Among Omaha's many attractions is the new salt water aquarium—the largest between Chicago and the West Coast—at the Henry Doorly Zoo. The River City Roundup and rodeo, when everyone dresses western, is another draw for both locals and visitors.

Events like this Mexican festival honor Omaha's broadly diverse ethnic population.

In the Old Market, Omaha's most popular gathering spot, produce is still sold on the street and locally owned shops and restaurants are going strong.

At the Rose, the children's theater is all professional and all enchanting. A regional center for the performing arts, Omaha also draws top touring companies performing Broadway plays.

In love with the out-of-doors, Omahans enjoy time with their families, leisure activities, and hometown events, like the NCAA College World Series.

116

"There is an incredible feeling among the clergy to work together. For the past two and a half years, Temple Israel has had a Catholic-Jewish dialogue, and we are constantly involved in black-Jewish dialogue. There is definitely a realization that scholarship is very important."

ARYEH AZRIEL, RABBI, TEMPLE ISRAEL

The Omaha Lifestyle:
COMPASSIONATE AND COMMITTED

A cold mist fell from the gray December sky, but it didn't deter vacationing Omaha police officer Adam Kyle from his mission–spending the week before Christmas on a billboard above one of Omaha's busiest intersections raising at least $10,000 a day for the Special Olympics. As fellow officers wearing Santa hats solicited donations from holiday shoppers caught in traffic, Kyle yelled his thanks through a megaphone. Kyle says he launched his crusade after participating in the Law Enforcement Torch Run for the Special Olympics for several years.

"I got hooked," Kyle says. "I saw what these children are like. The Special Olympics gives them a chance to develop friendships and opportunities in life."

Throughout his vigil, Kyle, a former paratrooper, slept in a hut equipped with a heater, water, a cot, a sleeping bag, a hanging light, and a portable toilet. Individuals and businesses covered all his expenses. Restaurants provided meals.

"That tells you something about this community," he says.

Indeed it does. Kyle exemplifies the concern for others Omaha residents mention as one of the reasons the quality of life in Omaha is exceptional. Among the other reasons are its strong neighborhoods, the outstanding educational system, and the spirit of generosity, manifested in Omahans' willingness to participate in charitable and religious activities. In Omaha, people personally identify with their community.

"Omahans have a strong sense of taking care of their own," says Barbara Haggart, executive vice president of the Greater Omaha Chamber of Commerce. "They feel a personal responsibility for their city, a sense of ownership."

For many Omahans, this "sense of ownership" begins with their neighborhoods and their vision of the good life.

120

O*mahans participate in outdoor activities throughout the year, but nothing beats the fun of summertime water sports on area lakes and the Missouri River.*

HOUSING AND NEIGHBORHOODS: SOMETHING FOR EVERYONE

To capture Omaha's quality of life, you must experience the diversity of its neighborhoods. Fasten your seatbelt; the tour is about to begin.

You will start your tour by the Missouri River in one of Omaha's oldest "new" neighborhoods, downtown. You will then explore the charming older neighborhoods just to the west before heading to the traditional ethnic areas of South Omaha, the African-American area of North Omaha, and finally the newer neighborhoods to the west. All contribute to the vibrant mix that is Omaha today—a city with something for everyone.

Tours of Omaha should begin near the Missouri River, because that's where the city took root. For generations, the neighborhoods near here have been ethnic enclaves of small but well-kept homes. Today, that's changing. Spurred by the success of the Old Market and the massive redevelopment of the riverfront, downtown is becoming an upscale urban enclave.

On South 13th Street, within a mile of the Old Market, stands a symbol of the new Omaha: a modern condominium development that rises high on a bluff with a spectacular view of the Missouri River and the downtown skyline. The compact, well-equipped units make ideal housing for singles and couples without children. Their impact on this

traditional, modest Czech neighborhood is obvious. The 13th Street retail district now includes antique shops and trendy pasta restaurants, as well as longtime businesses such as the colorful Bohemian Cafe.

There's evidence of new life throughout downtown. Former warehouses and the upper floors of office buildings and stores are being converted into luxury apartments and condos. The Old Market vicinity is expanding in all directions, apparent in the new gourmet restaurants, sidewalk cafes, shops, coffeehouses, bars, and art galleries opening on the fringes of the district.

Many of the people walking their dogs on the Eugene Leahy Mall or playing frisbee in Heartland of America Park live downtown. They like the casual, friendly atmosphere and the accessibility to centers of art and entertainment. Corporate jobs are a short walk away. Artists find loft apartments in former warehouses ideal places in which to live and work. No discount stores or suburban supermarkets intrude on the area's quaint brick streets, but there's a grocery store—solid evidence that residential living has taken root in Omaha's urban core.

As you head west on your tour, you gradually move through rings of development. And by the time the headquarters of Mutual of Omaha looms on the horizon, you have left Omaha's urban core and entered an area rich in history and architecture. To the north and south are the classic neighborhoods in which Omaha's wealthy developers lived their vision of the good life at the turn of the century.

At the top of Walnut Hill stands a symbol of this era, the magnificent twin towers of St. Cecilia's Cathedral. This lovely Spanish-style church is a treasure trove of original art and stained-glass windows. It speaks to an age when Omahans dreamed big dreams, so big that they dared to locate one of the nation's 10 largest cathedrals in what was then almost open countryside. Appropriately, the building faced west—the direction in which the city would grow.

Wealthy Catholics built stately mansions within blocks of the church, and some of Omaha's loveliest old homes still line historic 38th Street. In the quiet of an early morning, it's easy to imagine carriages pulling up to these well-preserved houses and especially to nearby landmarks like Joslyn Castle, home of the family that endowed Joslyn Art Museum. This stone castle surrounded by a Victorian garden is now owned by the Nebraska State Historical Society. Omaha brides seeking the perfect setting for a romantic reception often choose this elegant reminder of a more gracious era.

Today, the cathedral remains the heart of a lively neighborhood community. Its nationally recognized grade school is filled with more than 500 children in their red-plaid uniforms, many from homes within walking distance. The Cathedral Arts Project draws thousands of Omahans to its annual mid-winter Flower Festival and spectacular free concerts, like one that re-created the Vienna of Mozart's era.

Past and present mingle graciously in neighborhoods like Cathedral and the old Gold Coast to the immediate south. Younger families are attracted by homes with solid oak floors, beamed ceilings, and stained-glass windows, at prices they can afford. Many of these homes are being lovingly restored to their earlier splendor. One Victorian home has even been repainted in its original purple colors.

If the Cathedral area and nearby Dundee recall great dreams, South Omaha's historic ethnic neighborhoods recall another, equally magnificent vision: the dream of America. If Omaha had an Ellis Island, it would be South Omaha. To this large and varied area came thousands of people from every country of Europe. They built simple homes, not mansions, and neighborhood churches, not cathedrals, but they too achieved their dream of starting new lives in a better country. Walking these streets, one is reminded of the people who contributed their blood and sweat to building America.

For many immigrants, life centered on the packinghouses—once a massive area of cattle, hog pens, and slaughterhouses. The stockyards weren't scenic, but they offered employment to thousands of unskilled workers. There was no question what South Omahans meant when they talked about "the smell of money." The immigrants who labored in the heat and odor of those stockyards believed fervently in the value of work to build a better life—an ethic that still dominates Omaha today.

A portion of the stockyards and a few meatpacking plants remain, but a shopping center has been constructed in what was once the heart of the district. The high-rise Livestock Exchange Building is a reminder of the economic power this area and industry once exerted.

Yet even with the decline of the packinghouses, South Omaha remains a viable residential area of modest homes. Today's South Omaha has an increasingly Hispanic flavor along the 24th Street business district, where Mexican grocery stores and video stores have become prominent. Signs in Spanish are common. And, increasingly, there's an Asian accent. Next door to Duffy's Tavern, where both John and Robert Kennedy and other Democratic presidential hopefuls visited, sits a Thai restaurant. In South Omaha, the groups dreaming of a better life in America change, but the vision remains.

In North Omaha, the vision retains an African-American accent. While many African-Americans have settled throughout Omaha, many remain in their traditional neighborhoods in North Omaha. The area includes some of Omaha's most interesting churches, such as St. John's AME, an architectural landmark, and Salem Baptist Church, noted for its gospel choir, which made a gold record, and a girl's drill team that performs at numerous parades. The Great Plains Black Museum contains an outstanding collection of historical photos and other information about the contributions of African-Americans to the settling of the West and the building of Omaha. This area also has produced some of the nation's finest athletes, such as Baseball Hall of Fame pitcher Bob Gibson and Football Hall of Fame running back Gale Sayers.

Redevelopment efforts have been undertaken to combat physical and economic deterioration in North Omaha. New home construction and renovation have occurred in recent years, as well as the establishment of enterprise zones to provide employers with incentives to create jobs.

Some parts of North Omaha, such as Benson and Florence, were once independent communities, and they retain a small-town flavor and many of their own traditions. Florence is home to the historic Mormon Cemetery, where Mormon pioneers who died during a harsh early winter are buried. The cemetery and a Mormon genealogical center draw numerous visitors.

Not far from this historic site is a reminder of Omaha's longstanding military importance, Fort Omaha. Today it's a campus for Metropolitan Community College, but during the 1870s and 1880s, it was the headquarters for the army's military operations on the Great Plains. The fort's greatest historic significance, however, is in the area of human rights. Here Chief Standing Bear was tried and, for the first time, a Native American's rights were upheld. The restored home of Gen. George Crook, army commander during the trial of Standing Bear, is a monument to that era.

A drive through North Omaha takes a traveler back to the river. Gracious living in today's far north Omaha includes abundant outdoor recreation in the rugged hills overlooking the Missouri. Fine homes are nestled among the trees. Horse lovers, especially, are drawn to the area's scenic acreage. A large city park with a marina offers river activities. Neale Woods, owned by Fontenelle Forest Nature Center, protects a section of this land from depredation.

In contrast with the serenity of the hills of far north Omaha, West Omaha is constantly growing and changing. For most of today's Omahans, the good life means a home in one of the areas west of 72nd Street built since the 1950s.

About 85 percent of Omaha families are homeowners, higher than the national average. A national survey ranked Omaha at about the middle of the nation's cities in affordability, but it is actually even more affordable than those numbers suggest, since construction of numerous homes costing over $200,000 has raised the average price of a new home. According to realtors, middle-class families with children can easily purchase a modern home.

Some of the growth in luxury housing has been fueled by newcomers from more expensive markets who are able to reinvest in much larger and higher-quality homes than they previously owned. Affluent newcomers, especially, discover that their vision of the good life is much easier to attain in Omaha.

Many new neighborhoods boast extensive recreational facilities. One luxury residential area, for example, is built around a golf course designed by Tom Siekmann, a member of the PGA tour. Other developments surround Zorinsky Lake, Cunningham Lake, and Standing Bear Lake. In Candlewood, built around a manmade lake, residents can enjoy swimming, canoeing, paddleboating, and ice skating right outside their homes. Tennis courts, swimming pools, health spas and fitness centers, bicycle trails, parks, and other amenities are common in many areas built for today's active Omaha families.

Many of Omaha's newest and best employers are located in western areas, so that suburban residents can also enjoy the benefits of working close to home. These affluent new areas also have shopping malls and a variety of restaurants. West Omaha is definitely Omaha on the move.

While one of Omaha's greatest strengths is that its growth hasn't been stunted by restrictive annexation laws, the metropolitan area includes a number of rapidly growing suburban communities in Sarpy County, just south of Omaha. Omaha's "sister city," Council Bluffs, Iowa, retains its distinctive, historic character, while outlying communities on both the Nebraska and Iowa sides of the river offer traditional small-town ambience.

Whatever your vision—from contemporary urban to rural—Omaha has something to satisfy it. An excellent quality of life is possible for people in a wide range of income brackets and with a variety of lifestyles. Much of that has to do with the city's excellent schools, which are available to children in Omaha no matter where they live.

In Omaha you're never far from the city and never far from the country. The average rush-hour commute is still less than 20 minutes.

THOMAS HARVEY

In most cities, few jobs are more difficult than heading an inner-city high school. There have even been movies about heroic principals who succeeded. So why isn't Thomas Harvey, longtime principal of North High School in Omaha's urban core, waiting for the cameras? It's simple, he says. He's too busy having fun. ✦ "I love it," says Harvey. "It's fun to get up and go to work." ✦ Under Harvey's direction, North has been transformed from a school that students used to avoid attending into a math/technology magnet that *Redbook* magazine has cited as one of the seven most innovative high schools in the nation. ✦ During Harvey's tenure, North has more than doubled its enrollment, to more than 2,000 students, making it the city's largest high school; undergone a $20 million renovation of its 70-year-old building; created "classrooms of

the future" in English and geography, featuring fully networked computer access and instruction; developed advanced programs in math, technology, and engineering; and strengthened its ties with corporate Adopt-a-School partners, such as Union Pacific and Mutual of Omaha, resulting in scholarships and internships for graduates. ✦ A native of Louisiana, Harvey was recruited by the Omaha Public Schools from Grambling College as a junior high school football coach. He coached and taught physical education before moving into administration. He has nothing but praise for his adopted home. ✦ "I think Omaha is a tremendous city to raise a family in. It's one of the most generous cities I've ever seen. If there's a program or something that needs funding, you'll find support. People are unbelievable." ✦ Harvey says he's been impressed with the contrast

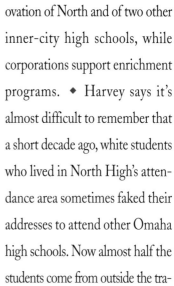

he sees between Omaha and the other cities he visits as a team member for the U.S. Department of Education's Excellence in Education program. ✦ "I travel to many districts in the western states. In comparing schools to those we have here, there's no comparison in areas of academic excellence." ✦ Harvey says that he's especially pleased with Omaha's mixture of private and public support for public education. A major bond issue financed the renovation of North and of two other inner-city high schools, while corporations support enrichment programs. ✦ Harvey says it's almost difficult to remember that a short decade ago, white students who lived in North High's attendance area sometimes faked their addresses to attend other Omaha high schools. Now almost half the students come from outside the traditional attendance area, and students from other districts have enrolled under a state-sponsored transfer program. North students have earned recognition in math and computer science, as well as in such non-high-tech fields as geography and journalism. ✦ Newspaper stories about North routinely feature its award-winning teachers, teams contesting for state championships, and students who have won awards. Recruiting students for the magnet program virtually takes care of itself. ✦ But Harvey isn't resting on his laurels. He talks about expanding services, increasing community involvement, and making sure that the highly computerized school (which has 600 computers) maintains its excellence. ✦ "I love every bit of it," says Harvey. ✦ The movie on Harvey and North High will just have to wait until he has time for it.

EDUCATION: NO SUCH THING AS A BAD SCHOOL

When asked why their quality of life is so high, Omahans often mention the quality of education. Businesses considering the Omaha area cite the schools as a major asset of the city. And the excellent education residents have received accounts for much of the area's reputation for having such a productive workforce.

Omaha places enormous importance on education. It simultaneously supports one of the nation's best urban school districts and one of its most outstanding private school systems. For an insight into the quality of education in Omaha, one must know something about the Omaha Public Schools' acclaimed magnet program.

Each year, about 3,000 Omaha families nervously wait to hear the results of a lottery, but the stakes have nothing to do with money. Will their children be among the lucky 500 selected for the Omaha Public Schools' (OPS) magnet program? Will they get the advantages of the enriched science curriculum at the King Science Center or the special computer and math instruction at MacMillan Junior High School? Never mind that these schools are located in old neighborhoods in Omaha's central city and that their programs were developed to further racial integration. What counts is excellence. Admission to all OPS magnet schools is so avidly sought that students are selected in the only fair way—in a random, citywide drawing.

Traditional values are evident in Omaha schools, where high school bands, debate tournaments, and science fairs are still popular.

The magnet schools have achieved their goal of promoting integration and in the process have helped foster excellence and national recognition for the Omaha Public Schools' approach to education. Former President George Bush selected Omaha as one of two cities nationally to kick off his America 2000 plan. Since the founding of Omaha 2000, civic leaders and school officials in cooperation with the Greater Omaha Chamber of Commerce have worked even harder to foster educational excellence.

Omaha's educational achievements are notable. Average graduation rates are 90 percent or higher in public school districts, a figure local leaders still find unacceptably low. They're pushing for as close to 100 percent as possible.

ACT and SAT scores of Omaha students consistently rank among the highest nationally. Each year, top Omaha high school graduates—many from inner-city public schools—are admitted to the nation's best colleges and universities, including Ivy League institutions. Some are admitted as sophomores because of the advanced placement courses they have taken. Recruiters say they like receiving applications from Omaha because the students are so well prepared. And to encourage educational achievement, each year the *Omaha World-Herald* selects an Academic All-State Team to give top students recognition comparable to that lavished on top athletes.

Terrel Bell, former secretary of education, says that Omaha has "perhaps the best urban school district in the country." NBC News and national magazines such as *Newsweek* have cited the Omaha school system as an example of the excellence that is possible in an urban district.

Part of the school system's strength is its size and the diversity of the neighborhoods it serves. Unlike many urban districts that are confined to low-income neighborhoods, OPS serves more than 40,000 students, from the Missouri River to Boys Town, in far west Omaha, south into Sarpy County. This geographic diversity ensures the racial and economic mix of students that makes meaningful integration possible.

For more than 20 years, the district has operated an integration program that relies heavily on voluntarism and allows all students a choice of at least two high schools. Academic and transportation incentives encourage enrollment in inner-city schools, such as North High School. North even attracts transfer students from suburban districts to its technology magnet program. Unlike urban districts that are shrinking, OPS continues to grow, building new schools in outlying neighborhoods.

The good news about public education in Omaha isn't restricted to OPS. The metropolitan area contains about a dozen public school districts, including the Millard Public Schools and Westside Community Schools, both located within city limits. Both have been cited for excellence and emphasize community involvement and educational innovation. Omahans like to brag that there's no such thing as a bad school district in the area.

One of the seemingly ironic aspects of Omaha's educational environment is that its excellent public schools are matched by an extensive, high-quality network of private schools that enroll about 15,000 students. Private school choices include Catholic, Lutheran, and Christian schools, a Jewish day school, and the nondenominational Brownell Talbott.

The vast majority of the private schools are Catholic, reflecting more than a century of commitment to high-quality education by the Archdiocese of Omaha. If the archdiocese were a school district, it would be among the five largest in Nebraska.

Residents of larger cities are sometimes amazed at Omaha's extensive Catholic school system. Omaha has eight Catholic high schools and more than 25 grade schools, and new grade schools are opening at suburban parishes. The Catholic high schools include both co-educational and single-sex institutions.

"I wish we had the choices you do," says a Denver resident who sends her children to Catholic schools.

Christian schools are growing rapidly. There are two Christian high schools, and several Christian elementary schools have waiting lists. Nebraska state law also permits home schooling, an option growing numbers of parents are selecting.

Since 1987, U.S. News & World Report *has rated Creighton University "one of the top colleges in the country."*

Regardless of what educational system they choose, Omaha parents are confident that their children are being well prepared for the future. Omaha businesses are actively involved in ensuring that this is the case. More than 250 businesses and service clubs participate in Adopt-a-School programs in various metro-area districts. Each year, Warren Buffett presents $10,000 awards to outstanding teachers in OPS. Individual businesses sponsor programs that send workers into the schools or bring students and educators into contact with industry. Special projects at schools readily get help from the community.

Omaha businesses recognize that the city's children are its economic future, and they are willing to invest time and talent as well as money in preparing them to be the next highly productive generation of Omaha workers.

Nebraskans invest heavily not only in elementary and secondary education but in higher education. Nebraska ranks in the top five states in per capita spending for post-secondary education and first in per capita spending for research. This willingness to invest in higher education is reflected in the higher education opportunities available in the Omaha area.

The metropolitan area contains nine colleges and universities with a combined enrollment of over 43,000. These include the University of Nebraska at Omaha (UNO), Creighton University, the University of Nebraska Medical Center (UNMC), Metropolitan Community College, Bellevue University, the College of Saint Mary, Grace University, Dana College at Blair, Nebraska, and Iowa Western Community College in Council Bluffs.

U.S. News & World Report has recognized Creighton as one of the "nation's best colleges" and UNMC as one of the top 20 comprehensive medical schools in the country.

UNO has a strong urban mission, which gives it a vital role in the city. In addition to making higher education available at an affordable price to thousands of Omahans who work full time, its Center for Applied Urban Research assists nonprofit and government entities with their research needs. UNO's numerous other strengths include a business college that is heavily involved with the Omaha business community and a doctoral program in education and public administration and a graduate program in social work. Fine arts play a prominent role on campus, and numerous community groups use the university's excellent theater. UNO students and faculty are even helping to excavate the lost city of Bethsaida in Israel.

Metropolitan Community College is a growing force in higher education in Omaha. It has a rich and varied program of both credit and noncredit courses, which are offered at convenient times at its four campuses. Students can take both entry-level college courses and two-year courses to help prepare them for jobs. Metro puts higher education within the reach of thousands of working Omahans.

From preschool to graduate school, education is big business in Omaha and a responsibility the community takes very seriously.

The University of Nebraska at Omaha provides a high-quality education to more than 15,000 traditional and nontraditional students.

Omaha is a generous community, and its generosity is a key element of the quality of life. Whether it manifests itself in the police officer who spends a week in the cold collecting for the Special Olympics or in individuals who raise money for the Red Cross's local tornado relief, Omahans have a history of helping those in need.

The generosity is expressed in both large and small ways. Jitu Suthar, a newcomer to Omaha, persuaded his boss at Shamrock Computer Resources Ltd. to ask employees to give to the *World-Herald*'s Good Fellows Christmas drive because he remembers the help he received from an elderly couple when he and his wife and two children were stranded on the highway while moving from Chicago.

"The couple opened its arms to us," Suthar says. "They called the police and drove us to our hotel. . . . People treat you like people here. It's a friendly place."

The *Chronicle of Philanthropy* ranks Omaha as one of the nation's 10 most generous cities in per capita and foundation giving to major charities. Omaha is home to one of the nation's 100 largest charitable foundations, Peter Kiewit Foundation, and many organizations have benefited from the Lied Foundation, which was founded by a former Omahan who donated his fortunes made from Las Vegas real estate. Warren Buffett has announced plans to leave his multibillion-dollar fortune to a foundation.

A United Way of the Midlands social service agency directory lists about 400 charitable groups. There isn't a major cause from AIDS to the Henry Doorly Zoo that Omahans don't support.

Omahans also take pride in the pioneering contributions they make in the area of human services. Best known is Boys Town, which started on what is still its main campus just west of Omaha and is now one of the nation's leading child care institutions, with homes for troubled children of both sexes in about 20 cities. It has changed a lot since the days when Spencer Tracy and Mickey Rooney immortalized Father Flanagan in the classic film, but Boys Town's spirit of helping neglected children remains the same.

Other Omaha programs that have gained national attention include Mad Dads, begun by Eddie Staton, which gets African-American men involved in combatting youth problems in the inner city. Omaha also was a pioneer in enabling mentally retarded citizens to leave institutions and live more productive lives in the community. The late Dr. Frank Menolascino of the Nebraska Psychiatric Institute gained international recognition for his pioneering efforts on behalf of the retarded.

Omaha continues to produce inspiring individuals like Joe Edmonson, an African-American quadriplegic who runs a wrestling program that teaches far more than just sports skills. Eli Dominguez, a junior high wrestler, says he benefits greatly from his involvement. "The biggest thing we learn is not giving up and discipline," says Dominguez. "Joe says that if you don't have above-average grades, you're off his team. He gives us lots of discipline and keeps us in line."

Edmonson enjoys support from powerful business leaders like Herman Cain, CEO of Godfather's Pizza, a talented singer who has given concerts to raise funds for the program. Cain got involved after a teen-aged janitor nicknamed Freight Train urged him to get acquainted with Edmonson.

Omahans strongly support programs that promote self-sufficiency, such as the

Employability Program at inner-city Sacred Heart School. From kindergarten on, children from disadvantaged homes begin exploring careers and preparing to succeed in them.

Two successful Omaha programs combine job training with meeting housing needs. With the strong support of Lozier Corporation and use of a manufacturing facility donated by Lozier, the Omaha Housing Authority teaches public housing residents how to fabricate building supplies.

Another grassroots housing program, Holy Name Housing, trains area residents in home-building skills by renovating neighborhood houses. The program began when the men's club of an inner-city Catholic church refurbished a neighborhood house and decided to keep the effort going. The renovated homes are sold to families at a reasonable cost.

"Holy Name Housing has kind of lifted up the entire area," says Tom LaHood, a long-time neighborhood and parish leader. "Now it's expanding into building new homes on vacant lots owned by the city."

The pragmatism Omahans show in human services is, to some extent, reflected in the city's religious community, which is notable for its absence of theological conflict and for its strong commitment to human service work. Omaha has more than 450 churches, temples, synagogues, and other houses of worship of 66 different faiths. All major world religions are represented. At least one-third of Omahans are Roman Catholics. Other major groups include United Methodists and Lutherans. But numbers alone do not fully reflect the city's religious climate and heritage. The number of Episcopalians, for example, is relatively modest, but they are very active. Trinity Episcopal Cathedral in downtown Omaha is the city's oldest continuous congregation and still holds services in a historic building with Tiffany stained-glass windows. For all its beauty, the cathedral is too small to hold the large group who attends the installation of a new bishop of Nebraska. The last two such installations have been held at St. Cecilia's Catholic Cathedral.

Omaha's 6,500-member Jewish community worships at four synagogues, including Temple Israel, another of Omaha's pioneer congregations. Omaha native Philip Klutznick, a former U.S. secretary of commerce, served as president of the World Jewish Congress. He also endowed a chair of Jewish civilization at his alma mater, Jesuit-run Creighton University.

Klutznick is just one of many Omaha Jewish leaders with strong ties to Creighton. One of the first editors of the university's student newspaper was Milton Abrahams, founder of the Abrahams, Kaslow & Cassman law firm. The university's first major capital drive during the presidency of the Rev. Carl Reinert, S.J., was led by Morris Jacobs, a founder of the advertising agency Bozell Worldwide, Inc. Jacobs had initially refused Reinert's request to head up the campaign, but Reinert, a remarkably forceful and persuasive man credited with almost rebuilding

*S*t. Wenceslaus Church, *in suburban west Omaha, originated in an inner-city neighborhood of Czech immigrants.*

Creighton after World War II, said he would pray until Jacobs accepted. Later that evening, Jacobs could no longer stand the thought of disappointing Reinert.

"Get off your knees, Father," he is reported to have told Reinert. "I'll lead your drive."

Like Jacobs, many Omahans are involved in volunteer work. Habitat for Humanity draws representatives of many religious traditions. In one recent partnership, a suburban Protestant church paired up with a Jewish congregation and an African-American church to build a home for a needy family. That's fairly typical. Catholics and Jews often head the Salvation Army's annual Christmas campaign, and members of congregations of all faiths work together at homeless shelters.

Omahans of many backgrounds celebrate their religious heritage. Church festivals offer thousands of people a chance to enjoy the Italian, Polish, Mexican, Croatian, Czech, and Greek cultures. There are also opportunities to pursue one's religious heritage through museum exhibits and interfaith dialogues.

Non-English-speaking Omahans and non-Christians find increasing numbers of opportunities to worship in Omaha. Some Catholic parishes offer masses in Polish, Spanish, and Vietnamese. There's a Chinese Christian Church and a Korean Assembly of God Church, as well as several Spanish-speaking Protestant churches. Omaha congregations include a Hindu temple, an Islamic Center, and a Zen Center. Ba'hai, Jehovah's Witnesses, Seventh Day Adventist, and other denominations are represented in the city, as well as nondenominational Christian congregations. There's also a church that ministers to Omaha's gay community.

Omahans tend to take their religious beliefs seriously, but they generally concede that same right to their neighbors. In Omaha, tolerance for diversity is a major part of the quality of life.

About 85 percent of Omaha families are homeowners, higher than the national average. Middle-class families with children can easily purchase a modern home.

Omaha: A City of Surprises

When people first think about coming to Omaha, they may be reluctant because they know nothing about it. After they've experienced Omaha's quality of life, they're reluctant to leave. That's Omaha in a nutshell.

Most people in Omaha aren't just passing through. This is where they are committed to living and raising their families. They feel a sense of identity with the city and invest in making it a better community. Omaha is a city that works because its leaders and people won't tolerate anything else.

The good life in Omaha takes in everything from its sophisticated, technology-based economy to its active cultural community. It includes the midwestern warmth and work ethic of Omaha's people and their commitment to providing their children with an excellent education. High-tech/high-touch. Omahans could not imagine life without either one.

As it looks with optimism to the coming century, Omaha is indeed a city of surprises, even to those who know it well.

People who want to buy the Big "O" are drawn to locally owned establishments, like MJ Java.

Although Omaha was one of the first cities to be entirely linked with fiber-optic loops, Omahans still maintain strong "old-fashioned" links to nature, their families, and their friends and a deep sense of spirituality.

"We work in crime prevention. The Police Department has been very supportive. In the past year, we've started 150 neighborhood watch groups. We see a snowball effect. The key is education and empowering people to do something on their own block."

JUDY JOHNS,
CO-FOUNDER, OMAHA NEIGHBORHOOD
COURAGE CITYWIDE

Newcomers are always
amazed at Omaha's wide
variety of attractive neighborhoods, both established
and new, that are safe, have
good schools, and offer a
warm sense of community.

138

*M*emorial Park, in the
heart of the city, has great
hills for sledding.

H*elping one another is what Omahans do best, making Omaha a very "hands-on" community.*

Volunteers help paint houses in an annual paint-a-thon.

O*mahans like to take part in and watch area sporting events. Kids grow up feeling that if they want to participate, there will be opportunities to do so.*

If someone had a great idea for a store, Sam Mercer and his family invited him to try it out in their turn-of-the-century buildings, paying what rent he could. From this simple formula was born the Old Market, one of the city's most popular attractions.

O*maha's growth was fueled by large influxes of immigrants, many from eastern Europe. Today, that ethnic heritage adds color and character to the city.*

The area's distinct seasons give Omahans a feeling of renewal four times a year as they change what they wear, what they eat, what they do for entertainment, and even what they read.

"Omaha is a great place for people and families. Its citizens believe in the future and plan for growth, by investing in both the infrastructure and the education of our youth. Entrepreneurial pioneers came to the Great Plains with ideas and dreams. They established new companies, many of which grew into international corporations and spawned new companies. Omaha is a place where people and businesses can still achieve their goals and dreams."

C. R. "Bob" Bell, president,
Greater Omaha Chamber of Commerce

Enterprise

GREATER OMAHA CHAMBER OF COMMERCE

A dynamic community that has experienced five decades of continuous growth. A national model for innovation in education. Working partnerships between business, government, educational institutions, and utilities. It's a foundation for success. Whether you're an individual, a start-up business, or a large company, whether you're already in Omaha or thinking of moving here, Omaha not only allows you to succeed, it helps you succeed. It's a city that loves winners and a city that wants to be number one. It's a city that supports individuals, companies, and organizations that have those same goals.

How does this happen? Newcomers repeatedly tell the Greater Omaha Chamber of Commerce that they are impressed by the friendly and supportive atmosphere. They are amazed by the willingness of people to share information, to offer help, to steer them in the right direction, even to help them get there. In Omaha you have access to elected representatives as well as to top business leaders. They all want to help remove barriers to your ability to sell your product or service and to grow your company. The Chamber calls it "Omaha: Access Success." It sets Omaha apart from other cities, and

it can make a difference in the lives of people and in the future of a business.

At the Greater Omaha Chamber of Commerce, an outstanding staff of professionals make up a team that historically has been recognized as one of the most effective among chambers in the country. The staff is dedicated to ensuring the success of businesses. There's a good reason it is so committed: Omaha is a city where commerce is the driving force. As a result, the Chamber is looked to as a leader in the collective efforts of business to ensure that the climate continues to allow businesses to succeed.

The headquarters of the Greater Omaha Chamber of Commerce, downtown, provides a front door for visitors and a meeting place for business people.

Omaha was founded and grew up as a center of trade, fueling the development of the western United States. As such, Omaha has traditionally had a wide range of businesses that serve a regional central U.S. market. In every era, the city's transportation and communications infrastructure was "state of the art," designed to facilitate the exchanges of goods and services. Throughout Omaha's history, the Chamber played an important role in making this happen.

The Omaha Commercial Club, later renamed the Greater Omaha Chamber of Commerce, was established in 1893. Initial efforts by the Chamber focused on ensuring that rail transport rates were competitive, but the focus rapidly expanded into key public issues of the time, from government reorganization to education to downtown redevelopment. A crowning achievement in the early years was the Trans-Mississippi and International Exposition, held in Omaha in 1898. It drew more than 2.5 million people.

Other early efforts by the Chamber led to the establishment of Ak-Sar-Ben, to help promote Omaha's image, and to the establishment of "Community Chest," a central collection for Omaha charities. The Chamber led the city's efforts to promote expanded transportation services, public safety, and the support of bond issues, pro-business legislation, and other efforts to make Omaha a better place for business and for people.

In the heart of the nation's largest agricultural region, Omaha played a key role in the development of that industry. The Chamber led in early efforts to establish a Grain Exchange in 1904 and the Omaha Hay Exchange in 1916. Omaha businesses market, finance, and

Heartland of America Park, on the Missouri River, features a fountain that rises 305 feet. Its light-and-motion display makes it a popular gathering place on summer nights.

manufacture inputs and equipment, test soils and vaccines, transport and process everything from raw commodities to frozen meals. The need for a sophisticated infrastructure for this global industry led the Chamber to press for advances at every level, from river navigation to international trade.

The Chamber also led efforts by the city to annex nearby communities, including state legislation that made annexation easier and "get-out-the-vote" campaigns to assure its passage. This aggressive annexation policy resulted in a city that is not strangled by surrounding communities with separate governments. The working partnership between Omaha's public sector and its businesses devel-

oped early and is today one of the strengths in attracting new businesses to the area. Today, the Chamber acts as the coordinator of a wide variety of "players" who work as a team to ensure that Omaha's business climate remains robust.

The Chamber's history mirrors Omaha's history because Omaha is a city of business. Today, the Greater Omaha Chamber of Commerce is leading efforts whose foundations go back to its early days. Omaha has seen its small entrepreneurial businesses become worldwide corporations. There is an understanding that the city's primary growth has come from the expansion of its home-based businesses and corporations. As a result, the Chamber consistently focuses on responding to the

needs, concerns, and dreams of Omaha-area businesses, whether they are just starting up or already large corporations. The combination of strong committees and an outstanding professional staff has resulted in an ability to respond quickly and effectively to business concerns, both individual and collective.

Legislation is a keystone of the Chamber's efforts to ensure a pro-business climate. Incentives for growth and development, as well as a tax climate that encourages business expansion, are at the top of the agenda. In 1987, the Chamber played a key role in a statewide campaign that significantly altered the state's tax structure and incentives. The results produced over $4 billion in investment and

Over one million people live within 50 miles of downtown Omaha. Here, I–480 enters downtown from Council Bluffs, Iowa.

30,000 new jobs, and these numbers are increasing each year. Chamber efforts target government spending levels, the need for consolidation and efficiencies in government, and "downsizing." Again, access to elected officials helps ensure that the government will be responsive. A survey of company CEOs found that over 60 percent have had personal contact with their U.S. senators and congressmen within the last year.

Success in passing legislative incentives to business growth led to business expansions that resulted in a 2.1 to 2.9 percent unemployment rate in the metro area, one of the lowest in the country. To assist local companies in recruiting the employees they need to meet the demands of their customers, the Chamber established a comprehensive program to help in long-term as well as short-term recruiting. Employing the latest in technology, print, electronic, and multimedia recruiting materials were developed, including a CD-ROM called "Access Omaha." The Chamber sends people to job fairs in cities where layoffs are occurring among the kind of employees Omaha companies need. It conducts campaigns to encourage young people to enter the technical trades in computer and engineering areas needed by area businesses.

Providing excellent educational opportunities for its young people and working adults was an early focus of the Chamber, and that emphasis continues today. Intensive efforts in the first decade of the 20th century led to the establishment of Omaha University (now the University of Nebraska at Omaha) and the University of Nebraska medical school in Omaha. Knowing that the greatest source of productive employees is Omaha's own youth, the Chamber has established exemplary efforts in business-education partnerships. It established the Applied Information Management Institute, a consortium of educational institutions and high-tech businesses that provides continuing education, research, and support for Omaha's rapidly

growing telecommunications and information technology industry. It established the Omaha Job Clearinghouse to help high school students find career paths in Omaha-area companies. It set up a pioneering program, "Omaha Work Keys," designed to assure that Omaha-area high school students were taught the skills needed by business. Working with the American College Testing program, "Work Keys" measures competencies of 10th graders against skills needed in Omaha's most prevalent jobs. Curriculum is then adjusted to assure that students graduate with all of the skills they need.

Each year hundreds of local businesses directly participate in Chamber programs and workshops and receive one-on-one assistance from various departments or volunteers in a variety of professions. Hundreds more work on legislation, the business climate, and quality of life issues that affect the entire community as well as their own company. It is all part of an ongoing commitment to business success as well as individual success by the Greater Omaha Chamber of Commerce. As one member put it, "If you haven't stopped in to see what the Chamber can offer your business, you are missing a real opportunity to grow your business."

Recognized as the place to go to get action, the Chamber is a draw for area business people. Top, left to right, are a Central Council meeting and a Buy the Big "O" Business Showcase booth; above, Chamber economic development staff members and a minority business award dinner.

FIRST NEBRASKA CREDIT UNION

When employees of more than 250 successful Nebraska-based businesses need convenient, low-cost financial services, they turn to their credit union first—First Nebraska Credit Union.

This Omaha-headquartered institution was organized in 1963 to provide financial services to employee groups that were not large enough to organize their own credit union, did not want the administrative responsibilities associated with managing a facility, could not provide the capital, or could not compete with other full-service credit unions and financial institutions.

Today, First Nebraska Credit Union is one of Nebraska's three largest credit unions. It serves over 14,000 members in the Omaha and Lincoln areas and has assets in excess of $30 million. The 1995 move into the Lincoln area is an indication of its growth and commitment to service in the future.

The credit union has a 14.5 percent capital-to-asset ratio, which ranks it among the strongest financial institutions in the nation.

First Nebraska offers financial benefits to employers for their employees through the ease of payroll deduction. Fraternal or social groups of five or more, relatives of members, and individuals who are active in the credit union movement are also eligible for membership.

Employers that have added First Nebraska services in the 1990s include First Data Corporation and Nashua Corporation in Omaha and Metromail and Centurion International in Lincoln. Other employers served include World Insurance, Physicians Mutual Insurance, Methodist Hospital, Immanuel Medical Center, and Builders Supply.

First Nebraska provides a wide array of financial services, including loans, checking accounts, savings accounts, children's accounts, IRAs, 24-hour-per-day electronic tellers, and ATMs. Accounts are insured by the National Credit Union Administration up to $100,000 per account.

Services being developed include home banking through personal computers, which credit union leaders expect to be the wave of the future.

"We know we can't be all things to all people," says President Rich Kounkel. "What we do, we do well! Transactions will exceed three million by year-end 1995. Earning our members' loyalty is our most valuable asset."

Norwest Bank has played a large part in Omaha's banking history. In 1856, Joseph A. Millard and Willard Barrows formed Barrows, Millard and Company, which later became United States National Bank. That bank not only survived the Depression but grew into one of the nation's leading banking operations.

In 1929, the Northwest Bancorporation acquired U.S. National Bank, and Banco became one of the leading bank holding companies in the Midwest. Banco's success was due in part to the unusual degree of diversification in the region's economy and to its locations in the seven state regions it served.

In 1983, Banco was renamed Norwest Corporation to expand its image and strengthen its presence throughout the Midwest. Today, Norwest is headquartered in Minneapolis and is the 11th-largest bank holding company in the United States.

In 1996, Norwest Bank Nebraska, N.A., is the third-largest banking institution in Nebraska. Norwest has 28 community banking offices statewide, of which 15 branches are in Omaha, including Ralston and Bellevue, and employs more than 1,000 staff in Nebraska.

Norwest offers a full range of community banking amenities, including personal and business loans, trusts, checking, savings, ATM cards, and money market accounts. Other banking services include products for businesses and institutions, cash management services, investment services, international banking services, and tax services.

Nationwide, Norwest is a $72.1 billion financial institution that has 694 community banking offices in 15 states. In all, more than 40,000 employees assist customers with their banking and financial needs.

Norwest stands as a symbol of strength and unity throughout the Midwest. Norwest has grown up with the city of Omaha and will continue to provide community banking services to the city for many years to come.

FIRST NATIONAL BANK OF OMAHA

ost banks record their progress in dusty ledgers filled with marching columns of assets, deposits, loans, and reserves. First National Bank of Omaha has books like that, too.

But its real history, aside from the bare bones of numbers and dates, is written across the Great Plains in steel rails, in the wagon ruts of the Oregon Trail, in the frothing wakes of river steamers, and in long, straight furrows through the prairie sod.

Drawing of the original First National Bank of Omaha building, 1863

For the figures in those ledgers describe more than the building of a bank. They tell much of the history of the building of the great heartland of America. First National Bank was here when it started—when the Pony Express stopped at the bank, when the Union Pacific started laying rails west, when the Civil War gave way to the great migration to the western wilderness.

Herman and Augustus Kountze started the bank in 1857 when they set up the Kountze Bros. Bank in a one-room frame building on a muddy street in the raw frontier town of Omaha. They did what bankers did in those days: issued their own wildcat currency, stewarded the dimes and dollars of their immigrant depositors, played a role in community affairs, and took chances in staking the early businesses, some of which grew into the corporate heavyweights of the 20th century.

The Kountzes saw what could lie ahead for this part of the country and were determined to be at the center of it.

irst National Bank of Omaha, along with its parent company, First National of Nebraska, with more than 46 locations in Nebraska, Colorado, Kansas, and South Dakota, has more than five million customers, $6 billion in assets, and over 4,000 employees. It is a top 25 VISA and Master-Card issuer and a top 7 VISA and MasterCard processor. First National of Nebraska has averaged more than 14 percent compounded growth annually since 1972. Its annual earnings have never decreased in the past 20 years and, on average, have risen by more than 20 percent every year.

In 1863, they applied for and received a national charter, thus becoming the oldest national bank from Omaha west.

The expanding territory the bank served expanded and prospered. So did the bank, by clinging to the same values and practices that worked so well for the other pioneers: hard work, thrift, trustworthiness, optimism.

As the rails went west, the farms provided their bounty, and the cities and towns of the region took root and became communities. First National Bank evolved from a two-brother operation into a corporation, and then into a provider of a bewildering variety of sophisticated financial services.

It is hard to envision now, when you read the billion-dollar numbers, visit one of the bank's towering office structures, or watch its telecommunications systems at work, that First National Bank started in a one-room building. And it takes a stretch to connect the bank that handles Fortune 500 companies with the bank that used to deal with trappers for their beaver pelts.

But it's the same bank—more than 130 years old and still doing essentially what the Kountze brothers did (minus the wildcat currency): stewarding the dimes and dollars of depositors, strengthening and supporting the community, and helping nurture the economy of the Plains.

You can read those dusty ledgers to learn the exact dates and numbers that chart the bank's growth and its evolution into the massive institution it is today. And as you read, you can see between the lines evidence of the faith the bank has always had in the people and institutions of its region—a faith that has never been shaken by war and depression, drought and disaster, good times or bad.

First National Bank of Omaha today

Member FDIC

COMMERCIAL FEDERAL BANK

Commercial Federal Bank is a major financial power among Omaha's banking institutions. Now, well into its second century of service, Commercial Federal dominates Omaha's mortgage lending activity. Built on a reputation for customer service and sound banking principles, Commercial Federal has grown so that in 1995 it had 17 customer locations in the Omaha area and more than 90 offices in its four-state service area.

With nearly $7 billion in assets, the bank, whose stock is publicly traded, ranks among the 17 largest retail thrift institutions in the United States.

Customers value the savings bank's convenient locations, its wide range of innovative financial services, and the employees' knowledge of financial products and their service-minded friendliness.

The bank offers several savings plans, including Individual Retirement Accounts, checking accounts, personal and mortgage loans, brokerage services, insurance, telephone banking, VISA and MasterCard, and automated teller machines and personal banking machines networked with more than 200,000 ATMs throughout the world.

Commercial Federal has grown from one part-time employee in 1887 to approximately 1,400 employees today. A look at this financial leader's history reflects the history of Omaha as well, for each has played a major role in the other's growth.

First known as South Omaha Loan and Building Association, Commercial Federal's roots are in South Omaha and the boom town climate that came with Omaha's

Commercial Federal's headquarters dominates the West Omaha skyline.

Nebraska's first drive-in banking facility, opened by Commercial Federal in 1953, was an immediate success.

status as a leader in the nation's meat-packing industry.

The association was organized with less than $10,000 in assets. By 1893, it needed a full-time employee and hired James J. Fitzgerald as secretary. Thus began a 64-year career for the 24-year-old Irish immigrant.

In 1910, the association changed its name to Commercial Savings and Loan. Commercial weathered the Great Depression in a spirit of partnership with its customers. Though the value of Omaha's homes plummeted by 40 percent and the savings and loan saw its assets decline from almost $4 million to $2.1 million, mortgage foreclosures were avoided as much as possible. Sometimes Commercial Federal would accept as little as $2 on a $20 monthly payment.

By the beginning of World War II, Commercial was growing again. Fitzgerald, who had retained the title of secretary since 1898, became president in 1943. His son, William F. "Wynn" Fitzgerald, who had joined the company in 1933, succeeded his father as president in 1955.

At the close of the Korean War, Commercial Federal showed a new spirit of leadership in Omaha. It financed entire housing developments for returning veterans, pioneered financial advertising on television, opened the state's first drive-in facility, computerized its entire operation, and opened branches throughout metropolitan Omaha and across Nebraska.

In 1972, Commercial received a federal charter and was renamed Commercial Federal Savings and Loan. By 1975, it had become the largest retail financial institution in Nebraska. At that time, the third generation of Fitzgeralds, William A. "Bill" Fitzgerald, was appointed president. Today he serves as chairman and chief executive officer. James A. Laphen has succeeded him as president.

Taking advantage of deregulation of the banking industry in the late 1970s, Commercial Federal began offering checking accounts, introduced a telephone bill-paying service, installed automated teller machines, and became the first financial institution in the country to provide the more sophisticated Personal Banking Machines in its lobbies.

In 1984, Commercial Federal issued stock to the public. During the 1980s, it also built an interstate network of retail banking offices reaching into Colorado, Oklahoma, and Kansas.

In 1990, Commercial Federal amended its charter from a savings and loan to a federal savings bank and adopted today's name, Commercial Federal Bank.

One of Commercial Federal's first offices in South Omaha

ACCENT SERVICE COMPANY, INC.

Partner with a Leader and Expect Success.

That's the invitation Accent Service Company, Inc. (ASI), extends to prospective clients and associates who want to achieve the same success that its clients and associates have enjoyed for over a quarter-century. A single man's dream of owning his own business has become an international network of accounts receivable recovery centers.

Years later, the dreams continue. If there isn't talk of a new product or service, or plans to open a new location, it just isn't a typical day at ASI. President and CEO Ron Wilwerding shares words of wisdom with a group of young ASI leaders: "You should be content, but never satisfied."

Many of the world's most respected companies entrust their receivables to one of ASI's four divisions:

Accent Service Company, Inc.— A premier provider of delinquent account collection and management services. Accent helps clients create, monitor, and refine accounts receivable recovery programs designed around organizational cultures, goals, and public images.

Accent Insurance Recovery Solutions— The forerunners of insurance claims recoveries, serving the entire benefits industry, including indemnity carriers, self-insured organizations, and third-party administrators. "Value-added service" is not a buzzword phrase to this unbeatable team of professionals, it's their middle name.

Advantage Receivable Solutions— Proven accounts receivable experts, offering customized receivable consulting, training, and innovative outsourcing programs. "Setting the benchmark of excellence in accounts receivable management."

Accent Service International— Excellence in international collections and credit reporting. "Whatever the language . . . we have the Accent."

ASI's generosity shows through in its civic and charitable activities. ASI associates are active in and serve on the boards of organizations such as the Greater Omaha Chamber of Commerce, the Girl Scouts, the Consumer Credit Counseling Service, the Ronald McDonald House, Junior Achievement, and Christian Urban Education Services. ASI plays an important role in improving credit education through the International Credit Association's "Train the Trainer" program for high school teachers.

Through the dedicated efforts of its astute leaders and associates, ASI will continue to enjoy a positive image as a first-class accounts receivable and cost-containment firm. Far and away, ASI is proudest of its people. "Everyone says their people are better; ours really are. You have to experience it to believe it," says President and CEO Ron Wilwerding.

Across the nation, 150,000 farmers protect their livelihoods with the help of Acceptance Insurance Companies Inc., the nation's third-largest crop insurer.

While corn is the largest crop covered, Acceptance also insures many other commodities, including spearmint in Idaho, cranberries in Michigan, rice in Mississippi, squash in Illinois, and canola in Montana and North Dakota.

Acceptance Insurance, headquartered in downtown Omaha, has 950 employees and offices in Council Bluffs, Iowa; Phoenix and Scottsdale, Arizona; Chicago; Kansas City, Kansas; and Burlington, North Carolina. It is one of five Nebraska-based companies traded on the New York Stock Exchange. Premiums rose from $86 million in 1990 to more than $500 million in 1995.

The company concentrates on writing specialty policies not generally emphasized by standard insurance carriers. In addition to crop insurance and traditional property and casualty products for rural America, its major insurance segments are:

- General Agency, which provides specialty automobile, surplus lines liability, and substandard property, complex products, and professional liability coverage
- Program, which provides transportation and workers' compensation coverage
- Non-Standard Automobile, which provides coverage for private passenger automobiles.

Acceptance was founded in 1979 by the late Gary O. Gross and Kenneth C. Coon, the current chairman and CEO. It has grown rapidly through strategic acqui-

sitions, joint ventures with other insurance managers, and new marketing partnerships.

Acceptance's most significant acquisition in the early 1990s was of The Redland Group, Inc., a leading writer of Multi-Peril Crop insurance and crop hail insurance. This acquisition gave Acceptance about 14 percent of the crop

insurance market and its national rank in the field.

Acceptance markets its insurance products through approximately 120 general agents and over 9,000 independent agents. The Company's insurance subsidiaries write business in 48 states, the District of Columbia, and the Virgin Islands.

MUTUAL OF OMAHA COMPANIES

More than 85 years ago, Mutual of Omaha set out in a modest way to provide health insurance protection to individuals and their families. Today, the Mutual of Omaha Insurance Company provides more individual health and accident insurance to Americans than any other company and is one of the largest group insurance organizations as well.

This leadership is supported by a strong financial base. The Mutual of Omaha Companies have total assets under management of more than $10 billion and a policyowner surplus of more than $1 billion. This surplus represents funds that remain after providing for obligations to policyowners and paying operating expenses.

Traditionally prudent management and fiscal policies give Mutual of Omaha the strength necessary to help protect its policyowners and clients for decades to come.

The company's experience and resources enable it to pursue new opportunities and challenges effectively in the rapidly changing marketplace.

As an aggressive and innovative developer of managed care networks, Mutual of Omaha works with leading physicians and hospitals to find ways to provide high-quality care in a cost-effective manner. Because Mutual of Omaha knows that the best health plan is one that helps keep people healthy, it is developing benefit plans that encourage doctors and patients to find health problems before they become serious.

In addition to their long-held strength in health benefit plans, the Mutual of Omaha Companies are increasingly emphasizing development and sales of non-health products, including life insurance, annuities, mutual funds, and other financial services products.

The Mutual of Omaha Companies have been leaders in Washington, taking an active role in discussions of health care reform. The companies support a variety of insurance reform measures that can make health care coverage available and affordable to as many Americans as possible.

Another kind of leadership is represented by Mutual of Omaha's longstanding commitment to the natural world, a commitment begun more than 30 years ago with the popular television program *Mutual of Omaha's Wild Kingdom*. Today, Mutual of Omaha's Wildlife Heritage Center provides cash grants to zoos and nature centers and awards scholarships to 30 colleges and universities across the United States.

Financial strength and a workforce committed to providing exceptional customer service have written the Mutual of Omaha Companies' success story. The next chapters already are being lived—in the companies' continuing quest for the most sensible, caring answers to problems that face our country and our natural world.

irkpatrick Pettis is the full-service, regional investment subsidiary of the Mutual of Omaha Companies, a relationship that provides customers with the assurance of strength and stability.

Founded in Omaha in 1925, Kirkpatrick Pettis is a midwestern door to Wall Street—but more important, it is midwesterners' door to many productive investment opportunities Wall Street may have overlooked. The Kirkpatrick Pettis Research

Department follows the performance of regional companies that have strong earnings potential. Some of these firms, which make excellent investments, probably wouldn't be known to investors who didn't have access to Kirkpatrick Pettis' knowledge of regional businesses.

Kirkpatrick Pettis is the leading underwriter of municipal bonds in Nebraska. In this leadership role, the firm ensures a steady stream of quality, tax-exempt bonds

for client portfolios and provides strong, knowledgeable financial advice to organizations and communities across the Midwest and Rocky Mountain regions.

In addition to the strong position it enjoys in regional municipal finance, Kirkpatrick Pettis offers individual and institutional investors a full range of financial options, including stocks, corporate bonds, mutual funds, money market funds, annuities and insurance products, insured certificates of deposit, and U.S. government securities. It also offers a choice of retirement plans ranging from IRAs and Simplified Employee Pension Plans for the self-employed to 401(k) plans for businesses.

The Kirkpatrick Pettis Trust Company assists clients with personal trusts and businesses with retirement plan trusts, while KPM Investment Management, Inc., offers professional money management assistance to individual clients and institutional investors, as well as groups overseeing company retirement plans.

At the core of the firm's business philosophy is an attitude toward customers that emphasizes partnership, close communication, and the building of long-term relationships. This attitude is summed up in the saying "We work with our customers, not for them." It is this traditional midwestern approach that has earned Kirkpatrick Pettis an enviable position in the region and beyond.

The professional trading staff at Kirkpatrick Pettis provides expertise in buying and selling stocks and bonds on all principal exchanges and over-the-counter markets. Kirkpatrick Pettis is a registered market maker in stocks of over 50 companies headquartered throughout the U.S.

PACKERS BANK

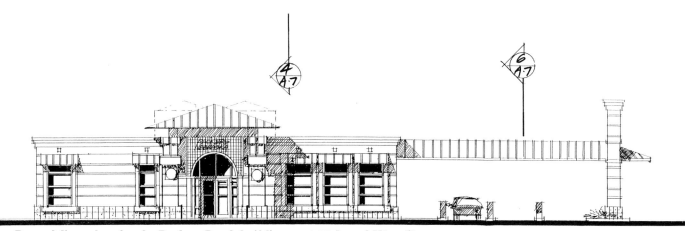

Remodeling plan for the Packers Bank building at 140th and West Center

Packers Bank is one of the driving forces in community hometown banking. For 105 years, Packers has built its products and services around people in the Omaha area. It is one of the few remaining "hometown" banks, and in times like these, people find that comforting.

THE PAST

The Packers legacy began in 1891 when the South Omaha branch of the Nebraska Savings Bank was reorganized and incorporated as the Packers National Bank. Packers was one of the most important additions to the banking community of Omaha, then known as "the Gate City." Packers was originally located at the southeast corner of 26th and N Streets in the main business district of South Omaha. The original officers were A. C. Foster, president; Samuel Cotner, vice president; and A. P. Brink, cashier.

By 1905, South Omaha's central business district had shifted to 24th Street, and in 1907, the bank went with it, moving its offices to 24th and O in a beautiful new building designed by Thomas Kimball, the renowned Omaha architect who also designed St. Cecilia's

Cathedral. This new location was ideal for both shippers and the stockyard workers. The building was sold in 1984 and renovated for offices and apartments. It was added to the National Register of Historic Places in July 1986.

A key bank employee whose years of service and dedication are unparalleled in the banking industry is Laddie J. Kozeny. Kozeny started his career with Packers in February 1923 at the age of 15 as the bank messenger. He has served in various positions, including as assistant cashier, assistant vice president, and vice president. He semi-retired in 1971, when he was named to the board of directors. In 1995, having celebrated his 89th birthday, he was still an active employee. Kozeny epitomizes the type of bank employee who has made Packers a major regional independent bank.

In July 1979, Packers moved to its present location at 24rd and L Streets. This new facility was completely remodeled from its original grocery store-type format and received a City Beautification Award. In its larger space, the bank continued to serve and promote the Omaha community and its growing number of loyal customers.

THE PRESENT

For more than a century, Packers combined its talents with those of the local community to build a better way of life. It has staked its future on the growth and progress of Nebraska. Packers continues to be a major supporter of education through its participation in the student loan program. It also co-sponsors the annual College Fair.

In August 1986, Edward A. Kohout became president. He continued to provide excellent leadership until his semi-retirement in August 1995. Kohout carried on the Packers philosophy that to be a good citizen the bank must serve four constituencies: customers, the community, employees, and stockholders. Kohout replaced Rodney P. Vandeberg from Falls City, Nebraska, as chairman of the bank's board.

During Kohout's presidency, Packers received recognition for its contribution in developing Corrigan Heights Senior Center and Elderly Housing Complex, and in 1986 it received the Omaha Chamber's Golden Spike Award for its outstanding contribution to the economic stability and growth of Omaha. Kohout remains very active in Omaha, serving as president of the Progress Development Corporation, president and director of the Omaha Industrial Park Development, director of the local Mercado Project, and a director of Omaha Small Business NetWork.

Always looking for ways to expand Packers' outreach, a small ATM network was added in 1990 and a southwestern loan production branch in 1991. In 1994, this location was replaced through the purchase of Nebraska National with a full-service branch.

THE FUTURE

Upon Kohout's semi-retirement, Tom Cover became president and CEO. Cover has served as chairman of the Chamber of Commerce in Council Bluffs. He has been president of the Industrial Foundation and is a member of the boards of the Boy Scouts of America and of the National Conference of Christians and Jews.

The local owners of Packers have made a long-term commitment to remain

Chairman Edward Kohout, Chairman Emeritus Laddie Kozeny, and President and CEO Tom Cover in the Packers boardroom at 24th and L Street

a major player in the Omaha community. Cover believes in Packers' philosophy of providing excellent banking service—a tradition that is often forgotten in today's era of big bank mergers and takeovers. This philosophy is based on the premise that quality instititutions last and that people who live in the community know the area best, understand the residents' needs, and know how to serve those needs.

Cover's plans include adding new technology and enhancements to the Packers product line. Info Express (a 24-hour account information line), a new bill-paying service, and a new trust account will be offered beginning in 1996. The southwestern location will be remodeled, and a community room will be added.

Packers will continue helping businesses and industries create new jobs. It will finance homes for growing families and education for their children. Packers is more than a banker. It is a neighbor and a friend.

Kozeny helped our grandparents. Kohout helped our parents and may have helped you. Now Cover will be here to help you and your children as the Packers tradition continues into the next century.

The Packers Bank building at 24th and O Streets is now on the National Register of Historic Places.

PHYSICIANS MUTUAL AND PHYSICIANS LIFE

In 1902, a salesman who sold physicians' supplies started a company designed to provide accident coverage to physicians and dentists.

Since then, Physicians Mutual and Physicians Life have built a foundation of stability and reliability based on superior service, innovative products, and conservative investment philosophies. And their principles, grounded in honesty and integrity, have remained unchanged for more than 90 years.

Today, with more than 1.1 million policyowners, Physicians Mutual is the 10th-largest individual accident and health provider in the nation. Physicians Life also is a significant power, with more than half a million policyowners and $2 billion of life insurance in force and growing. With Physicians Mutual attaining top ratings from insurance analysts Weiss Research (A+) and A. M. Best

(A+ Superior), it proves that the Physicians Insurance Companies are here to serve and endure.

In the mid-1990s, Physicians Insurance Companies surpassed a very impressive milestone: more than $3 billion paid in claims since their founding. Equally impressive, the companies pay more than $300 million a year in claims. Since the companies' beginnings in Omaha, Physicians Mutual and Physicians Life have made good on their promise— "We're Here When You Need Us"—every single day.

The Physicians Insurance Companies product portfolio reveals a diverse mix, including insurance for patients needing long-term care, persons with HIV or cancer, accident insurance, comprehensive hospital-medical and employer group plans, as well as whole and term coverage for people of all ages.

While the Physicians Insurance Companies have a history of providing quality hospital indemnity and life insurance coverage, they also look ahead and meet their policyowners' needs with exciting new products and services. VISTA annuities, for example, are a welcome addition for those seeking safe and secure investment options. Medicare Supplement policyowners enjoy such features as electronic claims filing and participation in a prescription drug program that guarantees them the best available price on prescription drugs.

President and Chief Executive Officer Robert Reed credits much of the success of Physicians Mutual and Physicians Life to the people of Omaha.

"Omaha is famous for the high work ethic of its workforce," says Reed. "It's the reason we're proud to be part of Omaha. Moreover, we're proud to be of service."

Corporate headquarters of Physicians Mutual and Physicians Life, at 2600 Dodge Street

WOODMEN OF THE WORLD LIFE INSURANCE SOCIETY

It started as a small mutual benefit society operated from one of its director's homes. Today, it's one of the nation's largest fraternal benefit societies and synonymous with one of Omaha's most visible landmarks.

Woodmen of the World Life Insurance Society has indeed grown up along with the city where it was founded in 1890.

The Society was founded by Joseph Cullen Root to provide its members with financial security and to foster fraternalism. The first life insurance certificates, which provided a $3,000 death benefit and a $100 monument benefit, were issued from the home of John T. Yates, the Society's secretary.

Today's Society has 856,000 members, who have nearly $29 billion worth of life insurance. Woodmen offers a variety of insurance products, including whole life, universal life, term and hospital supplemental insurance, and annuities.

As a nonprofit fraternal organization, Woodmen exists for the benefit of its members. The Society accomplishes this mission through a unique combination of business know-how and fraternalism.

"Providing insurance protection with fraternal benefits makes Woodmen more than just an insurance company," says national president John G. Bookout.

Woodmen has always placed a high priority on service to its members. Over the years, the Society has met members' needs by utilizing state-of-the-art technology in its business.

In 1983, Woodmen became the first insurance organization of its kind to make hand-held computers available to its field force. Three years later, the first laptop computers were issued to field associates. To meet the needs of the 21st century, the Society has installed high-tech imaging equipment and systems to handle the transmission of electronic applications to the Omaha headquarters from Woodmen representatives throughout the country.

The Society also continues its 105-year philanthropic tradition of helping members and their communities. The fraternal benefits for which Woodmen members are eligible include an orphans' care program, newborn benefits, youth and senior camps, and assistance for catastrophic illnesses.

In addition, members present U.S. flags to civic groups, donate equipment to fire departments, rescue squads, hospitals, and public parks, and provide assistance for senior citizens, the physically impaired, and orphans.

Woodmen's more than 500 home office associates now occupy several floors of the 30-story Woodmen Tower, which dominates downtown Omaha's skyline.

"Through our strength and stability, we are able to bring about a better way of life for our members, their families, and their communities," says Bookout.

GUARANTEE LIFE INSURANCE COMPANY

Founded in 1901, Guarantee Life Insurance Company, a wholly owned subsidiary of The Guarantee Life Companies, Inc., is a company with a proud past, a successful present, and a dynamic future.

With its headquarters in Omaha, Guarantee Life has been a prominent corporate citizen on the Omaha scene for nearly 95 years.

Guarantee Life was organized in Nebraska in 1901 as a mutual assessment association and became a mutual legal reserve life insurance company in 1931. It went on to become one of the 50 largest mutual companies in the United States.

The company, formerly known as Guarantee Mutual Life Company, celebrated another landmark year in 1995, when it successfully completed its conversion from a mutual life insurance company to a stock life insurance company, now trading on the NASDAQ national market under the symbol GUAR. At the time, it was one of fewer than 10 mutual life insurance companies to demutualize and the first in Nebraska. The company is now structured to maximize its financial flexibility, facilitate acquisitions, and position itself to grow, prosper, and flourish in the rapidly changing financial services business environment.

Guarantee Life is licensed in 46 states and the District of Columbia and provides insurance coverage and related benefits through approximately 200,000 individual and group policies issued to customers throughout the country. The company employs over 500 persons at its Omaha headquarters and in 20 regional offices across the country and is associated with more than 600 agents and several thousand employee benefit specialists nationwide.

Guarantee's Employee Benefit Division's products include life, accidental death and dismemberment, short- and long-term disability, and dental insurance, as well as voluntary products. The Group Special Markets portfolio consists of excess loss insurance for employers with self-funded medical plans and medical reimbursement insurance for business executives.

Individual Division insurance products include universal life, term life, and interest-sensitive whole life insurance and annuities.

Guarantee Life is committed to quality—quality products, quality service, and quality people. The company prides itself on offering sound value to its customers—value that enhances and safeguards their financial security. A commitment to service and a dedication to building strong, beneficial relationships with its customers and distributors is at the forefront of the company's philosophy. The company's motto, "Building Relationships

Chairman, President, and CEO Robert D. Bates

for Life," is an integral part of the company's culture. Guarantee Life is committed to providing service with a sincere, personal touch that caters to a customer's unique insurance needs, creates a strong bond, and builds lasting relationships—relationships for life.

Guarantee's business strategies are designed to anticipate, adapt to, and manage change. The company incorporates an innovative and disciplined management team, outstanding products and services, an enthusiastic workforce, rapid and accurate systems with a keen focus on technological development, and a commitment to understanding and anticipating customers' needs. Guarantee Life excels by providing quality insurance products that satisfy customer needs and service that exceeds customer expectations.

Formerly headquartered in downtown Omaha, the company moved west to Guarantee Centre in 1958 and is situated atop a sprawling, beautifully landscaped campus that was formerly Indian Hills Golf Course. The original building won several design awards and remains today one of Omaha's most attractive landmarks. A second tenant building was added in 1986. Continuing its steady pattern of growth, Guarantee added a third building to its campus in 1995 to accommodate its growing number of associates.

"Omaha is a great place to do business," says Chairman, President, and CEO Robert D. Bates. "There is a well-educated workforce with a solid, Midwest work ethic and people who really care."

Guarantee Life's strong commitment to the community is evidenced by its leadership and support of numerous community endeavors, such as the Greater Omaha Chamber of Commerce, United Way, Salvation Army, Brush Up Nebraska Paint-A-Thon, numerous civic organizations, and countless nonprofit organizations representing the arts, education, health and welfare, and various civic betterment projects. The company is an integral part of

Guarantee Life officers uncover a new corporate logo and sign.

a strong core of community leaders that are committed to Omaha's economic growth and the welfare and quality of life of its people.

Proudly headquartered in a thriving, vibrant, and friendly city, Guarantee Life has emerged as a new stock company, poised on the threshold of an even more productive future. Like Omaha, Guarantee Life is confident that the best years of its history lie ahead.

Guarantee Life's headquarters

As Omaha has grown, so has AAA Nebraska. An affiliate of the American Automobile Association, AAA Nebraska is best known for its motor club and travel services. However, its business ventures don't end there. That's just the beginning.

Starting in 1906 with a few hundred members, the motor club has grown into a statewide institution respected for its professional excellence, dedication to quality client service, and active role in community affairs. In addition to travel and motoring services, AAA Nebraska's diversified interests include publishing, computer services, insurance, and financial services.

More than 185,000 Nebraskans faithfully renew their AAA memberships each year, entitling them to dozens of exclusive benefits and services that appeal to anyone who drives a car. AAA Nebraska's emergency road service operators respond to nearly 85,000 emergency roadside assistance calls a year, and AAA auto travel counselors create personalized trip routings for about 32,000 families a year. But statistics alone don't tell the whole AAA Nebraska story.

Under the leadership of Robert F. Stubblefield, CEO and president, AAA has flourished in many ways as a result of its ability to offer its service expertise to others outside the state as well as outside the AAA network.

For example, in 1979, AAA Nebraska led the effort to create a travel and leisure publication that could be jointly used by AAA clubs in the Midwest. Formerly, each club produced its own magazine. The following year, *HOME & AWAY* magazine was born. This award-winning publication now reaches the homes of 2.6 million AAA members in 13 midwestern states.

One of AAA's most popular services is available to members and nonmembers alike. AAA Travel Agency, a full-service travel company, provides air ticketing, cruise bookings, group tours, and more from 16 locations across the state. Because of AAA's national buying power and partnership programs, world-renowned travel industry corporations such as Walt Disney World Travel Company, Hyatt Hotels, and Holland America and Carnival Cruise lines extend special privileges and savings to AAA travel agencies and their clients. Nationwide, AAA sales of travel products and services exceeded $5 billion in 1995.

In a search for computer services and programs that would launch AAA into the next century, AAA Nebraska decided to design a motor club software program that could be marketed to other automobile clubs across the U.S. and Canada. Automation, Inc., a wholly owned subsidiary of AAA Nebraska, has done just that. With a staff of 30 employees, Automation, Inc., is providing computer services and systems for motor clubs that reach more than four million members.

But there is more to this diversified giant. In 1948, the Motor Club Insurance Association was formed as an insurer of AAA member vehicles. This Nebraska AAA company has a long history of providing outstanding coverage at reasonable rates, making it the second-largest domestically based insurer in Nebraska. In more recent years, the association has expanded to include homeowner's, life, and health insurance coverage.

AAA's commitment to providing quality service to its members and clients has also meant a strong commitment to the state and communities it serves. Even in community service work, AAA's expertise has filled vital needs.

In 1920, AAA created the School Safety Patrol program to prevent pedestrian accidents in school zones. To address the need of a critical, future shortage of qualified automobile technicians, AAA sponsors the AAA/Ford Auto Skills Challenge, which during the past decade has offered nearly half a million dollars in scholarships to talented Nebraska students.

Looking to the future has been the key to AAA Nebraska's success. "In today's competitive marketplace, it isn't enough to provide a quality product," Stubblefield says. "We must understand and meet our clients' present needs as well as anticipate their future needs. Each day provides us with another opportunity to do just that."

AAA's fleet of emergency vehicles provides service 24 hours a day 365 days a year.

Empire Insurance Group is an Omaha-headquartered company that fills a specialized niche in commercial auto insurance. The Group is made up of four companies: Empire Fire and Marine Insurance Company, Empire Indemnity Insurance Company, Douglas Street Premium Finance Company, and Douglas Street Premium Finance Company of California.

Empire is nationally known for providing excess and surplus lines insurance to customers for whom standard carriers do not provide coverage. The company also delivers significant expertise to the commercial trucking and the auto rental insurance markets. It has experienced substantial premium growth over the last five years, has total assets of about $400 million, and has a current net worth of over $100 million.

Empire, which was founded in 1954 and employs about 300 people, receives top ratings from national rating services. It holds an A+ rating from A. M. Best, the most widely used rating organization in the insurance industry. The ranking reflects both management and financial results. For the past three years, Empire has been named to the Ward's 50 benchmark group for achieving outstanding financial results. Ward Financial Group is a highly respected management consulting and investment banking firm specializing in the insurance industry.

Empire's parent company, Zurich Insurance Group, has $67 billion in assets and is rated AAA by Standard & Poor's rating service. This signifies that the Zurich Group is one of the strongest financial organizations in the world. Empire, in turn, is the highest-performing company in the Zurich Group.

Empire prides itself on being a customer service-driven company that responds to the needs of a growing and changing marketplace. Strong partnerships with hand-picked distributors, including employees and a countrywide network of agents, make Empire very accessible to its customer base. Rapid, fair, and responsive claims service delivers consistent claims handling that surpasses customer requirements. These two elements combine to form the foundation on which Empire builds its superior reputation with its employees, with its customers, and within the insurance industry.

Nebraska Methodist Health System, Inc., brings together leading health care organizations from across the region to provide high-quality health care, excellence in education, and preventive health care information to residents throughout the Midwest.

Established in 1981, Methodist Health System was the area's first health system to offer a broad spectrum of services in response to the changing health care needs of the people it serves. Today, Methodist Health System is dedicated to providing residents of the region with the finest health care services and is noted for the distinguished physicians affiliated with the organization.

Methodist Health System includes the following affiliates: Nebraska Methodist Hospital, Jennie Edmundson Memorial Hospital, Methodist Richard Young, Nebraska Methodist College, Nebraska Methodist Hospital Foundation, Shared

Services Systems, Inc., as well as a network of outstanding primary care and specialty physicians and a variety of support services.

Methodist Hospital, which is regarded as one of the region's finest full-service hospitals, provides a wide range of educational, medical, and surgical services. Founded in 1891, Methodist Hospital is the leading obstetrical and cancer care provider in the Omaha area. Over the years, Methodist Hospital has been in the forefront of many medical advances and was the first hospital in Omaha to offer lithotripsy procedures and an outpatient surgery center.

Surveys reveal that Omaha households consistently rank Methodist Hospital as their first choice for hospital care. In addition, Methodist Hospital is a leader in several clinical specialties, including cancer care, cardiovascular services, cardiac rehabilitation, and diagnostic services. It has earned an outstanding reputation in many areas,

including outpatient and home health services, laproscopic surgery, neurosurgery, gastroenterology, ophthalmology, orthopedics, rehabilitation services, and urology.

Methodist Health System's affiliate hospital in Council Bluffs, Iowa, Jennie Edmundson Hospital, was founded in 1888 and serves approximately 250,000 residents in southwestern Iowa. Jennie Edmundson Hospital offers a broad range of inpatient and outpatient services and is also noted for its excellence in obstetrics. In 1995, Jennie Edmundson received "Accreditation with Commendation" from the Joint Commission on Accreditation of Healthcare Organizations (JCAHO)—an honor awarded to only 5 percent of the hospitals in the United States.

Both hospitals are members of the Voluntary Hospitals of America (VHA), one of the nation's largest not-for-profit hospital alliances, which offers cost-reducing purchasing programs. They also are members of Healthcare Partners of Mid-America (HPMA), a regional network of physicians and hospitals. Through this network, Methodist Health System and its affiliated physicians work cooperatively with insurers and other leading health care providers to offer high-quality, affordable health care to area employers and residents.

Methodist Richard Young (MRY), a full-service behavioral health system, has been providing progressive mental health care since 1931. Today, MRY provides a wide range of inpatient and outpatient services, including adult, child, adolescent, and geriatric programs.

Committed to working with other health care providers to enhance regional access to specialized health care services, Methodist Health System affiliates offer

As the area's first choice for hospital care, Methodist Hospital strives to improve the quality of life in the region through excellence in health care.

the largest network of outreach medical clinics in the region. These clinics improve the accessibility of specialty health care services to residents in rural communities and give the physicians on the medical staffs of Methodist Hospital, Jennie Edmundson Hospital, and Methodist Richard Young the opportunity to work cooperatively with local physicians.

Education is a key component of Methodist Health System. Nebraska Methodist College offers a variety of nursing and allied health programs, including a bachelor of science degree in nursing and a nationally recognized health promotion specialist program on the Nebraska Methodist College-Omaha campus and an associate of science degree in nursing program on the Nebraska Methodist College-Jennie Edmundson campus. Jennie Edmundson Hospital also offers a School of Radiography.

Within the Methodist Health System, patients benefit from a team approach involving both primary care physicians and specialists. Primary Care Resources

More than 200 of the area's physicians are affiliated with the Methodist Health System. Here, a Methodist family practice physician treats a young patient in his office.

(Physicians Clinic), the largest, private multi-specialty medical group in Nebraska, has grown to include more than 100 physicians in Nebraska and Iowa. Physician Resources, Inc. (Methodist Family Medical Centers), is a network of family practice clinics in Nebraska, Iowa, and Missouri.

Through Methodist Business Health, Methodist Health System affiliates are in the forefront in providing health care services to area businesses. Business Health includes the Methodist Employee Assistance Program, which serves clients throughout the United States. It also includes other preventive and educational programs, including a workers compensation managed care program called WorkComp Partners.

Community education plays an important role in the mission of Methodist Health System. Health Touch One, a free 24-hour telephone service offered by Methodist Hospital, Childrens Hospital, and Jennie Edmundson Hospital, is staffed by registered nurses who provide a wide range of general health care information to the public, including basic treatment information, wellness topics, hospital services, and physician referrals.

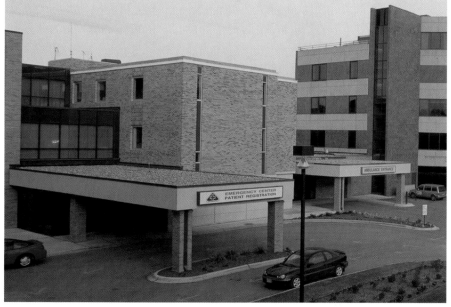

Serving more than 250,000 residents in southwestern Iowa, Jennie Edmundson Hospital in Council Bluffs joined Methodist Health System as an affiliate in 1994.

CLARKSON HOSPITAL

The more things change, the more they stay the same.

When it comes to Clarkson Hospital's commitment to delivering high-quality health care to residents of the Midlands, that well-worn adage rings true. The Clarkson of today is physically quite different than in 1869, when it was founded as Nebraska's first hopsital, but the mission is much the same. A multidenominational civic group created The Good Samaritan in that year to provide Omaha pioneers with a place to go when sick or injured, something the growing city did not have.

In the more than 125 years since then, the face of health care has changed in ways the Clarkson founding fathers could never have imagined, but the goal of providing the best possible health care remains. Today, Clarkson's services include primary care; oncology, cardiology, and pulmonary care; eye surgery; kidney dialysis; burn care; and renal and pancreas transplantation. Additional services include single-room maternity care and orthopedic and sports medicine services.

Clarkson has kept pace with technology, many times bringing new and innovative medical procedures or services to Nebraska and the Midlands for the first time, including:

- 1955 First cardiac catherization
- 1957 First kidney dialysis treatment
- 1958 First corneal transplant
- 1965 First kidney transplant
- 1975 First lens implant
- 1975 First CT scan
- 1982 First bone marrow transplant
- 1985 First heart transplant
- 1995 First 1,000 kidney transplants

By bringing new medical wonders to Omaha, Clarkson has brought thousands of Midlanders improved quality of life within convenient reach of home and family. The hospital also leads the way with innovation of a different sort—the delivery of new health care technology to small communities in the three-state area through its regional network of integrated health care providers. For example, Clarkson has dialysis centers in Council Bluffs, Shenandoah, and Harlan, Iowa, and in Grand Island, Keamey, and Baker Place in Omaha. Another example of Clarkson's outreach is its radiation oncology service in Shenandoah.

Closer to the center of the network, Clarkson West Medical Center, at 145th and West Center, with convenient, expanded hours, serves rapidly growing western Douglas/Sarpy Counties with comprehensive ambulatory care for everything from simple sore throats to emergencies. Services include primary care and specialty physi-

When it was founded in 1869, Clarkson was the first hospital in Omaha.

cians' offices, outpatient surgery, urgent care, physical therapy, sports medicine and occupational therapy, and CT services.

Another way Clarkson is providing convenient access to health care is through its expanding network of primary care physicians. Clarkson primary care physicians are located throughout the metropolitan Omaha area and in rural Nebraska and Iowa. Clarkson is also leading the way in the development of a physician organization—the Great Plains Physician Group (GPPG). GPPG is integrating independent physician groups with insurance partners and providers to improve quality and ensure consumer choice.

Clarkson is also noted for firsts in quality and choice as determined by independent surveys. Recently, its mortality rate was 9 percent below the national comparison standard, placing Clarkson in the top 20 Diagnostic Related Groups (DRGs) with 500 hospitals across the country. Also, a recent survey of referring physicians in a three-state area rated Clarkson the best area referral hospital in 13 of 14 medical specialty areas. By focusing on more efficient delivery and a length of stay 24 percent below

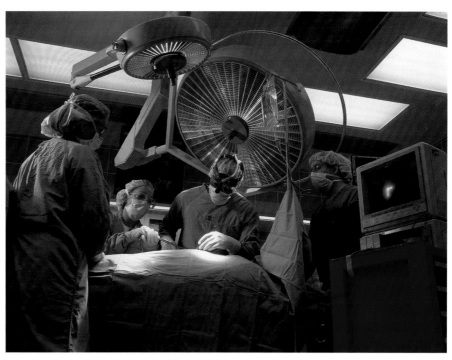

Clarkson provides both inpatient and outpatient surgery in 14 modern surgical suites in one area of the hospital. Outpatient surgery is also offered at Clarkson West.

the comparison group, Clarkson has also become a leader in reduced costs. Higher patient satisfaction is a result: in its survey of patient satisfaction, a majority rated the hospital "very good" or "excellent" in all categories.

Looking to the future, Clarkson is leading the region in health care reform by joining Columbia/HCA, the world's largest health care provider. Benefits of this new alliance will include an integration of physicians, hospitals, home health services, and other providers in an advanced health care delivery system.

By linking with other health care providers in this integrated network, Clarkson gains efficiencies in the delivery of care and enhances the quality of care while at the same time achieving cost savings. Clarkson is redesigning the shape of health care in the 21st century without losing sight of its original mission: to provide the best possible health care to the sick or injured. Clarkson has prided itself on living up to that mission for the past 125 years and can truly say, "The more things change, the more they stay the same."

Clarkson West Medical Center offers the expertise of Clarkson and the convenience of West Omaha. Services include primary care and specialty physicians' offices, outpatient surgery, urgent care, physical therapy, sports medicine and occupational therapy, and CT services.

TRADITIONS

Healing, teaching, and leading are among the rich traditions shared by Creighton University Medical School and Saint Joseph Hospital as, in partnership, they provide the highest-quality healthcare possible to Omaha and surrounding communities. Today's Creighton Saint Joseph Regional HealthCare System continues to fortify these traditions, nurtured over more than 125 years.

TRADITION OF HEALING

Healing has been a tradition at Saint Joseph Hospital since its humble beginnings in 1870, when the city of Omaha was itself only 16 years old. This tradition began when the Sisters of Mercy opened the doors of Saint Joseph's first hospital, a 28-bed, two-story frame structure. It continued when the building was purchased 10 years later by the Sisters of Saint Francis. The tradition continues today, as Saint Joseph operates a 404-bed, full-service, tertiary care hospital, more than 20 neighborhood clinics, and numerous outreach centers throughout Omaha and surrounding rural communities. Saint Joseph provides a full range of psychiatric services, meeting both inpatient and outpatient needs. The hospital has telephone and data links that provide information, educational resources, and medical referrals for the community it serves. And its Life Flight medical helicopter and other technological advances connect local rural communities with its facilities, which house some of the nation's leading medical authorities.

TRADITION OF TEACHING

Creighton University Medical School established the tradition of teaching in this partnership when it was founded in 1892. Creighton continues that teaching tradition as one of the nation's foremost educators of physicians and allied healthcare professionals. Here, students work side by side with some of the brightest minds in the country and prosper in an environment featuring the latest innovations in medical technology and treatment.

Since its inception more than a century ago, Creighton University Medical School has worked in partnership with Saint Joseph Hospital as its primary teaching hospital for training the healthcare professionals of tomorrow.

That partnership also includes continuing the Catholic teaching tradition. Creighton University proudly prevails as one of only five Catholic medical schools in the country.

Creighton's Jesuit Catholic presence flourishes today. The hospital boasts one of the largest pastoral care departments in the country, which emphasizes healing the whole person and the caring of all who come to its doors, regardless of race, color, creed, or ability to pay.

Today, as yesterday, Creighton's students and the community grow to understand that healing extends beyond the physical to the mind and spirit.

TRADITION OF LEADING

The Creighton Saint Joseph Regional HealthCare System is on the leading edge of medical research, technology, prevention, and treatment. It has often been a pioneer in developing or utilizing early advances in equipment and medical treatments for its patients.

Saint Joseph Hospital's Life Flight medical helicopter links rural and urban communities with Creighton Saint Joseph Regional HealthCare System's facility, housing some of the nation's leading medical authorities.

Today, it is home to state-of-the-art angiography equipment, used for interventional radiology procedures, saving lives and limbs by means that were once only dreams. It has attracted national and world-renowned authorities in many specialty areas, including:

Cardiology—where its leadership extends into rural outreach, providing the latest in education, treatment, planning, and clinical practices, as well as utilizing long-distance computerized monitoring;

Hereditary Cancer—where research originated decades ago by its dedicated physicians continues to redefine the field;

Osteoporosis—in which bone density studies and links with calcium and other substances are preventing what once was considered normal bone loss in the elderly while setting care standards for the world;

Trauma Care—where life-saving procedures are performed routinely and rural and local communities within a 150-mile radius in Nebraska and Iowa are linked via Life Flight medical helicopter to the highest-quality and most innovative medical technology and treatment;

Primary Care—where prevention is emphasized and physicians are the gateway to healthcare delivery in today's managed care environment.

The nearly 300 physicians in the Creighton Saint Joseph Regional HealthCare System have formed Creighton Medical Associates (CMA), a physician practice group, to combine the extensive resources of its multispecialty services

The distinguished medical personnel in the Creighton Saint Joseph Regional HealthCare System are dedicated to educating both patients and the community about the inner workings of their bodies and the best techniques for staying healthy.

into an allied organization. CMA will sign managed care contracts as the representative of the system's physicians, thereby more easily bringing its total healthcare package to the people of Omaha and surrounding communities.

Creighton Saint Joseph Regional HealthCare System has also formed a Physician Hospital Organization to better meet the managed care needs of the people the system serves.

The partnership of Creighton University and Saint Joseph Hospital is now linked with Tenet HealthCare Corporation, a national healthcare organization, providing the partnership with further expertise and financial stability so

it can remain strong in today's rapidly changing healthcare environment.

Within the Creighton Saint Joseph Regional HealthCare System, medical technology and treatment will continue to change, but its commitment to quality healthcare will not.

As the Creighton Saint Joseph Regional HealthCare System enters the 21st century, it pledges that its partnership will continue to forge new frontiers in medical advancements. It pledges to keep its healthcare focused on the people it serves and the quality of their well-being. It pledges to continue its rich traditions of healing, teaching, and leading. These form the legacy of its past and the promise of its future.

Two of Omaha's most respected health organizations have gone into partnership to meet Omaha's healthcare needs of the future.

Immanuel Healthcare Systems and Bergan Mercy Health System have formed Alegent Health, a nonprofit corporation whose goal is to develop integrated healthcare services to meet the diverse health needs and improve the health status of the people of the Midlands. Through this agreement, two strong, independent healthcare organizations have come together to create new programs and to provide more effective health services for the metropolitan area.

Both health systems have long commitments to the Omaha area. Since its founding in 1887 by the Rev. E. A. Folgestrom, a Lutheran pastor, Immanuel has grown into a fully integrated health system with more than 100 sites in Omaha, eastern Nebraska, and western Iowa. These sites include its northwest Omaha campus, at 6901 North 72nd Street, which includes an acute care hospital, a skilled nursing facility, retirement housing, a rehabilitation center, and a mental health and addictions recovery center.

In addition, Alegent Health includes physician clinics, family counseling centers, and physical therapy centers located in neighborhoods throughout metropolitan Omaha and the surrounding region. Immanuel Alegent Health is affiliated with the Nebraska Synod Evangelical Lutheran Church in America.

Across Omaha, Alegent Health Bergan Mercy is one of Nebraska's busiest medical centers. It was founded in 1910 by the Sisters of Mercy as St. Catherine's Hospital and Nursing School. When it relocated to its present location at 7500 Mercy Road, it was renamed in honor of former Omaha Archbishop Gerald Bergan. The medical center includes an acute care hospital, a skilled nursing facility, a respite care center, a wound care center, and medical office buildings. Additional off-campus services include outpatient surgery,

home care, adult day care, physical therapy, and urgent care.

Alegent Health Mercy Hospital, in Council Bluffs, Iowa, also is part of Alegent Health. Mercy Hospital, which was founded by the Sisters of Mercy in 1888, provides a wide range of medical services to the residents of western Iowa. These include acute care, inpatient and outpatient psychiatric and chemical dependency services, home care, and primary care.

By sharing their strengths and vision, these healthcare organizations have come together in Alegent Health to create a healthier environment for the entire community.

Alegent Health believes that quality healthcare must be available to all. It has developed two Neighborhood Health Centers in eastern Omaha to serve the needs of residents in medically underserved neighborhoods. The Neighborhood Health Centers provide primary care. They also emphasize health education and wellness activities.

Alegent Health Lakeside HealthPark, at 168th Street and West Center Road, exemplifies the newest concept in the delivery of healthcare. Lakeside provides one of the first fully integrated outpatient facilities available to residents of western Douglas and Sarpy Counties.

The HealthPark houses between 10 and 20 physicians in both primary care and specialty care areas. Other services include outpatient surgery, urgent care, laboratory and X-ray services, and physical therapy. Alegent Health Lakeside HealthPark places a unique emphasis on health education and healthful living. A large health educa-

tion center provides classes, screenings, and information on health topics. The surrounding site includes walking trails and fitness opportunities. The campus master plan calls for a fitness center and child care center.

Consistent with its vision of helping people stay healthy, Alegent Health has introduced the University of Healthy Living. This innovative "university" offers a full range of health education classes that

promote healthful behavior and lifestyles. Classes are offered throughout metropolitan Omaha. Because of Alegent Health's alliance with Mutual of Omaha, the university is able to encourage participation by offering some scholarships to Mutual HMO enrollees.

Through unity, strength, and dedication, Alegent Health's vision is becoming a reality as it creates a healthier tomorrow today.

For the latest in medical advancement and the highest quality of care, patients from Nebraska and throughout the country turn to the University of Nebraska Medical Center (UNMC).

UNMC is the place where more than 3,000 patients have received bone marrow, liver, kidney, small bowel, pancreas, or heart transplants since 1983. It's the place where more than 100 researchers are working together to find a cure for cancer and then sharing their knowledge to provide state-of-the-art cancer care in University Hospital and UNMC clinics. And it's the place where Torrey Johannsen, born weighing less than 12 ounces, received her start in life.

But UNMC is more than patient care. The health science center educates the majority of Nebraska health care professionals, and its medical research is known worldwide.

During the past quarter-century, UNMC has emerged as one of the top health science centers in the country, providing premier educational programs, innovative research, the highest-quality patient care, and outreach to underserved populations.

"We take our mission to care for the health of all Nebraskans seriously," says Carol Aschenbrener, M.D., chancellor of UNMC. "At the same time, we're pushing medical technology for future generations. We're also helping people learn to stay well. Because of UNMC's efforts, lives are saved. People are given second chances at living healthy, normal lives."

The University of Nebraska Medical Center's beginnings date to 1880 and the Nebraska School of Medicine. In 1968, the University of Nebraska united all the health sciences under one umbrella—the University of Nebraska Medical Center.

Through University Hospital, the Colleges of Medicine, Nursing, Pharmacy and Dentistry, the School of Allied Health Professionals, graduate studies, the UNMC/Eppley Cancer Center, the Meyer Rehabilitation Institute, clinical units, and the rural health network, UNMC first educates Nebraska's health care professionals. Then it provides them with opportunities for continuing education. More than 50 percent of the physicians, dental professionals, pharmacists, and allied health professionals practicing in Nebraska received their education at UNMC.

Health care professionals practicing in rural areas are linked to UNMC through SYNAPSE, a computerized health information network. As a result of their SYNAPSE connection, health care professionals throughout Nebraska can access UNMC resources—from its physicians, who are available for consultation, to information in the Leon S. McGoogan Library of Medicine.

UNMC's reputation as a leader in innovative research is based on its record of life-saving discoveries and advancements. For example, UNMC researchers discovered the gene that causes Marfan connective tissue disorder, which damages the heart and arteries. They were the first to develop a skin test to positively identify the syndrome. UNMC researchers were the first to use antisense technology to develop a process that effectively kills myeloid leukemia cells in a test tube. They also were the first to treat cancer patients with an antisense drug.

In addition, UNMC researchers tested a new drug that stimulates the production of red blood cells and platelets in patients who have undergone high-dose chemotherapy followed by a type of bone marrow transplantation.

The UNMC/Eppley Cancer Center

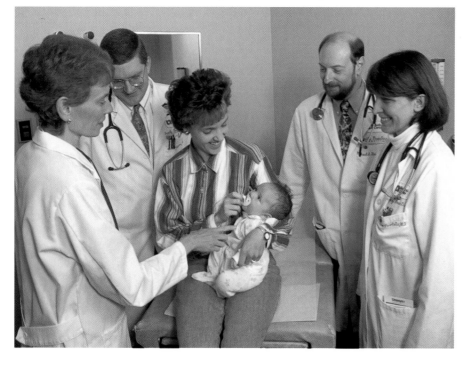

coordinates all cancer-related research and treatment at the medical center. Focusing on basic and clinical cancer research and educational programs, the UNMC/Eppley Cancer Center is a National Cancer Institute-designated basic cancer research center.

Through the development of new therapies and treatment techniques, UNMC continues to enhance its reputation as a health care organization that provides excellence in patient treatment and care.

With an eye on health care in the 21st century, UNMC's Lied Transplant Center aims to link transplant research with transplant-related care. UNMC is developing a new model of care for transplant patients—cooperative care—in which family members and friends help care for the transplant recipient in a home-style setting.

UNMC's efforts are attracting national attention. Among the recent awards bestowed on the medical center is UNMC's ranking of 21st among the top 40 cancer centers in the nation by *U.S. News & World Report* magazine. The magazine also has ranked UNMC's College of Nursing 27th out of the nation's 281 nursing schools that offer master's programs. Of the 29 Nebraska physicians listed in the most recent edition of the *The Best Doctors in America*, 24 are UNMC physicians.

UNMC, a nonprofit health care organization, follows its mission of providing medical care to the underserved and to those

in need. Last year, University Hospital provided $25 million in indigent care in Douglas County. UNMC's primary care clinics can be found in all areas of Omaha, including those underserved.

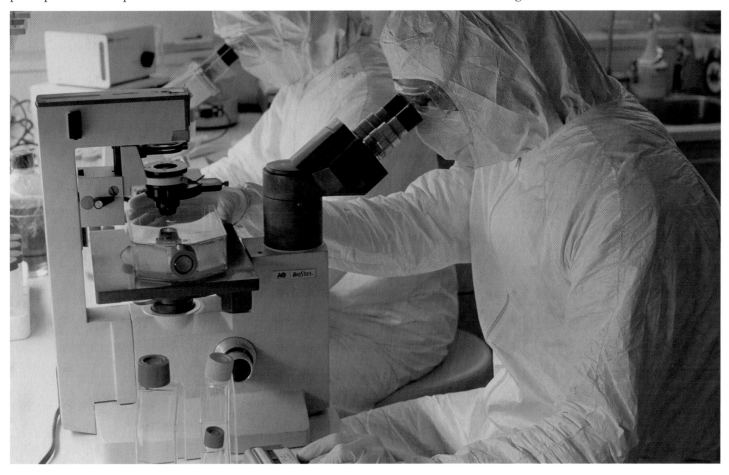

CHILDRENS HOSPITAL

Because children are not merely small versions of adults, they need special care, whether they suffer from a complex or unusual disease or require routine medical attention. Childrens Hospital was established in 1948 "so that all children may have a better chance to live."

This private 100-bed hospital specializes in meeting the special health care needs of children through a variety of integrated services in a health care network.

The hospital is fully accredited with commendation by the Joint Commission on Accreditation of Healthcare Organizations. It is the only pediatric specialty hospital in Nebraska and serves a five-state region. No child is refused treatment, regardless of ability to pay.

Services at Childrens Hospital include:

- a pediatric open-heart surgery program and a pediatric cardiac catheterization unit;
- one of the largest poison information centers in the country;
- more than 20 outpatient specialty clinics, several of which are on the leading edge of their respective areas, including one of only six helmeting clinics in the country;
- neonatal and pediatric intensive care;
- outpatient services and testing; and
- children's psychological services.

Childrens Hospital helps train the pediatricians of tomorrow by providing medical students at the University of Nebraska and Creighton University with pediatric and residence training. The hospital also provides pediatric training for all emergency medical technicians in Nebraska.

Childrens Hospital and its affiliated services are dedicated to meeting the needs of the entire child and of families affected by their children's health care problems. Special services include counseling, available at the Family Support Center, and Kids Care, an urgent care center that treats minor injuries and illnesses when regular doctors' offices are closed. Child Life Services helps families deal with the anxiety of a hospital stay. Pedi-Medical Equipment and Services, an affiliate of Childrens Hospital, provides home health care and medical equipment.

With its intense focus on children, Childrens Hospital and its network of pediatric health care services is one of the nation's leading pediatric health care systems.

WEST TELEMARKETING CORPORATION

West is the largest, fully integrated tele-marketing and interactive voice processing company in America. West designs, implements, and manages large-scale transaction processing and information services applications for Fortune 500 companies and large direct marketing organizations. Unlike its competitors, West offers integrated services to its clients within each of the three major industry segments of live operator inbound, outbound, and interactive call processing.

West's clients are successful, sophisticated marketers who collectively generate hundreds of millions of transactions each year. As more Fortune 500 companies and other large organizations focus on their core competencies and deploy targeted marketing techniques to build relationships with new and exciting customers, the need to outsource transaction processing applications to third-party service bureaus such as West will continue to increase.

In the future, increased competition will force companies to market their products and services more cost-effectively. Many companies are restructuring, flattening their organizations, while demanding more accountability for their marketing efforts as the costs of traditional marketing campaigns continue to rise. The outsourcing of direct marketing, data collection, order processing, and customer service activities is rising because service companies such as West have demonstrated that they are able to achieve better marketing results for lower costs.

Since its inception in 1986, West has invested millions of dollars in the development of proprietary operating systems, automated transaction processing facilities, and the most experienced management teams in the industry. Whether a client's application requires the use of inbound telereps for order capture/customer service, outbound direct marketing professionals, or interactive call processing, West is uniquely positioned to provide the integrated service solution.

West Telemarketing Corporation, in Omaha

When you're in Omaha on a business trip, you don't have to forsake the comfort of home. Clubhouse Inn, at 11515 Miracle Hill Drive, in the heart of West Omaha's rapidly expanding business corridor, offers extraordinary accommodations in a residential setting at an amazingly affordable price.

Clubhouse Inn, which is just west of Interstate 80, is less than half an hour from downtown Omaha and other major business locations. You may wish to schedule your meeting at one of the Clubhouse's conference rooms.

You'll never feel cramped in your spacious 14-feet-by-28-feet room. Other touches add to the comfort, such as a bathroom with a separate vanity area, a closet with full-length mirrors, a phone with a 25-foot cord, and a remote-controlled TV with premium movie channels. Roomy work desks, free local calls, long-distance access, and provisions for receiving incoming faxes are among some of the other features.

Free hot breakfast buffets, evening managers' receptions, including cocktails, and complimentary 24-hour refreshments are all signatures of Clubhouse Inn's amenities package.

The goal is to give guests a "home-away-from-home feeling."

At the home-style breakfasts, guests often mingle with each other. It's a great way to network with other business travelers tapping the opportunities of the expanding Omaha marketplace.

After a hard day, you can relax in the courtyard, where two barbecues have been set up on the patio by the pool. If you feel like it, you can cook your own food. Once a month, there's even "Steak Night," featuring a family-style filet mignon dinner—a perfect way to sample the classic taste of Omaha.

Being on the road isn't so lonely when you stay at an inn where staff and other guests get to know your name.

Frequent guests earn coupons for free nights in a two-room suite. Suites feature a dining area with a wet bar, microwave, refrigerator, and coffee maker.

You'll feel safe as well as comfortable at Clubhouse Inn, which uses the Ving Card Security Door Locking System. Without a key, hotel access is limited to the front door.

Next time you travel to Omaha on business, remember the Clubhouse Inn. It makes business travel almost a pleasure.

BORSHEIM'S

In 1870, Louis Borsheim opened a small jewelry store in Omaha. And for the next 78 years, Borsheim's remained a small jewelry store. Louis Friedman purchased Borsheim's in 1947. When his son, Ike, joined the operation a few years later, the stage was set for dramatic growth.

Borsheim's understands jewelry—but Borsheim's understands people even better. Borsheim's owners believed that if they offered people the greatest selection of jewelry, silver, china, crystal, watches, and other fine gifts available anywhere, coupled with extraordinary personal service and the absolute best value for every dollar spent, the business would prosper.

The owners were correct—beyond everyone's expectation. Why? Because Borsheim's kept its operating costs exceptionally low. Because it always paid cash (yes, cash) for every item in its inventory—so debt service costs were never passed on to customers. One other trade secret—Borsheim's never paid its sales associates on a commission basis. Instead, they were always compensated based on how well they served Borsheim's customers.

Through the 1950s and 1960s, Borsheim's business grew. More importantly, so did its reputation for value, selection, and very personal service. This was the most important factor in the expansion of Borsheim's in the 1970s. Sometime during that decade, Borsheim's became the nation's largest single-unit fine jewelry and gifts retailer.

By 1986, Borsheim's couldn't fit another earring into its downtown store. So it moved to its current 37,000-square-foot home in fashionable Regency Court.

Business quadrupled. Staff grew from a couple of dozen to over 300. The market grew to include all 50 states, North and South America, Europe, Africa, Asia, and Australia.

In 1989, Borsheim's sold the majority of its stock to Berkshire Hathaway Corporation, headed by renowned investor Warren Buffett. At the time, Buffett said, "I've long admired what you've accomplished together." And after the sale, Buffett issued strict instructions: "Forget this has happened—don't change a thing." Needless to say, Borsheim's has followed his advice.

Today, Borsheim's is headed by Susan Jacques, president and CEO. She began as a sales associate 13 years ago at Borsheim's and moved through the ranks as an appraisal writer, merchandise manager, fine jewelry buyer, and senior vice president.

Just as the late Ike Friedman did, Susan Jacques focuses on completely satisfying Borsheim's customers. And, as long as Borsheim's remains dedicated to its customers, they will undoubtedly continue to reward Borsheim's with their loyalty.

People who know fine jewelry and gifts come from the 50 states and six continents to shop at Borsheim's.

Redfield & Co., Inc., was founded in Omaha in 1883, the year Nebraskans traveled west for the first time via the Union Pacific Railroad.

Redfield found appreciative clients in the growing Omaha community. Among them were numerous county governments, for which Redfield did a great deal of their official printing. Today, more than a century later, Redfield still prints for many Nebraska counties and still uses high-quality metal type. But while it has retained its rich heritage and old-fashioned craftsmanship, Redfield has also become a leader in meeting modern communication needs.

In 1986, Redfield & Co., Inc., was purchased by Tom Beachler and Tom Kearney, who brought in a third partner, Dale Stephens, several years later. Former employees of a national computer forms manufacturer in Omaha, the new owners understand firsthand the business needs created by the technological revolution in communications. Building a rewarding environment for creative thinkers among their approximately 80 employees, they have diversified their operations and brought in the newest, most efficient state-of-the-art equipment.

While Redfield is expanding its boundaries into regional and national markets, valued long-time local clients are greeted with personal attention and benefit from the company's sophisticated new technology. Redfield provides many options for clients, including promotional mail, automated forms, commercial printing, labels, and numerous other custom-printed products.

Lining the halls in Redfield's 75,000 square feet of printing plants are service plaques honoring long-time employees. Some employees have dedicated more than 50 years to the business, and others have fathers who worked here before them. Expertise and experience go hand in hand at Redfield, where competitive prices, a "can-do" attitude, and sophisticated technology keep customers coming back time and time again.

Redfield's outstanding reputation leaves little doubt that this historic Omaha business will be around for at least another 100 years.

GARDEN CAFE

When busy Omahans get hungry for the kind of food fondly referred to as "home cooking," they're likely to head for the "garden"—the Garden Cafe, that is.

With over 200 homemade breakfast, lunch, and dinner menu items and cases brimming with fresh baked pies, muffins, tortes, breads, rolls, and cheesecakes, it's no wonder signs proclaiming "We Love Food" greet hungry customers at every entrance.

Founder Ron Popp remembers the cafe's early days in 1985, when the staff was only seven and he split his time in the kitchen between cooking and dialing home to his family in Iowa for all their favorite classic farm recipes. The Garden Cafe re-created those recipes, and today Aunt Ethel's Lemon Meringue Pie, LaVerne's Lasagna, cheesy Old-Fashioned Potato Casseroles, Dow City Cinnamon Rolls, and others grace the cafe's colorful menus and are customer favorites.

Having expanded from the original location in West Omaha's Rockbrook Village to locations across the Midwest, the Garden Cafe attributes its success to an exceptional staff. Popp says, "Our company mission statement is firmly rooted in providing tasty food in a fresh and clean environment by people who care." Garden Cafe employees across the years have proven vital to the growth of the company and "are a tribute to the Omaha community," Popp says.

Investing in the same community that has supported and championed its success is a large part of the Garden Cafe's concept. By donating to charitable fund-raisers, supporting various school activities, and heading community efforts such as Project Zebra, which raised over $75,000 to acquire, house, and feed three zebras for exhibit at the Henry Doorly Zoo, the Garden Cafe is able to return the support from which it has benefited through the years.

The commitment to service and quality is apparent throughout the bright and airy restaurants and within the pages of the diverse menu. Everything is fresh and recipe-driven. Offering an array of daily specials, steaming bowls of homemade soups, hearty breakfasts served anytime, and over 50 different bakery selections every day, it's easy to see why loyal customers have voted the Garden Cafe Omaha's favorite family restaurant for five consecutive years. The Garden Cafe also offers a full take-out menu, a variety of party rooms, and exceptional catering services.

Clearly, Omaha's Garden Cafe is the place for Old-Fashioned Foods You'll Remember.

The MEGA Corporation is Nebraska's leader in commercial and industrial real estate. Since its inception in 1980, the philosophy has been "MEGA Means Business . . . MEGA Gets Results." It works!

A full-service real estate firm, MEGA has expertise in brokerage services, property/asset management, facilities management, financial investment services, real estate consulting, site selection, and farm sales and management.

With the largest staff of experienced brokers and property managers in the industry, MEGA boasts the strongest team in Nebraska working to get profitable results for both clients and customers. Its knowledge of the market, coupled with dedication to professionalism and integrity, is the force behind MEGA's strength.

Commercial/Industrial Sales and Leasing
MEGA specializes in developing marketing strategies that will sell, lease, or sublease property quickly and profitably.

Property/Asset/Facilities Management
Whether full-service property and asset management or simply facilities management, MEGA utilizes state-of-the-art techniques to help owners maximize their returns.

Financial and Investment Services
MEGA Investment Services not only raises equity capital in real estate investments, but also provides investment analysis and counseling.

Real Estate Consulting/Site Selection
MEGA provides a variety of services, such as market valuations and analyses, designed to give clients the knowledge needed to make sound real estate decisions.

Farm Sales and Management
With nearly 30 years in the agriculture market, Mid-Continent Properties, Inc., a MEGA subsidiary, has the expertise in land valuation, management, and production techniques to sell and manage farms and ranches profitably.

The MEGA Corporation became Nebraska's premier commercial and industrial real estate firm by understanding the needs of businesses. The ability to determine exactly what the client is looking for in commercial real estate and the desire to find the best possible solution for all parties involved in the transaction have been the backbone of MEGA's success.

Whether a property owner in need of professional management services or a tenant looking for a location for its business, MEGA's clients know their needs are understood.

The MEGA Corporation is chosen by leading developers, investors, corporations, financial/insurance institutions, and professional organizations because **MEGA Gets Results**!

ALL MAKES OFFICE EQUIPMENT COMPANY

As America's retail landscape shifts from traditional downtown store-fronts to off-ramp "mega-stores," one Omaha institution stands firm, All Makes Office Equipment Company. Established in 1918, this fourth-generation family-owned business furnishes and equips the majority of Omaha's offices.

Located at 25th and Farnam, All Makes occupies two city blocks of historic downtown buildings and boasts one of the city's unique retail spaces. Floor-to-ceiling windows give drivers up Farnam Street a colorful view of a 50-foot mural depicting a bustling business day. Suspended from a two-story atrium are four life-size wire sculptures of "The Flying Briefcase Boys." Commissioned by All Makes, these "executives" soar through the air above the showroom.

"We've tried to create an inviting and dynamic space," says Larry Kavich, president and CEO of All Makes. "We're the opposite of a warehouse store. This is a big space, but it has personality."

Omaha businesses must agree. Since All Makes' inception, the company has experienced growth that shows no indication of slowing.

"A couple of things help us attract and keep customers," says Kavich. "One, we offer one of the largest selections of office furniture in the country. And two, we have a remarkable team of long-term employees who understand and practice true old-fashioned customer service."

Service. That's the word you hear most often when you talk to All Makes' customers, some of whom go back 50 years and keep growing right along with the company.

"We have actually seen some accounts grow from two people to Fortune 500 companies that employ thousands of people all over the world," notes Kavich. Indeed, as Omaha proves profitable for companies and steady growth occurs, so does demand for the space planning, interior design, and state-of-the-art furniture that keep a business running smoothly.

"We try to anticipate our customers' needs," says Kavich. "Every company has its own challenges. That's why we carry everything from the most flexible lines of new office systems furniture to quality pre-owned office equipment—something for

The southeast corner of All Makes' headquarters, at 25th and Farnam Streets, in downtown Omaha

every taste and budget." All Makes enhances its wide product selection by providing complete space planning and interior design services, as well as expert project management from start to finish.

Constant reinvestments in technology help All Makes lead the market in customer satisfaction, Kavich says.

"We've installed a new state-of-the-art, industry-specific computer system so that whether a business orders a single desk or a thousand workstations, it will benefit from the most prompt and accurate product ordering, job tracking, receiving, delivery, and installation in the industry," he says.

The firm traces its roots to Kavich's grandfather, Harry Ferer, who opened All Makes Typewriter Company in 1918 to sell typewriters and dictaphones. Ferer's son-in-law, Lazier Kavich, became president and CEO in 1940, and steered the company through triple-digit growth by acquiring huge inventories of surplus goods and reselling at discount prices to midwestern businesses in the throes of post-World War II expansion. Lazier's son, Larry Kavich, followed suit by

Right: All Makes' present and future. President and CEO Larry Kavich (right) with Jeff Kavich, Operations, and daughter Amee Zetzman, Finance, on the atrium stairs.

learning the business at his father's right hand. Larry Kavich became president and CEO in 1984.

All Makes has branch stores in Des Moines, Iowa, and Lincoln, Nebraska, and has become the region's largest provider of top-quality office furniture. The three All Makes locations employ 150 people and serve accounts across the country and in Europe, South America, and Canada.

"When Omaha customers branch out in the world, they often take the All Makes team with them," Kavich says. But while global in outlook, All Makes remains committed to its base in the Midwest.

"If I could lift up my business and relocate it anywhere in the country or in the world, I wouldn't move it an inch," says Kavich. "We're in a pocket of controlled growth. This isn't like a gold rush, but every year, the city stretches farther and farther."

When Harry Ferer opened his business in 1918, he could not have anticipated that the enterprise he started would one day become the largest office furniture dealership in the Midwest. He'd undoubtedly be pleased to find great-grandchildren Jeff and Amee managing affairs from 25th and Farnam and laying plans for All Makes' continued growth and success into the next millennium.

"I grew up around the dining room table talking about the values we held for the business—treating customers right and delivering what we say we'll deliver," says Kavich. "We've stayed centered on that philosophy—considering every customer vital to our business—and that's what drives our success."

An extensive selection of executive furnishings take center stage on the showroom's second floor, which features high ceilings, exposed beams, and colorful neon accents.

Fifty years ago, Travel and Transport was born as a two-person company located in the Securities Building in Omaha. Today, T&T is a 750-person company with 40 locations in the U.S. and around the world.

Travel and Transport is independently ranked among the top 10 largest travel management corporations in the United States. T&T is the largest employee-owned travel company in the U.S., as well as one of the largest employee-owned companies in Nebraska.

Travel and Transport initiated the Travel Careers Institute, an Omaha-based travel school, to educate people who love to travel and want to work in the industry. Travel and Transport has the nation's highest percentage of accredited certified travel counselors.

"Our people have made Travel and Transport what it is today," says Frank Dinovo, Jr., president. "Quality service begins with people, and we recruit, train, and retain only the best." Such quality is reflected in the firm's national ranking.

"Out of 32,000 travel companies, ranking number eight is quite an accomplishment," said Dinovo.

Sales for T&T have excelled as well. In 1995, sales reached the $350 million range. Being a healthy, debt-free company allows T&T to take advantage of many opportunities, including technological developments that are not always possible for competitors. Members of Travel and Transport's management information team work on automated quality control systems, have customized e-mail capabilities, and can provide domestic and international customers with on-line services.

Travel and Transport's Meeting Trends and Amerenhance divisions also maintain a commitment to quality. Meeting Trends is T&T's group, meeting, and incentive travel division. The Meeting Trends staff is committed to providing customized service, ensuring any meeting or incentive program unqualified success. Amerenhance, a credit card enhancement service, provides travel and travel benefits to major financial institutions across the nation.

Travel and Transport is proud to have its headquarters in Omaha. Travel and Transport also is proud to be able to provide Omahans with world-class service and to serve the needs of travelers around the globe.

When Omaha families seek quality merchandise at an affordable price, their first stop is often the nearest 1/2 Price Store.

The 1/2 Price Stores were founded in 1972 and have grown to 32 stores in eight states.

Currently, there are five stores in the Omaha-Council Bluffs area. Other Nebraska locations include Fremont, Lincoln, and Grand Island. There are also stores in Colorado, Illinois, Iowa, Kansas, Missouri, Oklahoma, and South Dakota. And company plans call for continued expansion.

In 1994-95 alone, the firm opened eight new stores, creating an additional 600,000 square feet of retail space.

The dominant merchandise assortments are composed of first quality department store national brands at 1/2 price. Also offered are exclusive and designer labels, as well as widely distributed brands, all at exceptional values every day.

The merchandise selection is targeted to meet the major needs of families: apparel, shoes, accessories, housewares, home furnishings, gift items, small electronic items, sporting goods, and toys.

Goals include bringing even more famous labels into the store to enhance the merchandise mix and introducing the 1/2 price concept to more regions.

Shopping hours are geared to meet the needs of families: 9 A.M. to 9:30 P.M. daily, including weekends.

When Omaha plays host to the nation, as it does each year for the College World Series, the guests are likely to check into a Holiday Inn.

The Holiday Inn Central, with 403 rooms, is an Omaha landmark that now houses the finest convention center in the Midwest. Its versatile facilities are used to host large state, regional, and national conventions, as well as such premier Omaha events as the CWS Kick-Off Dinner, the Child Savings Institute Gala, and the annual Omaha Press Club Ball and Gridiron Show.

The Palace Ballroom is the centerpiece of the convention facility. It has theater performance capabilities, including a full stage and sound and lighting systems.

The Holiday Convention Centre is also conveniently close to Hampton Inn Central, with 132 rooms, and the Homewood Suites hotel, with 116 of Omaha's finest suites. These three hotels, all part of the Omaha Hotel, Inc., group, permit organizations to host conventions for 3,500 people and banquet events for 2,000. The convention center is suitable for large trade and exhibition shows as well. Each year, it hosts such large high-tech exhibits as the Info Tech show and the Buy the Big O market show. Community activities rich in tradition, such as the Omaha Symphony Debutante Ball, also are on the convention center's busy agenda. A premier event hosted by the Holiday Convention Centre is the annual Berkshire Hathaway meeting.

Out-of-town guests with a variety of budgets can find high-quality accommodations through Omaha Hotel, Inc. Hampton Inn offers affordable comfort for corporate travelers and their families. For added convenience and economy, continental breakfast is served each morning in the lobby.

Travelers to Homewood Suites will find the 116 luxury suites meet all corporate and leisure needs. The lodge features a chalet-like atmosphere and is convenient for convention registration and meetings. An ample continental breakfast is served each morning, and appetizers and spirits are provided at the daily evening social hour.

Homewood also provides a welcoming retreat for newcomers to the Omaha area. It provides long-term lodging for families who are relocating or staying for an extended period. Movie star Robert Redford is among the celebrities who have called Homewood home during their stays in Omaha. Redford spent considerable time in Omaha while his son underwent transplant surgery at the University of Nebraska Medical Center.

Omaha Hotel, Inc., also includes the Holiday Inn Old Mill and the Hampton Inn Southwest. The company continues to expand with a new Holiday Inn Express project at 108th and L Streets. This facility will add 84 comfortable and affordable rooms to the Omaha hotel market.

The Holiday Inn Old Mill specializes in corporate lodging and meetings as

well as providing housing for small groups, family reunions, and groups in Omaha for sporting events. The Hampton Inn Southwest offers comfortable and affordable lodging at 108th and L.

Whether you're trying to organize a major convention or fund-raiser or a party for your parents' golden wedding anniversary, think Holiday Convention Centre and other Omaha Hotel, Inc., properties. These Omaha institutions are sure to meet your lodging and hospitality needs.

OMAHA PRINTING COMPANY

Omaha Printing Company is Omaha's largest and oldest commercial printer. Since 1858, it has been a leader in its industry and in the community.

Working with today's most advanced computer technology and automated printing presses, the company has earned a reputation for its high-quality, full-color printing. Its capabilities include computerized estimating, a state-of-the-art electronic prepress, four-, five-, and six-color Heidelberg Speedmaster presses, aqueous coating, a full-service bindery, and on-time delivery.

Omaha Printing Company will also provide its customers with a production schedule on every job, keeping them accurately informed on the status of their order. The company offers training to its customers on the basics of printing, as well as customized educational programs for their specific needs.

The company credits much of its overall stability and strength to its dedicated and skilled employees. No matter what the product, the most important thing Omaha Printing Company has to offer is customer service. Omaha Printing Company wants to assess your needs and help you determine how to achieve your goals.

Omaha Printing Company will develop the programs and services to make your job easier. The goal is to be a partner in the printing process, not just another vendor.

The company looks at customer service from a different perspective—yours.

Strong roots with a focus on the future

Omaha is the corporate headquarters for Pamida Incorporated and home to 700 of its 7,000 team members. Nonetheless, some Omahans may never have experienced Pamida's services.

The story is quite different in small towns throughout 15 midwestern, north-central, and Rocky Mountain states, where Pamida is the principal general merchandise retailer.

Pamida offers "hometown values," which is defined by three basic principles: offering quality brand-name merchandise at a value price, providing superior customer service, and supporting the needs of its communities.

Pamida stores are generally located in towns with trade area populations of fewer than 20,000. This unique market niche means that Pamida is the only general merchandise retailer in 82 percent of its markets.

Pamida's new prototype store is approximately 42,500 square feet, complete with new merchandise layouts, color schemes, inventory, and checkout technology.

Pamida's merchandise mix includes brand-name men's, women's, and children's apparel, jewelry, accessories, toys, home furnishings, stationery, domestics, seasonal items, and consumables. Pamida also operates a growing number of in-store pharmacies.

Pamida traces its roots to 1963, when the first Pamida store was opened in Knoxville, Iowa. Progressively, Pamida—whose name was formed from the first two letters of the first names of the founder's three sons, Pat, Mike, and Dave—made its mark as a prominent regional retailer.

Today, Pamida operates over 145 stores and plans to add 10 to 12 new stores each year. Total revenues for the 1994-95 fiscal year were $712 million, which represents an 8.2 percent increase over the previous year.

Pamida is listed on the American Stock Exchange under the ticker symbol PAM.

A new prototype Pamida store was opened in October 1995 in Blair, Nebraska, just 20 miles north of Omaha.

ConAgra, Inc.

ConAgra is a diversified international food company headquartered in Omaha. ConAgra operates across the food chain around the world. The company's products range from convenient prepared foods for today's busy consumers to supplies farmers need to grow their crops.

ConAgra Facts

- Second-largest food company in the United States
- Annual sales: More than $24 billion
- More than 90,000 employees
- Operations in 27 countries
- Employer of 6,000 people across the state of Nebraska

ConAgra's Nebraska Heritage

ConAgra's roots are in Nebraska. The company has been headquartered in Omaha since 1922. ConAgra was founded in 1919 in Grand Island, Nebraska, when four flour mills consolidated and incorporated as Nebraska Consolidated Mills (NCM). In 1922, NCM relocated to Omaha. By 1971, NCM had outgrown its name and changed it to ConAgra, Inc. "ConAgra" was derived from the Latin words for "with" and "land" and signified the growing company's past and future "partnership with the land."

Trusted Brands

ConAgra is the good name behind the good names. Some of ConAgra's brands have been around for a century or longer— Hunt's, Wesson, Armour, Swift. The more than 50 ConAgra brands include Healthy Choice, Banquet, Van Camp's, Orville Redenbacher's, Marie Callender's, Peter Pan, Butterball, Swiss Miss, and La Choy. Of the 50-plus ConAgra brands, 21 brands have annual retail sales exceeding $100 million. ConAgra markets over 4.5 billion packages of branded food products per year, equivalent to over 12 million consumer purchases every day and 140 purchases per second.

Food Processing Technology

ConAgra is proud to contribute to Nebraska's position as a major locus of food-processing technology and management. In Omaha, ConAgra food technologists develop new food products at ConAgra's Charles M. "Mike" Harper Food Product Development Center on the ConAgra campus. The state-of-the-art product development lab-pilot plant facility is the centerpiece of ConAgra's $80 million campus, located in downtown Omaha along the Missouri riverfront. The campus, built in 1989–90, was the result of innovative Nebraska legislation that encourages businesses to create jobs and invest in Nebraska.

ConAgra and several ConAgra companies are headquartered on the campus. More than 1,000 people work at the campus, and the number of campus employees continues to grow.

ConAgra in Nebraska

Outside Omaha, across the state of Nebraska, ConAgra employs close to 4,000 people. Many ConAgra companies have operations in Nebraska. ConAgra's total economic impact on Nebraska is estimated to be more than $500 million.

To help support the high quality of life people enjoy in Omaha and throughout Nebraska, the ConAgra Foundation contributes millions of dollars each year to more than 100 programs, foundations, and associations representing educational, environmental, health and welfare, civic, artistic, and other community endeavors.

Omaha and Nebraska are important to ConAgra. In Omaha and across the state, ConAgrans are helping to feed people better in many ways—day in and day out.

I n 1954, a momentous advance in American food preparation took place in Omaha: Swanson invented the frozen TV dinner.

The original "Turkey" dinner included turkey, cornbread dressing, gravy, peas, and sweet potatoes in a three-compartment aluminum tray. The price: 98 cents.

The dinners were an immediate hit with consumers. The original production run of 5,000 dinners became 10 million by the end of the first year.

This giant step in food-processing history laid the groundwork for the growth of one of modern Omaha's most important food-production facilities. In 1955, Campbell Soup Company purchased the Swanson Company. Campbell's

began strengthening and greatly expanding operations at the downtown Omaha plant.

It added new product lines and has invested millions in keeping the plant state of the art. Most notably, in 1993, Campbell's completed a multimillion-dollar expansion and renovation program that added 37,350 square feet for a total of 491,000 square feet.

Since 1993, the Omaha plant has been Campbell's largest frozen food operation. Twelve production lines, employing more than 1,400 workers, prepare over 200 different products that are distributed to all 50 states, the Bahamas, Bermuda, Canada, and Mexico.

Product lines include Swanson

Dinners, Hungry-Man Dinners, Fun Feast Kids Dinners, and Swanson Lunch and More varieties. Also produced are Campbell's Food Service frozen entrees and frozen soups.

Campbell's Midwest Distribution Center is located 15 miles southwest of the Omaha plant, just two miles from Interstate 80. The center can service all points of distribution in the continental United States within three days. It has 13,500 pallet spots in the 123,730-square-foot facility.

Campbell officials praise the quality of their Omaha workforce, which contributes to the success of operations. In 1990, the Omaha plant won the company's prestigious "World Class Manufacturing Award."

VALMONT INDUSTRIES, INC.

Headquartered in Valley, Nebraska, about 20 miles west of Omaha, Valmont Industries, Inc., is a global leader in designing and manufacturing engineered metal structures for use in various applications, including infrastructure development, communication, construction, and industrial products. Valmont leads the world in mechanized agricultural irrigation systems, enhancing food production while conserving and protecting our natural water resources. Valmont also produces a broad range of energy-efficient lighting ballasts.

Valmont is celebrating its 50th anniversary in 1996. It started in 1946 as Valley Manufacturing Company, producing various farm implements, including elevators, front-end loaders, clod busters, and accessory items. Many of these products were private labeled for Sears Roebuck & Company, as well as being distributed under the Valley name.

Today, the farm implements are gone and Valmont has been transformed into a multinational, publicly owned corporation with 1995 sales of over half a billion dollars. The company's 13 manufacturing facilities are located throughout North America and Europe and, most recently, in Shanghai, China. Valmont's worldwide employment totals 3,800, including 1,400 at the Valley location.

Infrastructure development, road expansion, and urban renovation are taking place worldwide. Valmont participates in these markets by manufacturing a variety of metal structures, including poles used in highway lighting and traffic signal applications. Geographically dispersed manufacturing facilities throughout

Valmont manufactures a variety of metal structures, including electrical transmission poles that are used to distribute energy throughout the world.

the world provide high-quality products with just-in-time delivery.

Valmont also produces communication towers. Use of cellular telephones is expanding more than 50 percent each year. With each new coverage area or "cell" requiring a tower, and the development of "personal communication systems," the opportunities ahead for Valmont are significant.

As worldwide consumption of electrical energy continues to rise, Valmont produces the structures to transmit and distribute power throughout the world. Many existing wood and metal lattice poles are being replaced with Valmont's steel structures for better appearance, greater reliability, and more efficient use of space.

Valmont creates custom steel tubing in a wide array of types, shapes, and sizes, all made to precise customer specifications. Most of this tubing is used by other manufacturers as components within finished products. Valmont's manufacturing flexibility meets customers' just-in-time requirements.

Valmont's mechanized irrigation systems utilize the latest in structural engineering and computer controlled water application techniques. Valley® mechanized irrigation systems produce consistently higher yields while using significantly less water than traditional gravity flow or flood methods. Using less water also helps protect the groundwater from potential contamination. Valmont founded this industry in the early 1950s and continues to lead it 40 years later.

Driven by energy conservation, the lighting ballast market is undergoing an evolution from magnetic to electronic products. Valmont produces a complete line of ballasts that include both electronic and magnetic.

Valmont is a world leader in the manufacture of lighting and traffic poles for streets and highways.

Computerized controls and precision water application enable Valley® mechanized irrigation systems to increase yields while using up to 50 percent less water than traditional flood irrigation methods.

Modern Equipment Company

When Omaha drivers head to their jobs downtown, passing through the Jefferson Square area without a second glance, no billboards on Modern Equipment Company's buildings scream "Official Boat Rack Supplier for the Atlanta Olympics."

However, rowing clubs throughout the nation recognize the quality of this Omaha-manufactured product, which is being used in the 1996 Summer Olympics. It also is used by colleges such as the U.S. Naval Academy, the University of Pennsylvania, and the University of Wisconsin.

It's just one of the many reasons Modern Equipment Company (MECO) has averaged over 20 percent growth per year over the past 20 years.

MECO, which occupies several industrial buildings over three city blocks in the 20th and Cuming Streets area just north of downtown Omaha, produces one of the nation's most complete lines of nonmechanical heavy-duty industrial material handling and storage equipment.

Its self-dumping hoppers, pallet racks, cantilever racks, drum-handling equipment, hand trucks, and cylinder storage equip-

ment are sold only to dealers, who, in turn, sell them to businesses and industries in all 50 states. The 50 largest Fortune 500 industrial companies all use MECO Omaha products.

MECO was founded in 1907 as the Omaha Folding Machine Company. For over 50 years, it manufactured newspaper folding machines used all over the world until they became obsolete. The firm still receives an occasional request for parts. Later, the company added a line of drum-handling equipment and, eventually, storage racks and other products.

The company dates its spectacular modern growth to 1975, when Dick Johnson purchased the firm and became its president and CEO. "This company had always been known for its quality products and just needed to get out and become more widely recognized throughout industry," says Johnson.

Today's MECO prides itself on:

- its high-quality fabricated steel industrial products;
- an almost fanatical determination to meet customer shipping deadlines;
- a skilled workforce of dedicated employees; and
- reliability and integrity throughout all aspects of its operations.

For years the company has maintained a "never-miss" policy on shipping orders on time. For 2,282 consecutive workdays, it was able to boast that this was true. But alas! Even the longest streaks have to end.

In 1994, a lightning strike caused a day-long power outage that left workers unable to weld, paint, or move materials between floors. The firm missed promised shipping dates on a handful of noncritical orders.

Installation of a custom-designed MECO pallet rack at a major manufacturing facility

MECO immediately began a new daily string of meeting shipping commitments.

MECO's strategic location just 10 minutes from Eppley Airfield and even less from Interstates 29 and 80 is a major asset for both receiving raw materials and shipping finished products by truck. Sheets and bars of steel and steel tubing are delivered to the firm. Steel is cut, formed, punched, welded, and painted, emerging as products American industry requires to function.

Customers are unaware of how MECO has touched their lives. It happens every day—at least indirectly.

For example, it's likely that some of the food on grocery store shelves formerly sat in a distribution warehouse or packing plant equipped with MECO storage racks. The same goes for hundreds of other household products, including furniture and appliances.

Like so many other Omaha employers, MECO takes great pride in the high quality of its workers. It believes in hiring good people, training them, and paying them well. This earns their loyalty

Examining a MECO racing shell boat rack at the United States Naval Academy are Rick Johnson, vice president of MECO, and Ken Shaw, of Fred Hill and Son Company.

and helps explain their enthusiasm for serving their customers. That devotion is shared equally by plant, office, and sales force employees.

MECO's location near downtown is convenient for many of its manufacturing employees who live in adjacent areas.

MECO officials, including Vice President Rick Johnson, have been leaders of the Jefferson Square Industrial Park organization. The group encourages the economic development of the area, which includes about 180 businesses employing several thousand people.

"This is a great area because of the access to transportation," says Rick Johnson. "It's a hub of manufacturing."

MECO officials see no end to the opportunities for growth. Upcoming years probably will see an increase in exports as major U.S. dealers distribute more MECO products to customers in Europe and elsewhere. One MECO customer, a large New York dealer, has already discovered that MECO products are attractive to his European customers.

The company also is considering further product diversification, as well as establishing additional facilities in the United States.

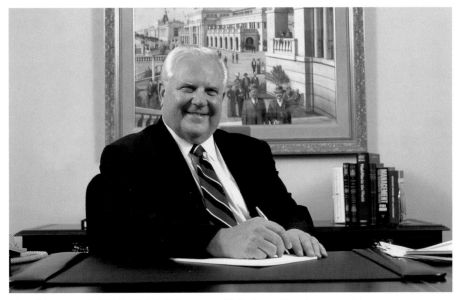

President and CEO Dick Johnson of Modern Equipment Company

CAMPOS CONSTRUCTION CO.

The definition of the word "Omaha" is "those who go against the current." Campos Construction Co. is a shining example of the definition of Omaha. Started in 1977, Robert Campos, founder and president, began building the foundation of the company during a time when many companies in the construction industry were broadcasting nationally a five-year forecast of doom and gloom for the industry. With only $500, Bob Campos decided to jump right in and fill the void.

What Campos knew that many others had forgotten has become the cornerstone of Campos Construction Co. and remains the central underlying reason for the company's growth and success, as best stated by Bob Campos:

I knew I could build a business that would allow me to provide for my family if I could hold true to four simple principles and make them the center of my business. *First is honesty.* I never wanted to receive money I had not earned, and many times I gave money back for jobs completed under cost when it was not expected. *Second is integrity.* People respect you when you do what you commit to doing; they find they can depend on you, and that comfort zone is important. *Third is consistent quality.* For me, a job is not complete until I have a personal feeling of pride. The finished product of my work represents me; it must be my best. *Fourth is community service.* It's easy to say you want a better life for yourself and others, but the real difference shows up when you become seriously committed with active involvement. Omaha is a great place; it has become that because people get involved in the work of making it so.

"Honesty, Integrity, Quality, and Community Service"

Campos Construction Co. has come a long way from its humble beginnings in 1977. The national publication *Hispanic Business* recently listed Campos Construction Co. as one of the largest and fastest-growing Hispanic-owned businesses in America. Additionally, the Greater Omaha Chamber of Commerce and KPMG Peat/Marwick Accounting Company listed Campos Construction Co. among the 25 fastest-growing companies in Omaha.

The primary focus for Campos Construction Co. is commercial buildings, offices, retail complexes, and some metal building design. The company has received many awards and national recognition. The pride and history of our nation was entrusted to Campos Construction when the company was selected to construct the President Gerald R. Ford Conservation Center. Campos also restored the homes of three other U.S. presidents: Harry S. Truman, Herbert Hoover, and Abraham Lincoln.

The company's depth in highly experienced professionals and completed major projects has created a new launching pad of growth opportunities. The company recently entered into a joint venture agreement, with multi-future venture understanding, alongside one of the 100 largest construction companies in America.

With the future bright and the workloads increasing, do not think for one moment that Robert Campos is going to be found stuck only in some office or at some construction site. Expect him and the Campos Construction Co. to remain actively involved in the betterment of life for all Omahans.

Oriental Trading Company (OTC) is known as the company that sells "fun." This Omaha-headquartered and founded company is an industry leader in the sale of value-priced toys, novelties, and giftware, as well as home and garden decor, through mail-order catalogs and other distribution channels. Examples of its inventory include such enduring and popular items as slinkies and Chinese finger traps.

"For more than 60 years, we've been selling fun, the kind of stuff that makes you say, 'Hey, I had one of those when I was a kid,'" says OTC President and CEO Terry Watanabe.

Despite all these fun items, OTC is a serious, rapidly growing business that employs nearly 3,000 people and has been featured in *Forbes* magazine and *USA Today*. Forbes described OTC's marketing as "about as sophisticated as it can get." OTC ranked 36th on *Catalog Age* magazine's 1995 list of top 100 catalogs.

OTC was founded more than 60 years ago. The company is headed by Terry Watanabe, who began working for his father when he was six years old and became president and CEO at age 20. Watanabe built OTC from a carnival and circus supplier into the industry leader it is today. OTC now operates 13 facilities in Nebraska and Iowa, comprising more than 1.5 million square feet. Every year, OTC designs, produces, and publishes more than 25 different catalogs.

OTC has broadened its product line, moving into the areas of home and garden decor. *Terry's Village* is a catalog that offers customers a higher class of decorations and gifts for the home with value-oriented prices. OTC's latest addition to its product expansion is the acquisition of *David Kay*, a popular garden decor catalog.

While the majority of OTC's business is done through consumer catalogs, the Commercial Sales Division expands the market to businesses that buy toys and novelties in bulk. Areas of business include Redemption, which provides merchandise for businesses that redeem tickets for children's prizes; restaurants and hotels that offer kids meal packages; and special gift shop markets, like zoos and museums.

From slinkies to floral swags for the home, Oriental Trading Company offers something for everyone.

LOZIER CORPORATION

According to *Display and Design Ideas*, it's the nation's largest supplier of retail store fixtures and accessories. It has received honors and been named "Vendor of the Year" by many major retailers across the country.

It has been a key supplier and helped develop such emerging retail markets as discounting, catalog showrooms, automotive parts, mass retailers, office, computer, pet, and sporting goods superstores, and discount drug and supercenters.

Lozier Corporation.

For the past 40 years, this Omaha-founded and headquartered company has been synonymous with quality manufacturing, customer service, and social responsibility.

Lozier began modestly in 1956 with 25 people and Omaha manufacturing facilities totaling 20,000 square feet. Originally the firm was called the Gordon Lozier Company. The company changed its name to Lozier Line Manufacturing Company before becoming simply Lozier Corporation.

By the mid-1990s, Lozier had expanded to more than 2.4 million square feet of manufacturing space in five cities, including Omaha, and had sales of over $300 million. The firm employs about 2,500 people.

Omaha facilities include the main office, with a product showroom, two manufacturing plants, and a distribution center. The company also has

plants in Alabama, Missouri, and Pennsylvania.

Lozier's standards for design, quality, and service revolutionized the fixtures industry and are relevant today. They include features that give merchants more usable shelf space, are easy to assemble and install, and permit merchandising flexibility and tighter shelf spacing.

Lozier optimized structural design by using high-strength materials in the right places, thus eliminating needless bulk, weight, and cost. The firm also led the way in service with the first direct-sell sales force, product inventory, and broad-based product lines.

Front-room products include modular steel display shelving and accessories (the

Christmas family project is funded entirely by employees and supports over 20 North Omaha families during the holidays. In addition, the company and the Lozier Foundation support these and many other community programs.

Allan Lozier, the son of the founders and the current active owner, designed the original fixture line and established the business philosophy based on better products at a lower cost with customer service as the lifeblood of the business. He became company president at the age of 26 and is a member of the Omaha Business Hall of Fame.

Lozier, who originally wanted to be a scientist, says that the keys to his business success are related to science: "Curiosity, impatience, a thirst for knowledge. Even as a businessman, I thirst to know what's going on. I always want to know more than anybody else."

industry standard), high-performance display shelves, wire displays and accessories, wood showcases and counters, tubular garment racks and softlines systems, and pharmacy systems. Backroom products include storage shelving, cube savers, wide spans, and pallet racks.

Lozier also is an industry leader in its commitment to safety and the environment. Since 1984, all Omaha facilities have been members of OSHA's Voluntary Protection Program. Lozier is one of only 180 companies nationwide to hold OSHA's star rating.

Lozier Corporation also participates in the Environmental Protection Agency's 33/50 Program, a voluntary initiative that promotes reductions in direct environmental releases and off-site transfers of 17 high-priority chemicals. Lozier also has a waste minimization program that focuses on reducing waste from raw materials and on recycling.

Lozier employees have a strong sense of civic responsibility. Their active participation in the community and their volunteer efforts support many people through such programs as Meals on Wheels, Brush Up Nebraska, the Cans Festival (Omaha Food Bank), the Red Cross Bloodmobile, and Adopt-a-School partnerships. An annual

AG PROCESSING INC.

Farmers and their cooperatives throughout the Midwest and Canada have a devoted partner in food production in Ag Processing Inc., headquartered in Omaha.

Ag Processing, which was formed in 1983, is dedicated to providing a competitive outlet for stockholders' agricultural products while providing stockholders a fair rate of return through increased net worth.

Ag Processing (AGP) manages the business while adding other operations to produce a combined performance that generates levels of profitability capable of sustaining the long-term growth of the company.

The firm is directly owned by over 340 local cooperatives representing over 350,000 farmers in 16 states. In addition, 11 regional cooperatives throughout the U.S. and Canada are stakeholders. Ag Processing is:

- the largest cooperative soybean processing company in the world;
- the third-largest supplier of refined vegetable oil in the United States;
- one of the leading manufacturers and developers of pet food; and
- the third-largest commercial feed manufacturer in North America.

Ag Processing sells over 10,000 tons of soybean meal every day. It also stores more than 40 million bushels of grain.

Soybean processing remains AGP's core business. AGP ranks fourth in the U.S. in terms of combined soybean capacity from its seven plants. The plants purchase the equivalent of 350,000 acres of soybeans each month for processing.

Ag Processing processes soybean meal into soy flour and grits. These products can be found in bread and in many baking products and meat products, such as sausages and ground beef. AGP is adding a sealed-bag line of soy flour to help its efforts in new market areas.

AGP purchases, stores, and markets all grains. It is both owner and major stockholder in two grain businesses—AGP Grain Cooperative, with more than 200 stockholders, and AGP Grain, Ltd. These firms operate elevators and terminals in North Dakota, Minnesota, Indiana, Ohio, Kansas, and Nebraska with a combined grain storage capacity of 40 million bushels.

AGP also is one of the nation's leading manufacturers and developers of private-label pet foods. Its branded products include Sir John's Choice, Gainer,

Denis Leiting, chairman, Ag Processing board (left), and James Lindsay, CEO

Pathfinder, Kitty Kream, Top Dog, and Kennel Kruncher. The firm exports pet food to markets in Mexico, Europe, and the Pacific Rim as well as the United States.

AGP pet food plants in Lincoln, Nebraska; Bern, Kansas; and Dexter, Missouri, are certified by the American Institute of Baking—a testimonial that AGP plants meet strict sanitation, production safety, and hygiene standards.

Production and marketing of food for all species of livestock is another major AGP enterprise. AGP's Consolidated Nutrition, L.C., headquartered in Omaha, is the third-largest commercial feed manufacturer in North America. Its brands include Supersweet Feeds, Supersweet Animal Health, Master Mix, Tindle Mills, and Masterfeeds. Masterfeeds is headquartered in London, Ontario. Consolidated Nutrition operates a modern research center in Decatur, Indiana.

AGP works to expand its customer base in the vegetable oil industry with value-added products. It expands its presence in the food business through partnerships and long-term agreements with major food companies.

The food service industry is a strong outlet for finished products from AGP's vegetable oil refineries. This vegetable oil supplies the producers of such items as barbecue sauces, salad dressings, mayonnaise, margarines, cookies, crackers, potato chips, baked goods, bottled oils, and canned shortenings, as well as a variety of snack foods. Several less noticeable uses for vegetable oils are in cosmetics, paints, resins, and pharmaceutical products.

AGP is in the forefront of developing markets for soybean oil-based industrial products. It has formed Ag Environmental Products, LLC, to research, develop, and market industrial soybean oil-derived products such as biodiesel. A new corn-processing facility at Hastings, Nebraska, will process 30,000 bushels of corn per day into fuel ethanol and feed byproducts.

In all its various business groups, AGP contributes to making thousands of products that both enrich life for consumers and help keep America's family farms viable and productive.

AGP knows that farmers have a big job in producing the nation's crops. They need AGP as their partner in turning those crops into profitable commodities.

STRECK LABORATORIES, INC.

One of the most important components enabling a physician to provide high-quality patient diagnosis is the accurate performance of the instruments on which he or she relies for the measurement of patients' blood samples. An Omaha-based firm plays a major role worldwide in ensuring such accuracy.

Streck Laboratories, Inc., has gained worldwide recognition as an innovator of hematology quality-control products. It currently manufactures 25 percent of the hematology reference controls in the United States and 35 percent of the controls worldwide. It is the largest supplier of hematology reference controls to Japan.

Streck has been a pioneer in its business since its founding by Dr. Wayne Ryan in 1971. Dr. Ryan, a biochemist, was instrumental in developing and patenting a number of first-time quality-control products.

These became necessary with the development of automated instruments to ensure correct counts on patient specimens. Until the 1960s, blood cells were counted manually using a microscope.

In the mid-1970s, Streck began manufacturing reference controls for the automated hematology instruments that were introduced into the clinical laboratory market. Since then, Streck has become a leader in the development of control products for instruments that measure the various parameters of whole blood—red cells, white cells, platelets, hemoglobin, and so on. Streck products can be found in hospitals, physicians' offices, and clinical research laboratories.

Streck's research and development program is the cornerstone of the firm's steady growth. In recent years, its innovative capabilities have resulted in the diversification of the company's product lines into the fields of chemistry, histology, and immunology.

Streck products are sold throughout the United States and 42 countries worldwide. Customers purchase products directly from Streck or through a network of independent distributors.

Streck's growth is reflected in its workforce of more than 225 employees and the expansion of its physical facilities to a new location in the Brook Valley Business Park in suburban LaVista.

In 1995, Streck launched a two-phase building program that included the construction of a 23,000-square-foot manufacturing facility and warehousing space. By the end of 1996, the firm expects to complete an additional 127,000-square-foot building that will house research laboratories, manufacturing and warehouse facilities, and administration and headquarters offices.

DAN WITT BUILDERS, INC.

Dan Witt Builders, Inc., is often ranked as Omaha's top home builder and one of the best in the nation.

A survey of 3,000 consumers by *Omaha* magazine gave Dan Witt the top local ranking. Even more impressive, the National Association of Home Builders has applied for the firm to receive the Total Quality Housing Award. This would recognize Dan Witt Builders as one of the top 10 home builders in the U.S. The award is the Malcolm Baldrige Award of home building.

The firm's projects include such notable developments as Linden Estates II, Huntington Park, Walnut Ridge, and Pacific Springs.

The firm operates as a design-build team, handling all the details of the home-building process from the beginning, rather than the traditional method of selecting the lowest bidder to construct a previously designed home. Dan Witt Builders believes that this traditional method causes quality to suffer—the last thing anyone building a dream home wants.

"We can find the ground and then help design a home to fit that home site," says Witt. "We have the knowledge and experience that will save the customer countless headaches along the way. It's a much better way to build a home."

The secret to Witt's success starts with enormous attention to detail. He personally conducts an 18-point interview with prospective buyers to ensure that he understands their desires. Complimentary plot maps and new construction kits are available at any time. Each detail of the construction phase is tracked through a series of computerized checklists that everyone from apprentice carpenters to job superintendents must initial and keep on file. Subcontractors also are required to sign off on checklists.

Dan Witt Builders works closely with N. P. Dodge Co., one of Omaha's largest real estate firms. N. P. Dodge and one of its agents, Jeff Rensch, are committed to helping prospective buyers build a Dan Witt home.

Dan Witt is proud of its system, which has helped it gain its reputation for quality, but Witt recognizes that systems are no better than the people who follow them.

"The carpenters, craftsmen, and other workers are the real heroes who have built this company into what it is today," he says. "They take a great deal of pride and ownership with them to their jobs each day. Every one of them thinks like the customer."

Jeff Rensch and Dan Witt

Courtesy of Omaha Works

When Western Electric opened one of its factories in Omaha in 1958, its parent company, AT&T, was virtually the nation's telephone industry. The new plant, known as the Omaha Works, manufactured products for what was then the Bell System.

Dramatic changes have occurred in the communications business since the Omaha Works opened its doors, including the breakup of the Bell System and, more recently, AT&T's decision to split into three separate companies.

Yet the Omaha Works—now part of Lucent Technologies—has endured all the transitions. In fact, the Omaha Works is thriving, approaching $1 billion in annual sales worldwide.

Thanks to the adaptability and flexibility of its 3,400 employees and their firm commitment to quality and service, today the Omaha Works plays a key role in the emerging global information industry in which phones, computers, TVs, and fax machines are part of multimedia systems that meet advanced information needs.

Courtesy of Omaha Works

Top photo: Robotic machines assemble the components for plug-in unit protectors and test the final product. Above: Production associates perform final quality checks on components used in telephony cabinets.

A state-of-the-art numerically controlled punch press stamps precision parts that are configured for optimum space use, keeping scrap levels and costs down.

Courtesy of Omaha Works

The Omaha Works is situated on a 340-acre site near 120th and L Streets in southwest Omaha. It has a $140 million annual payroll and occupies two million square feet of floor space that includes an employee career/education center that boasts one of the plant's state-of-the-art computer classrooms, a library, and study labs. Developed and funded in partnership with the International Brotherhood of Electrical Workers, the center was designed to ensure the Omaha Works a leading role in the telecommunications market by enabling the company to continually improve its employees' skills and knowledge.

The plant is recognized as a world-class manufacturer, having earned registration to ISO 9001. This means that its quality system meets the strict requirements set forth by the International Organization for Standardization.

The rating is important as an increasing number of global customers require that companies be ISO registered before doing business with them. The rating also translates into more business opportunities and a better future for the Omaha Works and the Omaha community.

The Omaha Works manufactures products that are different from those it made in its earlier days. Products have been expanded beyond telecommunications items into data communication, video, and audio systems that fall into three main groups:

- Outside products include metal cabinets and electronic housings, connectors, tools, and distribution terminals. These range from sophisticated digital loop carrier equipment to broadband communications equipment that pulls together the fiber-optic, coaxial, and copper cable needed to provide interactive video services.
- Interconnection products include building entrance, central office, and station protectors that safeguard the communications network from problems like power surges. Also included in this group are SYSTIMAX® Structured Cabling Systems (SCS), integrated communications cabling (distribution) systems for voice, data, and video networks within a building, factory, or campus of buildings.
- Electronic wire and cable products include a new generation of wire and cable products that carry not only voice signals for phone systems but also data and video cable for specialized applications in computer systems, instrumentation, and local area networks (LANs).

The Omaha Works formerly sold its products and services only within the U.S., but today the company is cultivating a strong international customer base, shipping its products worldwide as countries expand or upgrade their communications networks. About 30 percent of the plant's annual production is exported.

Attention to growing global competition has not detracted from the Works' involvement in the Omaha community. Omaha Works employees are major donors to the annual United Way/CHAD

Leading-edge computer classrooms broaden learning opportunities for Omaha Works employees.

campaign and are active supporters of numerous other charities and drives. The Works has contributed various grants to benefit Omaha, including $150,000 to develop high-technology classrooms at the University of Nebraska at Omaha. The Works also has awarded more than $500,000 in grants to increase the supply and improve the quality of child and elder care services in Omaha.

The plant also is firmly committed to safety and protecting the environment. In 1994, it achieved OSHA's top honor for workplace safety—one of just 113 businesses in the U.S. to claim Star Status.

Since its opening in 1958, the Omaha Works has demonstrated a commitment to excellence and a willingness to change to meet the challenges of new technology and a global economy. In the process, it has contributed significantly to the growth of the Omaha community. Together, they will continue to grow in the future.

Top photo:"Stems" of drawn copper wire used in electronic wire and cable products made at the Omaha Works. Above: Double-twist stranders twist single wire into precise pair configurations for broadband applications.

OMAHA PUBLIC POWER DISTRICT

The Omaha Public Power District (OPPD) has built a reputation for leadership in its community and in the utility industry. That reputation is based on ongoing efforts to provide quality service on a daily basis and on efforts aimed at everything from improving the air we breathe to encouraging business growth in Omaha and southeast Nebraska.

OPPD's mission statement is simple and straightforward: "To provide reliable electric energy and energy services at the lowest reasonable cost." OPPD's success in fulfilling this mission helps explain why Nebraskans remain enthusiastic about public power.

OPPD is a business-managed utility that was organized in 1946 as a political subdivision of the state of Nebraska—the nation's only state with all-public power.

A public corporation, OPPD receives no tax support of any kind. Its policies and electric rates are established by a publicly elected board of directors. As a public utility, OPPD emphasizes public service and community development in addition to providing energy.

OPPD serves nearly 270,000 metered customers (a population of well over 600,000 people) in 53 communities and surrounding rural areas in 13 southeast Nebraska counties. The cost of electricity for residential customers is consistently well below the national average. The utility also offers competitive, innovative rates and a solid power supply for commercial and industrial customers.

OPPD operates two coal-fired baseload generating facilities and one nuclear generating plant. These units provide a total baseload generating capacity of 1,705,400 kilowatts. OPPD also has more than 300,000 kilowatts of peak generating capacity for use when the demand for electricity is highest. A good mix of coal, nuclear, and natural gas generating units results in both economy and reliability for customers.

Innovative technology also helps OPPD maintain a reliable power supply for its customers even during adverse weather conditions, which can include windstorms, ice storms, heat waves, and an occasional tornado.

A 55,000-square-foot tornado-resistant Energy Control Center houses the main functions needed to coordinate the production, transmission, and distribution of electricity for OPPD customers.

The center contains storm-support facilities and advanced computer and other systems that allow operations to continue in spite of inclement weather. For example, OPPD operates an Automated Trouble Call System programmed with information that helps crews quickly pinpoint service problems in the event of serious storm damage. OPPD's computer link to the National Lightning Detection Network, which helps the utility better mobilize power restoration personnel, also is located in the center.

Reliability is further enhanced through OPPD's membership in the Mid-Continent Area Power Pool, an organization of utilities in nine states and two Canadian provinces established to promote regional power-supply stability and economy.

All of these elements, combined with committed personnel, produce an average system reliability of more than 99 percent.

According to the Utility Data Institute, over the past few years, OPPD's coal-fired Nebraska City Station has consistently ranked as one of the most economic steam electric power plants in the nation. OPPD also operates North Omaha Station, another coal-fired plant, and Fort Calhoun Station, a nuclear power generating facility.

Chemists at OPPD power plants test water quality regularly to ensure compliance with environmental regulation.

Such dependability boosts OPPD's economic development efforts, which include providing customers with detailed information about electric rates, energy availability, site availability, and other energy-related services.

OPPD is an environmentally sound power generator. It is active in the Climate Challenge Program, a joint effort of the U.S. Department of Energy and the electric utility industry initiated to produce voluntary reductions in emissions of greenhouse gases. Several efforts support OPPD's goal of reducing emissions of carbon dioxide, including the following:

• efficiency improvements at fossil-fueled power plants, which reduce both emissions and coal requirements;
• promotion of fly ash, a power plant waste product, as a substitute for cement in concrete; this ultimately reduces emissions from the production of cement;

• implementation of the Residential Energy Conservation Program, which promotes use of high-efficiency cooling and heating systems;
• commercial energy audits to help large commercial customers use energy more efficiently; and
• recycling of transformer oil, scrap metal, and paper.

OPPD also sponsors the planting of more than 12,000 trees each year. Since 1990, funds provided by OPPD have helped dozens of civic groups, schools, and other nonprofit organizations plant more than 75,000 trees and shrubs throughout southeast Nebraska.

OPPD's focus on good corporate citizenship is apparent in numerous other community-service programs. For example, it sponsors an energy assistance program that helps needy customers pay energy-related expenses. In partnership with

the local chapter of the American Red Cross, OPPD raises and distributes approximately $80,000 a year to those in need.

OPPD offers a free energy advisor telephone service, which provides customers with a wide variety of energy-related information. It also sponsors programs to help children and senior citizens who encounter emergency or potentially dangerous situations. Through the Buddy Alert and Gatekeeper programs, those who need emergency assistance are encouraged to contact OPPD field crews, who use their two-way radios to call for help.

One of OPPD's primary strategic goals is to be a customer-oriented business. The utility works to fulfill that goal by providing quality service to its customers and support to its southeast Nebraska community.

Transmission and distribution line dispatchers make use of an Automated Trouble Call System that enables faster electric service restoration following storms.

MIDWEST EXPRESS AIRLINES

In 1994, travel from Omaha's Eppley Airfield became faster, more convenient, and decidedly more comfortable with the inauguration of service by a 10-year-old Milwaukee-based carrier—Midwest Express Airlines. Since May of that year, Omaha-area travelers have been treated to an exceptional level of service at competitive coach or discounted fares, a combination not found with any other U.S. carrier. This combination is at the heart of the airline's slogan, "the best care in the air."

From Omaha, Midwest Express serves many major cities throughout the U.S. and offers the only nonstop service to Los Angeles, Milwaukee, New York/Newark, San Diego, and Washington, D.C. Convenient connections are also available through the airline's uncongested Milwaukee hub to Atlanta, Boston, New York/La Guardia, Philadelphia, Toronto, and other destinations.

This convenient schedule of nonstop, direct, and connecting flights is one of the keys to the airline's success in Omaha and gives business travelers a selection of flights designed to fit their needs while making it easier for inbound travelers to reach the city. But what most endears the airline to frequent travelers is what happens when they step onboard.

Every Midwest Express DC-9 jet is reconfigured to carry one-third fewer seats than on a normal coach flight, resulting in rows of wide, two-across seats with plenty of legroom and no middle seats. As an added touch, each seat is upholstered in rich leather. Passengers find them comfortable, and so do the experts. Midwest Express seats have consistently been rated as the most comfortable coach seats in the sky by a leading consumer report.

The remarkable inflight experience continues with the airline's food service, which often includes a full breakfast, a delicious lunch, or an inventive light snack, depending on the length and departure time of the flight. All meals are served on china with stainless flatware and linens. It's a far cry from peanuts. The airline spends more per passenger than any other on its food service. As a crowning touch, meals are served with an offering of complimentary wine or champagne.

One small addition to the Midwest Express's menu has achieved almost legendary status. On some flights, chocolate chip cookies are baked onboard, and served warm, to the unexpected delight of smiling passengers.

Supported by a friendly and courteous staff both in the air and on the ground, Midwest Express service ranks high with Omaha travelers and has attained national recognition as well. Readers of *Condé Nast Traveler* magazine, as well as those of a leading national consumer report magazine, named Midwest Express the number-one U.S. airline. The carrier was also rated best in the U.S. by the prestigious Zagat Airline Survey.

Midwest Express award-winning service is offered at a full range of coach, one-way, and discounted roundtrip excursion fares. Tickets are available for purchase through any travel agency or through the airline's reservations department.

Midwest Express began operation in 1984 and is headquartered in Milwaukee, Wisconsin. The airline went public in September 1995 and is publicly traded on the New York Stock Exchange under the ticker symbol MEH. Astral Aviation, a wholly owned subsidiary of Midwest Express, operates Skyway Airlines, the Midwest Express Connection, the regional airline partner of Midwest Express.

KMTV is Omaha's CBS affiliate. It broadcasts Midlands news, information, and weather seven days a week, including weekend mornings. Led by anchors Loretta Carroll and Michael Scott, KMTV (Channel 3) broadcasts more local news and information than any other Midlands television station.

Such leadership is characteristic of the station, which has had a proud tradition in local news since its founding in 1949. In all areas of broadcasting, KMTV chooses to lead. It is dedicated to common goals to ensure customer satisfaction and community excellence. It is staffed by creative individuals with the courage to care for one another. KMTV's goal is to be the most successful multimedia provider in Omaha.

KMTV leads in the vital area of weather forecasting. Its Forecast Center provides forecasts to radio station KFAB News/Talk 1110, as well as to KMTV's television audience.

KMTV is the Midlands home of the Easter Seals and Muscular Dystrophy telethons. The station is the exclusive source for *The Tom Osborne Show*, broadcast in association with University of Nebraska football. KMTV is especially proud to be the exclusive broadcast member of the College World Series corporate home team. Beginning in the fall of 1996, the station will broadcast Big 12 Football.

Channel 3 takes its responsibility to educate the public seriously. It produces and broadcasts *LifeQuest* in association with the University of Nebraska Medical Center. Children enjoy *Miss Jean's Storytime*, produced in association with Lutheran Ministries. Sunday morning features interviews on *Face the Midlands* and a minority affairs program, *Common Ground*.

KMTV's annual "Friendly Advice" seminar has trained more than 1,000 local not-for-profit volunteers to get results for their groups by using positive media relations. The seminar is held each January.

The annual Mid-America Partners Program reaches out to thousands of Midlanders with public service projects ranging from Warm Hearts (an October coat collection for needy children) to *Women of Mid-America*, a vignette series broadcast each summer. KMTV also is involved with such services and events as the Omaha Business Hall of Fame, the Omaha Public School Familyness Town Hall, and the River City Roundup Parade.

At KMTV, leadership and service combine for outstanding television and a better community.

KMTV's Loretta Carroll and Michael Scott are the anchors at Channel 3—the Midlands News Channel.

SITEL CORPORATION

W hen businesses nationwide need top-quality telemarketing services, their first choice is often SITEL Corporation.

SITEL creates, manages, and conducts large-scale telephone-based direct sales and customer service programs on an outsourced basis for many Fortune 500 companies.

Since its founding in 1985 as an 800 answering service with only 12 phones, this Omaha-headquartered company has grown to be one of the nation's leading independent providers of direct sales and customer services. It operates several state-of-the-art facilities across the United States and employs thousands of skilled professionals. In June 1995,

SITEL completed its initial public offering, making it the first publicly traded, independent telemarketing company.

During a four-year period in the early 1990s, revenues grew at a compound annual rate of 37 percent and earnings grew at a compound annual rate of 58 percent. The firm expects to maintain its rapid growth rate throughout the decade.

SITEL has achieved its leadership in direct sales and customer service by developing industry-specific operating divisions such as insurance, finance and banking, telecommunications, and publishing. This divisional structure enables SITEL to group its talents into specialized areas, offering customers the most effective and experience-based teleservicing solutions available in today's market.

The senior management at SITEL has over 200 years of collective direct sales and customer service experience, providing the utmost in customer service and proactive account management and ensuring the success of its clients and their programs.

The secret to SITEL's growth and success is service. At SITEL, customers don't have to settle for a cookie-cutter approach. The firm custom-designs fresh, innovative, effective strategies and solutions geared to meet each organization's specific marketing needs.

Telemarketing can benefit customers in many ways. It can increase response to an important direct mail campaign, identify high-quality leads, boost customer service and retention, and maximize cross-sales. SITEL's success reflects its expertise in all aspects of direct marketing campaigns, from scripting to training to list management and quality assurance.

The key to effective sales and customer service is a powerful and persuasive

script. If a customer doesn't already have one, SITEL will develop it. SITEL has the expertise to create scripts that will enhance any marketing campaign. SITEL also knows that scripts often need to be changed while the campaign is in progress. Knowing what to change can often make the difference between a program's success and failure.

Even the best script will be effective only if the people delivering it are competent and service-oriented. SITEL is especially proud of its intelligent, proficient, hard-working representatives. These staff members undergo in-depth market- and product-specific training so they can listen to and respond to questions with the utmost thoroughness and attentiveness.

SITEL operates a model quality assurance program. Experienced sales supervisors coach, motivate, and provide immediate feedback to all telemarketing representatives. Quality assurance representatives continually monitor performance and results to keep customers apprised of progress and to ensure customers the highest quality standards in the business. SITEL's emphasis on quality is reflected in everything from its training programs to its state-of-the-art automation.

The firm's investment in telemarketing automation is second to none. Recent developments in technology enable SITEL to maximize both the number of calls-per-hour and sales-per-hour opportunities, so the emphasis is

on conversion. All software programs are custom-designed and proprietary.

SITEL's mission is "to deliver superior results to our clients through inbound, outbound, and interactive telemarketing services." SITEL has become a nationally recognized telemarketing service bureau as well as a locally known corporation. Over the past five years, SITEL has been recognized by *Telemarketing* magazine as one of the nation's five largest service bureaus and by the Omaha Chamber of Commerce as one of the city's 10 fastest-growing companies.

Top industry leaders across the nation have lent their names, logos, and reputations to SITEL and rely on SITEL to represent them in a way in which they would represent themselves. SITEL is proud of its track record of repeatedly producing innovative, cost-effective, industry-specific marketing solutions and strategies for its customers. In every industry it serves, SITEL sets new standards!

STERLING SOFTWARE

Sterling Software is one of the nation's largest software firms. The Information Technology Division of Sterling, headquartered in Bellevue, Nebraska, has over 300 Omaha-area employees. The division specializes in software products and professional services for commercial, state and local government, and federal customers. Sterling's offerings include:

- electronic image management (EIM) and work group solutions;
- electronic commerce integration with EIM and database management systems (DBMS);
- network integration services from the mainframe or servers to the desktop; and
- client/server technology and object-oriented software development.

The division's leadership in these technologies is based on a quarter century of outstanding performance as a major Department of Defense contractor. Now expanding its offerings to the commercial sector, the division possesses a breadth and depth of experience to provide customers with practical solutions to paperless office operations.

Sterling Software is a premier provider of electronic commerce products in the United States. It is superbly positioned to integrate EIM work group solutions with electronic commerce. It can provide end-to-end solutions to electronic commerce requirements. Its technical resources, second to none, are complemented by strong project management. Most important, its mature methodology marshals all resources available to ensure project completion, on time and on budget.

Many companies can reduce their long-term costs substantially by making the transition to a client/server system. Sterling's nonproprietary solutions center on software applications and interfaces that work in concert with the underlying hardware, regardless of the hardware vendor or vintage. Sterling offers the largest independent UNIX technical staff in the Midwest. This staff possesses hands-on experience with many environments, including HP, Digital, and SUN.

Sterling attracts top professionals through its state-of-the-art technology, its comprehensive benefit packages, and the opportunity to share in a progressive company.

With laboratories equipped with multigenerational technology that can emulate customers' environments, the firm develops, modifies, and maintains software quickly and accurately. Its low Midwest overhead allows it to provide customers with practical solutions at attractive, highly competitive prices.

In an era when many defense contractors are forced to downsize, Sterling's Information Technology Division has been singular in its capability to grow within the Heartland. Sterling Software is a company on the move in Omaha and throughout the nation.

HunTel Systems is a diverse family of businesses, each with its own unique products and services. It has successfully combined the strength of a reliable midwestern workforce with today's sophisticated technologies.

Granddaddy's (Emory C. Hunt, Sr.) vision in 1912 gave birth to the legacy that has become HunTel Systems. He passed his pioneering spirit on to Emory, Jr., who nurtured the young firm through the middle of the 20th century. Today, that same spirit lives on in the third generation in Richard Hunt and Hugh Hunt. Their fresh and innovative management style has earned them the respect of their associates, their customers, and their peers.

Business has expanded beyond the core local exchange telephone service called HunTel Telephone Properties. Through diversification and rapid growth, the firm has spread its wings to develop the focus that will guide it to the future. HunTel Systems delivers products and services to customers coast to coast and throughout the world.

HunTel CableVision brings cable television to rural Nebraska communities. HunTel Engineering provides communication engineering services throughout the Midwest. Mid America Computer Corporation is the largest communications service bureau of its kind in the country. Concrete Equipment Company manufactures the premier product line in the concrete production industry.

Professional Forms, Inc., offers business forms and a sophisticated system of forms management. HunTel Communications, Inc., is Omaha's business telephone and computer networking specialist.

In each of its diverse businesses, HunTel's people hold the key to the future. HunTel's philosophy can be summed up in three words: dedicated to quality. Remarkable for its diversity and unique in its breadth of services, HunTel Systems soars into the 21st century.

DATA DOCUMENTS

orms automation is growing rapidly in today's high-tech business environment. The demand for greater efficiency, accuracy, and speed in the flow of information has prompted many companies to consider incorporating forms automation software into their systems as an alternative or supplement to traditional paper-and-ink forms.

Few companies have been better positioned to take advantage of that growth than Data Documents®.

For over 35 years, Data Documents has been a leader in the development and

marketing of products and services designed specifically for the management of business information.

Today, Data Documents, with headquarters in Omaha, is one of the nation's largest producers of custom forms, pressure-sensitive labels, and forms management systems. These systems enable its large corporate customers to enhance productivity and reduce costs associated with managing information.

The company's Odyssey Integrated Services[SM] program provides customers with comprehensive forms and information

management services on either a fully outsourced basis or in combination with existing in-house customer programs.

Services are supported by Data Documents' proprietary software and include workflow reengineering, process analysis, forms design, inventory and warehouse management, internal and external electronic transactions, and disaster recovery. Customers choose which service modules best meet their needs. Data Documents provides complete training, customization, and consultative support to ensure maximum benefit.

Data Documents also has established a leading position in the rapidly growing pressure-sensitive label market. Through its continuing involvement with customers and third-party vendors, the company has developed numerous label innovations, such as airline baggage tracking labels and combination label/form products. Many of the company's products have been developed to satisfy customers' increasingly variable information needs, such as inventory control barcoding for manufacturing, retailing, and distribution businesses.

Since its founding in Omaha in 1958, Data Documents has expanded nationally. The company has 11 manufacturing plants and more than 70 sales offices in the U.S. and employs 1,250 people. Data Documents' common stock is traded on the NASDAQ National Market.

Data Documents understands the dynamics of information and the technology required to manage it. The firm has helped customers maintain peak performance in their information management systems.

Data Documents offers a unique blend of products and services aimed at helping customers boost productivity and control costs within their information systems.

The first step when checking in at a Hyatt Hotel anywhere in the world is usually a 1-800 call to Omaha.

From Hyatt's highly sophisticated Worldwide Reservation Center at 98th and Q, nearly 250 representatives handle more than seven million calls a year, booking 76,000 rooms in 164 hotels in 34 countries.

Whether the guest will be staying at a Hyatt Hotel in Texas or Tahiti, the request for service is handled by the Omaha center, which has received the prestigious Esprit Award from *CIO*, a magazine for information executives.

The Reservation Center opened in 1972 with a staff of 14 and no computer system. It handled 575,000 calls during the first year.

Today, the center's SPIRIT Central Reservation System easily handles more than 200 million transactions annually. Representatives can access a wide range of information on all Hyatt properties, including rates, the availability of baby-sitting services and cable TV, and the distance between the hotel and the airport. Travel agents can book rooms directly through links with major airline reservation systems and receive instant confirmation.

Since SPIRIT went on-line in 1990, Hyatt's bookings have increased 25 percent annually with no increase in the average length of the call.

Hyatt's plans call for ever more sophisticated personal service. For example, regular customers will have their calls handled by the same "personal reservationist" each time they call. Improved graphics will let representatives view city maps and pictures of rooms at each Hyatt property so they can answer questions more easily. Even now, Internet users can view

Jodi Falcone, executive assistant and a 10-year veteran of the Hyatt Reservation Center, demonstrates Hyatt's SPIRIT Central Reservation System.

pictures of some Hyatt properties and rooms on their PC screens.

Hyatt knows that the success of its reservations business depends on Omaha's high-quality workforce, as well as sophisticated technology. The Worldwide Reservation Center is recognized as an excellent place to work; benefits include tuition reimbursement after six months of service and complimentary accommodations at Hyatt hotels.

In addition to handling calls from travel agents and guests, Reservation Center staff members provide a wide range of customer services. For example, members of the Service Assistance Department act as liaisons between guests and hotels, answering questions and resolving problems. The Consumer Affairs Department responds to guest comments. The 1-800 Check-in Desk allows Hyatt guests to check in to hotels over the telephone and to receive their room numbers before they arrive.

A 1-800 call to Hyatt in Omaha buys travelers a world of enjoyment.

Twenty short years ago, it might have been difficult to imagine sophisticated telecommunications companies sprouting up on the prairie around Omaha. But a few pioneers recognized Omaha as a natural breeding ground for the world's most advanced telecommunications industry.

Two of these pioneers were Steven and Sheri Idelman, who established Idelman Telemarketing in 1986.

Today, Omaha is recognized as the center of the telemarketing industry worldwide, and the Idelmans are known nationally as founders of the telemarketing industry. The explosive growth of Idelman Telemarketing parallels the growth of the telemarketing industry in the United States.

• Sales from telemarketing have grown from approximately $130 billion in 1985 to more than $600 billion today. This does not include Wall Street transactions, which add another $200 billion a day.

• Employment opportunities are increasing faster in the telemarketing industry than in any other area of business. In 1995, there were more than 4.5 million people employed in telemarketing, and industry experts project that as many as eight million will be employed by the industry by the end of this decade.

• Telemarketing, once used only for simple lead generation and sales campaigns, is now employed for a wide range of highly sophisticated sales and customer support operations, including complex customer service programs, help lines, and sales and database marketing efforts.

• Nearly every Fortune 500 company employs telemarketing in support of its sales and/or customer service functions.

Nurturing a service industry like telemarketing from entrepreneurial infancy to a confident and prosperous maturity requires the development and standardization of management practices that are consistently effective.

Idelman Telemarketing has been a leader in developing and refining the management techniques that have helped the industry mature and gain in stature. As a result, the company has become the largest outbound telemarketing service agency in the country, based on billable minutes. Its inbound division is among the fastest-growing inbound telemarketing service agencies in the U.S., and telemarketing management practices developed at Idelman Telemarketing are now considered industry standards throughout the world.

Today, Idelman Telemarketing is known as ITI Marketing Services and has 22 facilities in six states and more than 3,000 workstations. The company employs more

than 7,000 people and is led by a professional management team headed by President and Chief Executive Officer Brent Welch. The company provides both inbound and outbound telemarketing services for programs directed to consumers as well as businesses. It also provides bilingual telemarketing services and interactive and insurance support.

ITI Marketing Services has been cited many times for its commitment to integrity and quality in telemarketing. In 1994 and 1995, ITI was awarded *Telemarketing* magazine's MVP Quality Award, a top industry accolade. ITI is the only non-employee group to have received the Sprint Consumer Services Group President's Award for quality customer service. And in 1994, ITI was the recipient of a special commendation from the U.S. House of Representatives' Subcommittee on Telecommunications and Finance for its pro-consumer policies and procedures.

ITI's growth and achievement have occurred in large part because of the company's recognition that, fundamentally, telemarketing is a "people business." According to Brent Welch, "We know that the success of the programs we run for our clients, and consequently our success, depends in large measure on the people we have in our centers. Our quality processes begin with our recruitment philosophy of seeking, hiring, training, and retaining the best people in every market in which we operate."

ITI is committed to being the highest-paying company of its kind in every community in which it has a facility, thus attracting bright, talented people. From there, the company concentrates on intensive, ongoing training programs and provides a comprehensive employee

benefits package that includes health insurance and profit-sharing for even part-time employees. This, in turn, helps to improve the quality of life in communities such as Omaha where ITI is a significant employer.

ITI Marketing Services provides additional value that greatly enhances Omaha's quality of life. ITI gives substantial financial support to many community organizations, including the Special Olympics and United Way. Beyond strictly financial support, ITI executives serve on the boards of numerous nonprofit organizations.

ITI strongly supports the education arena by sponsoring public television and Adopt-a-School programs in several states.

The next decade for ITI Marketing Services will take the company into the 21st century. To position the company to best capitalize on its leadership image and evolving technological developments in marketing and communications, Golder, Thoma, Cressey, Rauner, Inc., of Chicago recently acquired a majority equity interest in ITI. Golder, Thoma, Cressey, Rauner, Inc., is a private equity firm with a long record of investing in leading-edge companies in high-growth industries with strong management teams.

According to Welch, "ITI Marketing Services will continue to be headquartered in Omaha. The management team that was responsible for our growth thus far will continue to lead the company into the next century. ITI Marketing Services will continue to be a leader in telemarketing and telecommunications."

PKS INFORMATION SERVICES, INC.

KS Information Services, Inc., is a world-class information services company headquartered in Omaha. The company provides customers from coast to coast, large and small, with their own large-scale, high-performance computing environment 24 hours a day, seven days a week. PKS also offers systems integration services to help customers define, develop, and implement cost-effective information systems.

The PKS computer center was engineered to ensure fault tolerance and to enable scale economies in hardware, software, people, and so on. The first point ensures nonstop operation for customers. The second virtually guarantees more cost-effective computing services than most organizations can deliver themselves.

In conjunction with offering computing services, PKS manages a wide-area network (WAN) on a nationwide basis. The company is also engaged in the design, installation, and maintenance of high-performance local area networks (LANs) and multitiered distributed architectures that use the latest hardware and software technologies.

PKS's business is driven by its quality service commitment. PKS backs its commitment to total customer satisfaction by adhering to a comprehensive and organization-wide service management process that enables continuous measurement and monitoring of all technical services and deliverables—always with an eye on exceeding the customer's expectations. The PKS Service Management Process is founded on the Quality Assurance Institute's Quality Implementation Model and the 14 quality principles of Dr. W. Edward Deming for service-oriented businesses. This process emphasizes establishing service levels unique to each customer and thereafter measuring actual performance against those levels.

PKS's infrastructure and Service Management Process are designed to meet the highest performance standards—those of its customers. Under the terms of PKS's Base Level Services, dedicated resources are appropriated to meet each customer's unique requirements. In providing support services, PKS does not

make distinctions according to account size. Every customer receives the same high-quality service. In addition, PKS's contractual agreements stipulate base-level and incremental-level service fees so customers are always aware of their computing costs. A customer's base-level services include:

- **Computer operations and telecommunications management and support.** Monitoring and response; job/task start, recovery, restart, and rerun; and management and maintenance of all computing and telecommunications equipment.
- **Scheduling, maintenance, and support.** Management and maintenance of the job/task scheduling process; coordinating and verifying of production job/task schedules; and monitoring of job/task schedule queues, processing activity, and performance.
- **Storage management.** Managing and maintaining the disk storage subsystem; monitoring error statistics and taking corrective action; and monitoring utilization and performance.
- **Tape management.** Management and maintenance of the tape storage sub-

system; management of off-site archiving procedures; and coordination of external tape processing procedures.
- **Help Desk services.** A 24-hour customer support center staffed by operating and network systems technicians who provide immediate response to customer problems and requests for service.
- **System software services.** Installation, maintenance, and troubleshooting of all system software and performance of system generations for specific customer requirements.
- **Technology planning and change management.** Monitoring customer service levels; planning, coordinating, and monitoring changes to the technical environment; forecasting resource requirements and providing technical guidance for customer project initiatives.

The PKS systems integration organization develops a unified architecture of hardware, software, and communications technologies in order to meet the customer's specific design, operational, and management objectives. The company offers a turnkey service that includes the design, development, acquisition, technical

integration, implementation, training, and support necessary for successful completion of a customer project.

PKS provides customers with professional software developers and the most advanced software development technologies available. Acting as an extension to the customer's in-house staff, PKS can address a broad range of customer requirements, such as converting, replatforming, reimplementing, or replacing of systems. One such offering is PKS's *Suite 2000* service, which facilitates the conversion of programs and applications so that date-related information is accurately processed and stored before and after the year 2000.

Better service and better value are the result of PKS's total focus on integrating capital, technology, and expert people. PKS Information Services, Inc., has combined these key components in a unique way for the benefit of organizations seeking to enhance their value chain.

First Data Corporation

First Data Corporation (FDC)—a giant in the information processing industry—employs more people in Omaha than in any other city. Of the company's 37,000 employees, about 6,500 call Omaha home.

The largest part of FDC—called the Card Services Group—began as First Data Resources in a small office at 72nd and Pacific Streets more than 25 years ago. Today, First Data Corporation is a leader in a variety of industries.

In 1995, FDC grew immensely. The company merged with competitor First Financial Management Corporation in one of the world's biggest mergers that year. The merger allows for opportunities that are just surfacing in the global payments marketplace.

That marketplace is being driven in large part by consumers' demand for more ways to pay for things and easier access to their funds. FDC clients want to meet those consumer needs. The new FDC has the size, scale, and resources to ensure that they do.

Chairman and CEO Ric Duques, who is based at the company's headquarters in Hackensack, New Jersey, says "working with clients, we can shape how business is transacted in the United States and around the world; how people purchase and pay for goods and services; how they transfer funds; how they gather, store, and utilize information; how financial institutions adapt to the world of electronic commerce; and how the Information Highway works as a thoroughfare and not a roadblock."

With the merger, FDC's estimated $3.6 billion in revenues place it about 320th on the Fortune 500 revenues list. The $14 billion value placed on it by shareholders—what is known on Wall Street as its "market capitalization"—makes FDC about the 70th-largest company in the U.S.

But even as the company expands deeper into the global marketplace and plays a greater role in how consumers the world over pay for things, its roots remain firmly planted in Omaha. FDC remains committed to providing good, sound jobs in a city where it's proud to have a major presence.

The company also is committed to maintaining a diverse workforce; providing a safe and healthy workplace; and creating an environment that values individuality, respect, and open communication.

The units that make up the new FDC—both inside and outside Omaha—together serve some of the largest names in the financial services, health care, hospitality, insurance, and public utility industries, as well as in federal, state, and local governments.

These units include FDC's Omaha-based Card Services Group, a world leader in third-party transaction card processing. The Card Services Group processes more than 3.3 billion credit card and merchant transactions and 1.1 billion bank card statements yearly. In recent years, the unit has expanded to the oil, retail, and private label card markets. In addition, the unit

provides a full range of merchant processing services through its acquisitions of Card Establishment Services and Envoy. FDC also processes card transactions internationally through Basildon-based FDR Limited in the United Kingdom and Sydney-based FDR Australia.

Three other FDC units are headquartered in Omaha. FDC's Teleservices is the sole provider of operator and customer support services to MCI, the nation's second-largest long-distance company. Teleservices operates five voice centers throughout the U.S.

Call Interactive is a leading provider of interactive voice services. The unit's patented technology enables its customers to interact with as many as 10,000 callers in 90 seconds. Call Interactive handles music video requests for MTV and has executed marketing programs for some of the country's best-known brand-name products.

First Data InfoSource provides critical information retrieval and management services to the collections, financial, insurance, retail, and direct marketing industries through its integration of several databases

of more than 96 million U.S. households and 10 million businesses.

Other FDC units and their locations include Integrated Payment System, Inc., of Englewood, Colorado; First Data Investor Services Group, Boston; Nationwide Credit, Atlanta; CES/NaBanco, Sunrise, Florida.; Western Union Financial Services, Inc., Paramus, New Jersey; TeleCheck International, Inc., Houston; International Banking Technologies, Atlanta; First Image Management Company, Atlanta; First Health, Atlanta; and MicroBilt, Atlanta.

Good partners make a world of difference. With the right partner, life can be rich and fulfilling.

That's the type of partnership U S WEST and Omaha have enjoyed for years.

As a major player in the connections business, U S WEST helps customers share information, entertainment, and communications services in local markets throughout the world.

But there's no market quite like Omaha. A state-of-the-art infrastructure, coupled with a favorable regulatory environment, have been the springboard for a wide range of the newest telecommunications services.

Multimedia services began in Omaha. U S WEST TeleChoice® services provide interactive television programming via fiber-to-the-curb, thus giving Omahans a potential array of information and entertainment options.

Omaha was the first U S WEST city with a ubiquitous Integrated Switched Digital Network (ISDN). The network provides digital connectivity throughout the world for Omaha businesses. Their business is better because it's so easy to communicate and share information.

ISDN helped launch another first in U S WEST territory—the PC/Phone^{SM} trial. U S WEST PC/Phone service lets users plug personal computers directly into telephone sets. The service turns an ordinary phone into a virtual office.

Omaha enjoys a high development of self-healing network services. Local businesses can count on trouble-free telecommunications because the network automatically detects trouble and reroutes traffic.

The favorable regulatory climate and advanced communication capabilities have enhanced Omaha's position as the telemarketing capital of the world.

A host of additional services made their debut in Omaha, including Priority Ring, which assigns a certain ring to callers you decide you don't want to miss, and Call Rejection, which lets you determine who you do want to miss. And Omaha was the first U S WEST location and the second city in the nation to identify the name and number of the calling party through Caller ID service.

Omaha and U S WEST—it's a partnership that works!

When industries nationwide consider locating in Omaha, they often get their first view of Omaha through the "lens" of Rainbow Video Productions.

The firm has prepared the video picture for a Greater Omaha Chamber of Commerce CD-ROM used as a tool to recruit new employers and high-tech workers. The project packs text, photos, audio, and video onto a computer disk. The disk contains more than 1,700 still images and graphics, 45 videos, over 70 audio recordings, several databases, and thousands of words of text.

Ironically, this "Omaha" company is actually located on an acreage in southeast Lancaster County, Nebraska, because Rainbow founder Phil Troupe, who lives next door to the studio and offices, prefers country living. Clients don't care where the firm is based as long as Rainbow's production work maintains its outstanding quality.

Rainbow Video is the only production company in Nebraska to offer clients the D-3 digital-tape format. Since 1981, the firm has been producing video presentations for local and national markets, ranging from 30-minute documentaries to 30-second TV commercials. It handles all aspects of video projects, including concept development, research, scripting, videography, graphics design, editing, and duplication.

Rainbow's facilities include a large studio, a video edit suite, a computer- graphics suite, an interactive multimedia suite, a video library, and offices.

Rainbow has provided camera crews and editing facilities for visiting broadcast networks and syndicated programs. Clients have included ABC, CBS, A&E, and NBR, among others.

Rainbow's diverse clients include medical facilities, agriculture-related companies, manufacturers, financial institutions, retailers, research facilities, educational institutions, and government agencies.

Rainbow has attained national status as a video production firm by developing relationships with Nebraska clients that have national connections. It has active sales and marketing programs in both Omaha and Lincoln.

Tess Fogerty

"Technology in Creative Hands"

INACOM

Today's corporate executives view information technology not just as a tool to process information but as a key competitive advantage for their companies. They are looking for a single source to help them maximize their information technology investments and control the ongoing costs associated with the life of their systems. That's what the professionals at Inacom offer corporate customers.

Omaha-based Inacom, founded in 1982, has become one of the premier technology management services providers to national and international corporations. Inacom, with offices in every major U.S. market and affiliated offices throughout the world, offers logistical, support, and integrational services, including computer and communications systems from the world's leading technology companies, including AT&T, Compaq, Cisco Systems, Hewlett-Packard, IBM, Intel, Microsoft, and many more.

Inacom professionals work with business customers to determine the best technology systems for their workforce. The Inacom solution for one company could be a global computer network, backed by onsite professional staff to help maintain, upgrade, and inventory every unit in the company. Another customer may require a mobile solution for its traveling sales force, including cellular phones, long-distance services, and

notebook computers to provide the company's travelers with a virtual office environment anywhere in the country.

Regardless of the systems solution need, every step in the Inacom process is backed by ISO 9001 quality standards, the most rigorous quality certification in the industry. Fully automated distribution centers, located in Omaha as well as on the East and West Coasts, ship the systems directly to the desktop of each employee. Inacom technical experts then provide ongoing seamless support for the entire voice and data system.

The more than 2,000 worldwide employees of Inacom are committed to their customers and their communities. In Omaha, the company is a major employer and key corporate sponsor of a variety of social services, arts, and civic efforts. In addition, employees are encouraged to volunteer their time to support community betterment organizations.

Inacom is proud of its innovative efforts to help customers get the most from their information technology investment.

UNION PACIFIC

When the Union Pacific linked with Central Pacific to create the nation's first transcontinental railroad in 1869, workers drove the famous Golden Spike to commemorate the momentous achievement.

Little did the Irish crews who set out from Omaha after the Civil War know that the genuine "golden age" of railroading would be more than a century in the future—in the 1990s.

Today's Union Pacific is proud of its heritage of having helped build the West. It's keeping that heritage alive in building today's West, using some of the industry's most advanced technology.

Today's Union Pacific Railroad stretches over 22,800 miles of track in 23 states. It also is the major U.S. rail link to Mexico.

It has 35,800 employees, about 10 percent of them in the Omaha-Council Bluffs area, where UP has been headquartered since President Lincoln signed the Pacific Railroad Act in 1862.

Throughout this century, Union Pacific has been one of the nation's most profitable railroads.

In 1994, Union Pacific Corporation, the railroad's parent company, ranked eighth among the nation's 50 largest transportation companies, according to *Fortune* magazine. It had revenues of $9.1 billion, about two-thirds stemming from the railroad. If the railroad had been ranked separately, it would have placed 11th among transportation firms.

Ever since E. H. Harriman purchased a bankrupt Union Pacific in 1897 and com-

pletely rebuilt the railroad, it has been noted for its outstanding maintenance and technological sophistication.

Appropriately, one of the finest examples of that technological sophistication is named after Harriman and located in Omaha. The $50 million Harriman Dispatch Center, which was constructed in the renovated historic freight house where Harriman purchased UP, is the largest and most sophisticated rail command center in the world. From here, dispatchers control the operations of more than 1,200 trains a day across the UP system.

Union Pacific also operates the world's largest switchyard, the massive Bailey Yard in North Platte, Nebraska, the operating hub of the railroad. Here, incoming cars are sorted into new trains

for destinations all over the country. During peak periods, the switchyard handles 125 trains a day.

Ironically, one of Union Pacific's greatest problems in the mid-1990s was keeping up with the rapidly increasing demands for its service. It is one of the nation's leading carriers of coal, grain, soda ash, and intermodal freight.

Union Pacific has met the increasing demands of its customers by double and triple tracking in especially busy corridors such as central Nebraska and by increasing the flow of its unit trains. The busiest segment for Union Pacific is from O'Fallons (west of North Platte) to Gibbon, Nebraska.

Technology helps Union Pacific route trains and cars most efficiently. The railroad uses one of the nation's largest fiber-optics transmission networks to control and monitor rail traffic. Union Pacific now emphasizes meeting the transportation needs of "just-in-time" manufacturers who want cars on time, not early or late.

Union Pacific also uses the latest in technology to communicate with its widely scattered workforce. It is one of a handful of major corporations to have its own corporate television network. In 1995, that system had 100 downlink sites. Every Union Pacific employee is within 40 miles of a downlink.

Union Pacific has even reentered the passenger train business by operating daily commuter trains for local authorities. Metra in Chicago carries about 109,000 riders a day, while Metrolink in Los Angeles carries 3,300 riders daily.

Union Pacific has always been noted for being one of Omaha's most outstanding corporate citizens. Union Pacific Foundation makes grants totaling about $1.2 million a year in Nebraska, about $1 million of which is given to Omaha educational, social service, and health programs.

UP's civic mindedness has given it another distinction. It's the nation's only railroad to help operate a professional baseball team. UP joined Warren Buffett and Walter Scott in purchasing the AAA Omaha Royals to help ensure that Omaha remained the home of the College World Series.

Reminders of the major role Union Pacific plays in Omaha are everywhere—from Kenefick Park and the Union Pacific Historical Museum to announcements of Union Pacific scholarship winners or UP participation in the Omaha public schools Adopt-a-School program or UP sponsorship of "nights" at the Omaha Symphony, Opera Omaha, and other cultural institutions.

If it had not been for the coming of Union Pacific, Omaha might have remained just another small Missouri River community. UP continues to play a crucial role in the area's economic development, quite apart from its $180 million local payroll.

In a very real sense, they've grown up together: Union Pacific and Omaha.

Cox Communications

As one of the nation's telecommunications centers, Omaha is at the crossroads of the Information Superhighway. And as one of the nation's leaders in communications for more than a century, Cox Communications is Omaha's recognized leader in providing for the community's total communications needs.

Once known only for its superior cable television service, which remains the company's core business, Cox Communications has built a fiber-optic network that positions this multidimensional business to deliver a wide range of cutting-edge products and services throughout the Omaha area. Its advanced fiber-optic technological platform allows Cox to offer Omahans one-stop shopping for video, voice, and data communication.

Since the company started a newspaper business in Ohio in the 1890s, Cox has successfully pioneered through all of America's developmental stages in the world of communications. The Cox Fiber Network in Omaha is the logical progression for a company whose path has included the frontiers of newspapers, radio, broadcast television, and cable television.

In 1995, Cox broke new ground by demonstrating personal communications services (PCS) technology in the state of Nebraska for the first time ever. That event showcased the marriage of Cox's fiber-optic system and wireless telephone technology.

And Cox's participation in the Sprint Telecommunications Venture holds promise for incorporating long-distance and local wireline telephone service into the company's array of offerings.

While these "high-tech" advances assure Omaha of being at the forefront in the competitive field of information technology, Cox Communications bases its success on a foundation of simple, basic concepts. The company's three-part vision sums them up best.

Cox takes pride in being the industry model for customer service . . . a pacesetter in delivering state-of-the-art technology . . . and a valued, caring part of the community.

Cox is not the only communications company exploring the world of information technology. But Cox's customer service sets it apart from the crowd. The company has reaped numerous customer service awards locally, regionally, and nationally.

"Customer-driven" best describes the Cox attitude toward serving the people of Omaha, which is why the Omaha cable system has been lauded for such practices as its 24-hour service; the scheduling of installation and service appointments in convenient two-hour time windows; and its one-call service, where transferring a customer call is out of the question.

As if these service initiatives were not enough, Cox-Omaha continued to be a trailblazer in 1995 by launching its Cox WireLink service, a residential telephone and cable wire maintenance program that saves Omahans more than $1 million every year on their telephone bills.

Cox LocaLink is another unique twist offered in Omaha. LocaLink is a 21-channel level of service offered at no charge to subscribers. With LocaLink, vital information services are provided with ease to Omaha homes that need them most.

These and many other customer service practices that are standard procedures at Cox reflect a dedication to the community. But Cox does not contain its

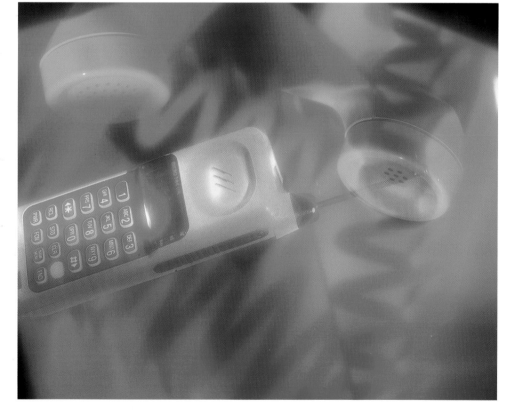

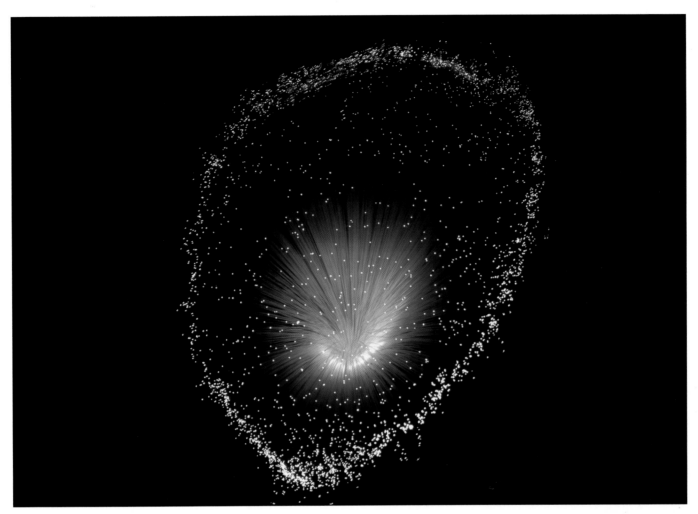

care for the community within its business operations.

The company and its more than 250 employees are deeply involved in community service of all kinds. From the most visible, such as Cox's substantial contributions to and assistance in the annual Muscular Dystrophy Association Telethon, to behind-the-scenes participation by Cox employees on boards and civic groups all over Omaha, Cox is a critical part of the community fabric.

And Cox's commitment to education in Omaha is unparalleled in the business community. Cox provides free cable service to every Omaha school and supports that courtesy service with an ongoing program of innovative classroom activities that are made available to educators at no charge. Cox's partners at Harrison School, Ezra Millard School, and Northwest High School stand out as models in the use of educational technology in the community.

Finally, a unique investment in the community that only Cox makes is the dedication of local television programming services for public use and enjoyment. 02TV (Cox Channel Two), Cox's independent cable channel, blends the best of locally produced programs with popular nationally syndicated shows. Omaha Lancers hockey, Omaha Racers basketball, and Omaha Royals baseball are just a few of the many "exclusives" that make Cox the cable television provider of choice.

Cox weaves these elements—technology, customer service, community involvement—to give Omahans what they expect in a modem telecommunications company.

Omahans demand—and Cox Communications delivers—the best new fiber-optic technology available anywhere, presented with honest, old-fashioned dedication to the customer as boss and a deep-rooted investment in the community.

And that's what makes Cox Communications Omaha's recognized leader in total communications.

BAIRD HOLM

Companies from major corporations to entrepreneurial start-ups have a legal partner in the firm of Baird, Holm, McEachen, Pedersen, Hamann & Strasheim, one of the largest law firms in Omaha.

Baird Holm, which traces its origins to 1873, is proud of its long record of excellence and professional leadership nationally and particularly in the Midwest. Today, the diversity and extent of Baird Holm's practice sets it apart from other firms.

The firm not only has recognized expertise in traditional areas of the law but also in technology and intellectual property. Such expertise is critical to today's companies that are technology-based or that rely on technology. The firm is expert in handling licensing transactions, developing programs to protect and enforce intellectual property rights, registering copyrights and trademarks or service marks, and raising capital and managing acquisitions.

At Baird Holm's core is its large and highly varied civil practice. This practice includes expertise in employment and labor relations; franchising; insurance; health care; litigation; mediation and arbitration; banking and finance; securities and general corporate law; tax, environmental, real estate, and bankruptcy law; and creditors' rights.

With attorneys licensed in Nebraska, Iowa, and six other states, Baird Holm seeks to match legal experience with each client's requirements and budgets. The firm's goal is to provide prompt, effective, and professional services. It is proud of its responsiveness to each client's needs and goals. It believes that understanding the unique nature of each business and the "ins and outs" of what clients do is essential in providing high-quality legal services.

Clients of all sizes are welcome. Baird Holm represents a range of clients, including small start-up companies, family-owned businesses, large publicly held corporations, large government and nonprofit entities, and individuals. Baird Holm has successfully served clients in industries such as telecommunications, manufacturing, wholesale, retail, finance, health care, education, insurance, entertainment, broadcasting, agriculture, and the service sectors.

Baird Holm's attorneys keep current with developments in their fields. They appreciate the trends and forces affecting their clients' businesses. They don't just react to current problems; they plan for the future so as to provide clients with an effective response to their needs.

Baird Holm's goal is to be a key resource in the management and success of its clients' businesses.

Much has changed since the firm opened in 1873, but Baird Holm's commitment to the highest standards of professional service for its clients has certainly been maintained.

Since 1966, Dana Larson Roubal and Associates (DLR) has maintained a clear focus on serving clients. DLR professionals listen to a client's facility needs and define better solutions. Adaptable. Cost-effective. Responsive. Each of these terms characterizes DLR projects.

Fast-track schedule requirements? DLR completed an 86,000-square-foot corporate office building in only 14 months using fast-track construction techniques.

Need passage of a bond referendum for educational facility improvements? DLR has a community awareness program that since 1991 has been used to pass more than 26 bond referendums representing over $150 million in construction for Nebraska, Iowa, and surrounding communities.

Changing requirements affecting your health care facilities? For the past eight years, DLR has worked with major health care providers in completing over 200 projects, from interior renovations to the design of a 75,000-square-foot medical office building.

Looking for national expertise in criminal justice facilities? Federal agencies around the nation have turned to DLR for its experience in designing law enforcement centers, county correctional facilities, jails, federal penitentiaries, and the General Service Administration's new $48 million federal courthouse in Omaha.

Interested in sports facility design? DLR has designed and built over 13 major league training facilities and minor league stadiums with combined budgets of over $136 million.

A national network of multidisciplined firms, DLR is an employee-owned corporation with headquarters in Omaha and offices in 12 other U.S. cities and Mexico. With over 370 professionals providing architecture, engineering, planning, and interior design services, DLR is certain to continue to grow and diversify with its clients into the 21st century.

Serving clients nationwide from the DLR office in Regency

ABRAHAMS, KASLOW & CASSMAN

For over half a century, Abrahams, Kaslow & Cassman has been one of Omaha's most respected business law firms. The firm began in 1940 when Milton R. Abrahams and Ben E. Kaslow, both Creighton University law school graduates, combined their legal practices. In 1949, the two were joined by Frederick S. Cassman, a Harvard law school graduate. The three original partners and their successors have earned a reputation for providing high-quality legal services and for serving the Omaha community through their involvement in significant professional, civic, and charitable activities.

Over the years, the attorneys of Abrahams, Kaslow & Cassman have contributed time and effort to a wide variety of nonprofit and civic organizations,

including the Omaha Public Library, United Way, the Omaha Board of Education, Joslyn Art Museum, the Greater Omaha Chamber of Commerce, the Omaha Airport Authority, Father Flanagan's Boys' Home, the Omaha Community Foundation, Fontenelle Forest, the Jewish Federation of Omaha, the National Conference of Christians and Jews, and the Small Business Association. The Abrahams branch public library is named in honor of Milton Abrahams, in recognition of his long service on the board of trustees and his generous donations to the Omaha Public Library and its foundation.

Members of the firm also are active in the Omaha, Nebraska, and American Bar Associations. Of particular note, Terrence

P. Maher is vice chair of the Electronic Commerce and Communications Committee of the Section of Business Law of the American Bar Association.

Today, the firm includes more than 20 attorneys with a broad range of expertise and experience in representing businesses in a wide variety of industries, including banking, data processing, retail, mortgage servicing, health care, meatpacking, processing and distribution, restaurants, telemarketing services, direct marketing services, trucking, publishing, store fixturing, credit card processing, real estate development, real estate and equipment leasing, rehabilitation services, dairy processing, independent electric power production, cattle feeding, mass transit services, and securities.

Attorneys in the firm's business department regularly assist clients with a large variety of legal matters, including business formation and entity selection, securities issues, commercial transactions, business sales and acquisitions, financing issues, real estate sales and acquisitions, franchising, and tax matters. Other primary areas of practice in the business department include banking law, bankruptcy, employment law, municipal law, intellectual property law, employee benefit plans, and executive compensation arrangements. In addition, several of the firm's attorneys have extensive experience in technology law matters.

Abrahams, Kaslow & Cassman also has a very experienced and active litigation department. The firm's attorneys handle a wide variety of litigation matters, including contract disputes, commercial claims, wrongful-discharge and other employee matters, mortgage foreclosures, landlord-tenant matters, environmental and land-use controversies, and personal injury claims.

Partners John Herdzina (left center) and Randall Hanson (right center) meet with Howard Hawks (left), president and chief executive officer, and Ronald Quinn (right), vice president and chief financial officer, of Tenaska, Inc., an international private sector electric power generation company, to discuss legal issues related to the construction of a 586-megawatt electric energy plant and complex near Dera Murad Jamali, Pakistan.

The attorneys at Abrahams, Kaslow & Cassman continually strive to bring clients cost-effective legal services in a timely manner. The firm has made significant investments in technology to increase efficiency and client service and has fully automated its offices. All professionals and staff members have networked computers and e-mail and voice mail, as well as access to a large variety of CD-ROM research materials. The firm is committed to continually updating its technology to remain on the leading edge of client service.

Abrahams, Kaslow & Cassman is a member of Commercial Law Affiliates (CLA), a select association of independent medium-sized law firms in over 200 cities around the world. CLA accepts only one law firm in each geographic area for membership, and Abrahams, Kaslow & Cassman is the only member of CLA in Nebraska. All CLA firms have broad-based commercial and business practices and are recognized for high standards of ethics, accountability, client service, and tech-

Partners Howard Kaslow (right center) and Harvey Cooper (left center) meet with Pamida, Inc. Chairman and Chief Executive Officer Steven Fishman (left) and Executive Vice President Frank Washburn (right) to discuss an upcoming real estate closing. Abrahams, Kaslow & Cassman has represented Pamida, a retailer with over 150 stores in 15 states, for more than 30 years in a wide variety of legal matters involving the areas of corporate, securities, litigation, real estate, and employment law.

nical legal proficiency. When legal effort is required in another state or country, Abrahams, Kaslow & Cassman can assist

clients by coordinating the delivery of services through CLA member firms.

Each attorney at Abrahams, Kaslow & Cassman is committed to serving the firm's clients by providing the highest quality legal services possible, by exhibiting the highest degree of ethical conduct, by continuing the firm's tradition of efficiency and responsiveness, and by caring about its clients as individuals.

Partners Ronald Parsonage (left center) and Teresa Beaufait (left) meet with SITEL Corporation Chairman and CEO James Lynch (right center) and Executive Vice President Edward Taylor (right) to discuss SITEL's $42 million initial public offering of the telemarketing company's common stock, which was completed in 1995 with the assistance of Abrahams, Kaslow & Cassman.

LEO A DALY

Leo A Daly is an internationally recognized planning, architecture, engineering, and interior design firm headquartered in Omaha. It has U.S. offices in Atlanta, Washington, D.C., St. Louis, Houston, San Antonio, Phoenix, Los Angeles, and Honolulu, as well as international offices in Hong Kong, Tokyo, Dubai, Madrid, and Berlin.

The firm, which began more than 80 years ago in Omaha, currently has nearly 700 dedicated design and engineering professionals on staff—alumni of more than 100 colleges and universities. It has received national and international design and engineering awards and citations.

In addition to architectural and engineering services, the firm has in-house capabilities in the fields of community and land planing, master planning, space planning and programming, and program management.

Daly projects have been completed in more than 50 countries, the 50 U.S. states, and the District of Columbia. Project types range from individual condominiums to entire new communities; airline terminals to zoos; underground command centers to high-rise corporate offices; elementary schools to universities; health care clinics to full-scale medical centers; and day care centers to computer centers. Clients include nations, local government agencies, corporations, industry, and profit and nonprofit institutions.

The firm was begun by Leo A. Daly, Sr., in 1915. It was headed by his son Leo A. Daly, Jr., FAIA, from 1952 to 1981. Since his father's death in 1981, Leo A. Daly III, FAIA, RIBA, RAIA, has served as chairman and president.

Continuing the firm's awareness of emerging trends, Daly has altered its services, organization, and practices to suit current business, government, and social climates. Most of the firm's clients—corporate, institutional, and government—are business oriented. They expect businesslike associations and returns on their investment in professional services. The firm shares this concern for the practical aspects of the business world and uses diligence and ingenuity to fulfill client expectations.

The firm gained early fame in the 1930s for planning the large campus of historic Boys Town near Omaha. During and after extensive wartime work in the 1940s, the firm developed the team concept, perhaps its most durable contribution to the design field. This innovative approach to project organization brought architects, planners, engineers (structural, mechanical, and electrical), and interior designers together for the first time to collaborate as members of permanent project teams. The team approach equipped the firm to handle the large, challenging assignments for which it is now known around the world.

Design of U.S. government defense-related projects initiated major firm growth in the 1950s and '60s and reflected Daly's expertise in high-technology defense facility design. This growth continued during the 1970s when the fields of education, health care, and research offered the company opportunities to direct its design experience to projects for institutions, industry, and commerce. The firm continues today as a world leader in the design of technologically demanding facilities.

The Daly firm has also been a leader in the design of the rapidly growing aviation industry since the early 1960s, when its development of the first underground jet

Creighton/St. Joseph Medical Center

air-start fueling facilities eliminated the need for runway-crowding fuel and air trucks.

Over the past five years, the firm has designed more than $1 billion worth of new airport facilities around the world. Current projects in this field include the new terminal complex at Washington, D.C., National Airport, the multiconcourse expansion of Seattle-Tacoma International Airport, and the revolutionary new 25-story air traffic control tower at John F. Kennedy International Airport in New York City.

Leo A Daly has been active offshore since the late 1950s and established its first permanent overseas office in Hong Kong in 1967. In the succeeding 28 years, Leo A Daly Pacific has grown to become a leading provider of architectural, engineering, and program management services in the region. It has completed projects throughout Asia and the Pacific Basin. Internationally recognized clients include IBM, American Express, Citicorp, Kodak, and Motorola. Among the firm's significant Hong Kong-based clients are Swire Pacific Ltd. and Cathay Pacific Airways.

Current international projects include program management and design involvement for a major (more than $100 million) office tower to be built in downtown Hong Kong; design of a new airport terminal in the Philippines; and two $50 million office towers planned for the United Arab Emirates.

Major projects under way in Daly's Omaha corporate headquarters include a $175 million expansion of McCarran International Airport in Las Vegas, design of the FAA's new air traffic control tower for Washington, D.C.'s National Airport, and the renovation/expansion of downtown Omaha's civic auditorium complex.

U S West Building, formerly headquarters of the Northwestern Bell Telephone Company

HDR, INC.

HDR's headquarters in Omaha

HDR is looking for ways to deliver services in the future, including design-build, privatization, and international consortiums.

That's the way Francis Jelensperger, HDR's chief executive officer, sums up the goals of this nationally recognized full-service corporation that provides engineering, architecture, and construction services. HDR, Inc., which is headquartered in Omaha, was founded here in 1917 as the Henningson Engineering Company.

Since then, it has expanded nationwide. Today, it employs nearly 1,600 people at 40 offices. About 400 employees are in Omaha. HDR, Inc., which has been owned by the French company Bouygues, S.A., since 1983, includes three operating companies:

- HDR Engineering, Inc., HDR's engineering company, which provides water/wastewater, transportation, and waste and energy services;

- Henningson, Durham & Richardson, Inc., HDR's architectural/engineering company, which specializes in the design of health care, justice, and science and industry facilities; and
- Huffle PM, Inc., which provides project management, lender services, building evaluations, relocation services, and consulting on matters pertaining to general construction.

HDR strives to be the nation's highest-quality architectural and engineering firm for its clients, employees, and shareholders.

HDR Engineering, Inc., has completed projects in many states and other countries. Projects include design of sections of the Boston Central Artery, the largest civil works project in the U.S.; design of a wastewater treatment plant for fast-growing Las Vegas; and development and implementation of a plan for handling and disposing of Chicago's solid waste. Locally, HDR helped Douglas County resolve a gas migration problem with a closed landfill.

Henningson, Durham & Richardson specializes in the design of health care and justice facilities. Its science and industry program includes work in science labs, manufacturing, and universities. One of the company's three major design centers is in Omaha.

Some of HDR's most noted projects have been undertaken in Omaha or other parts of Nebraska. These include work on Methodist Hospital, the Bergan Mercy Medical Center, Joslyn Art Museum, and the University of Nebraska.

HDR's reach is worldwide. It has projects completed or under way in 50 states and 30 foreign countries.

Lovgren Advertising was founded in 1978 and has built a reputation as a solid, forward-thinking business. It has all the elements of an award-winning company—talented creative people, experienced account staff, media, production, and technology.

"What sets us apart is our desire, our passion, for the success of our clients. We become part of the client's team, shaping strategies and executing the communications needs for concrete results," said Linda Lovgren, president.

RESULTS ARE THE DIFFERENCE

Results are always the best evidence of accomplishment. Lovgren Advertising took on the challenge of helping a new bank credit card enter an already crowded and fiercely competitive market segment. Lovgren participated in forging the marketing strategy. Then it designed and produced direct-mail, print, and outdoor advertising, launching a campaign that, over a five-year period, landed the credit card among the top 50 issuers in the nation.

Another client, a major insurance company, implemented a plan to become a public company. This meant the company would be changing its name and corporate identity along with all of its marketing materials and administrative forms. Lovgren Advertising became a team member for both operations and communications in the transaction process. It was the agency's responsibility to orchestrate the redesign of the corporate image and work with the client's internal divisions to coordinate the image transition as well as revise all materials.

A third case history involves a bank that was undergoing major internal changes while competing banks in the communities where it had branches were

experiencing significant ownership changes. The bank's marketing director retained the services of Lovgren Advertising to help implement a new image, develop competitive products, design training for the staff, and create highly visible promotions. The results from the year included a 44 percent increase in savings accounts, an 11 percent increase in checking accounts, and the acquisition of two major business alliances.

The agency has experience with a broad spectrum of accounts. These are long-term business relationships in which Lovgren Advertising collaborates on strategy, advertising, and public relations implementation and provides many other communications support services. Lovgren's seasoned staff, along with the effective use of technology, allows the company to do outstanding work for clients across the country.

Marketing is not only competitive by nature but the companies that are in the field are also very competitive. Knowing that, and knowing the philosophy behind Lovgren Advertising, it's no wonder that the founder's favorite quote is "If you don't make dust, you eat dust."

CLARKSON COLLEGE

Programs in medical imaging, radiography, physical therapy, occupational therapy, business administration, and health services management are all among Clarkson College's offerings.

The pioneers who founded the Bishop Clarkson School of Nursing in 1888—Nebraska's first nursing school—would be amazed if they could visit Clarkson College today.

The school is still providing state-of-the-art instruction in nursing, and it still maintains its traditional focus on health. However, the key word that describes today's Clarkson College is "diversity."

This private, regionally accredited institution is educating health care professionals of all ages and backgrounds to meet the rapidly changing health care needs of the future.

Clarkson College, located in a modern six-story tower in central Omaha, offers outstanding undergraduate programs that prepare students for careers as nurses, physical therapist assistants, occupational therapy assistants, and radiographers.

There's even a bachelor of science program in business administration tailored for the health care industry. Today's marketplace offers opportunities to health care professionals with broad-based business knowledge.

In addition, Clarkson College offers graduate programs leading to the master of science in health services management and the master of science in nursing, with majors in administration, education, and family nurse practitioner roles. Continuing education programs provide opportunities for health care professionals to develop new skills and knowledge and to remain current with advances in their professions.

Since 1990, Clarkson has been providing distance education. Students receive course materials in audiotape, videotape, and/or printed formats. Faculty follow up in telephone conferences or by using the college's computer bulletin board system, supplemented by library support via mail.

Clinical experiences for distance learners are provided in the summer on campus, utilizing the modern, high-technology hospitals in the Omaha area.

Clarkson seeks to meet the individual learning styles of its 650 students. Whether students learn best by doing, hearing, or seeing, they have opportunities to practice new skills in labs and in *real* health care settings, to participate in lecture/discussions, and to use interactive video and other media in the Educational Resource Center. Computer-assisted instruction is an important focus of the college. Several large computer labs are dedicated to student use.

The college contracts with 96 different agencies in the Omaha/Council Bluffs area to expose students to as many different situations and health care facilities as possible.

Students work in home health care, schools, skilled nursing, long-term care, and acute care/hospital settings. The diversity of environments, systems, and programs prepares graduates to step confidently into any health care organization.

Clarkson College is committed to giving each student an extraordinary amount of individual attention. The student/faculty ratio is 10:1. Faculty members are nationally recognized and active in their professional organizations.

About 85 percent of Clarkson College students receive some form of financial aid. Scholarships, grants, loans, and work-study arrangements are available.

Flexible scheduling with both day and evening classes enables students to meet the demands of work and family. Students may also choose to attend classes year-round (three semesters) to receive degrees sooner. Eight-week courses allow students to pursue twice the number of courses in a semester, thus reducing the time in college.

Clarkson's flexibility has resulted in a diverse student body that includes men and women in their mid- to late 30s, many of whom are working on second degrees. Still others are recent high school graduates. Rural and urban America are represented, and there is a rich ethnic mix.

Applications are accepted anytime during the year. Prospective students are judged on their academic work and scores on the ACT/SAT examinations.

For more than a century, Clarkson College has been helping the people of the Midlands lead healthier lives. Even with all of Clarkson's exciting changes, that's a mission the school's founders could still identify with.

METROPOLITAN COMMUNITY COLLEGE

Metropolitan Community College is training today's workforce for the jobs of today and tomorrow. The college's goal is to provide an affordable, accessible, high-quality education to residents of Dodge, Douglas, Sarpy, and Washington counties in Nebraska.

Metro opened its doors in 1974 in a renovated warehouse. Today, the college consists of three main campuses: Elkhorn Valley, Fort Omaha, and South Omaha. In addition, education centers are located at the Sarpy County Center in LaVista and at the Fremont Center in Fremont. Metro takes its classes to many other sites as well, including Offutt Air Force Base and business, community, and public centers. Wherever learning is important, you'll find Metropolitan Community College!

Metro's focus is on providing area businesses, industries, and organizations with highly skilled technical and professional employees. All campuses offer well-equipped microcomputer laboratories, learning centers, and libraries. Students can choose from more than 100 programs in business administration, computer and office technologies, food arts and management, horticulture, industrial technologies, nursing and allied health, and visual and electronic technologies.

Metro accommodates the needs of working students with easy registration, convenient class times and locations, distance learning and telecourses, free parking, skills assessment, counseling, and other services. Credits transfer to many four-year institutions.

More than 43,000 credit and noncredit students are enrolled at Metro, making it the third-largest college in Nebraska. Yet its classes are kept small so students can learn more. Most classes average around 15 students.

The Continuing Education Division offers the community classes in professional development, computer software, English as a second language, allied health, foreign languages, arts and crafts, travel, home improvement, and sports, as well as children's events. At Metro, there are classes to fit everyone's interests.

Metro's industrious Workforce Development Group can customize training for businesses and other organizations, conduct skills assessment and job profiling, and offer licensure and certification exams. Workforce Development can provide expert trainers to conduct sessions at convenient times and suitable locations for busy employees. Metro's goal is to help businesses improve their productivity in an increasingly competitive world.

Metro graduates excel in the workplace. Eighty-five percent of the college's graduates are employed in their fields of training, and 97 percent remain in Nebraska. These achievements make Metro a proud member of its community.

As it continues to strive to meet the needs of business and the community, Metropolitan Community College will seek to enhance the quality of life in the areas it serves.

The Catholic community of Nebraska traces its roots to 1838, when exploring missionaries visited the area. Catholics built their first church in Omaha in 1856.

Established as the Diocese of Omaha in 1885 and raised to an archdiocese in 1945, the Archdiocese of Omaha comprises more than 14,000 square miles in the 23 counties in northeast Nebraska. Under the leadership of Archbishop Elden Francis Curtiss, 154 parishes serve more than 205,000 Catholics.

The Catholic Diocese, committed to God through Christian faith and hope, maintains a strong dedication to the dignity of each person and to family life as the foundation of the community and society. From the earliest days of the territory until the present, a Catholic presence has exerted noteworthy influence on the life of Omaha and northeast Nebraska.

Schools are a hallmark of the vibrant Catholic commitment to provide young people with high-quality education and personal formation, which prepares them for value-centered lives of service. Seventeen high schools and 61 elementary schools in the archdiocesan school system educate 21,000 students annually. Tuition aid programs valued in excess of $150,000 assisted 1,550 students in 1994-95.

Catholic Charities reaches more than 45,000 persons annually through various social service and charitable assistance programs in Omaha and rural Nebraska. Battered women and their children find support and safety at a shelter; persons struggling with alcohol or chemical dependency find needed help through counseling, support groups, and residential programs; couples in troubled marriages and disrupted families receive guidance and insight from dedicated counselors. Without regard to religion, race, age, or income, Catholic Charities offers hope and vital assistance.

A nationally recognized Family Life Office provides premarital preparation and education, programs and support group assistance for widowed and divorced persons, grief coping for children through adults, as well as training for lay family ministers in the parishes across the archdiocese.

Catholic social ministry is active through support programs and active outreach for the disadvantaged in urban and rural settings. Parish-based groups and programs provide an important presence in the local communities.

The Archdiocese of Omaha has a long history and a proud legacy in Omaha and northeast Nebraska. Archbishop Curtiss, the priests and religious, and thousands of Catholic laywomen and laymen look to the future with faith and hope. Catholic presence and action will continue to be a good neighbor, an effective leader, and a committed provider of service and hope in northeast Nebraska into the 21st century.

Many visitors to Omaha call the city one of the nation's best kept secrets. They're astonished at all there is to see and do, the quaint neighborhoods to explore, the great shopping, and the many fine restaurants.

But word is getting out. Each year, more than two million people visit Omaha. This translates into an economic impact of over $600 million a year—an amount that is rising rapidly annually.

The addition of new luxury hotels, more world-class attractions, and upscale restaurants ensure that Omaha's popularity with tourists will continue to grow.

Since its establishment in 1981, the Greater Omaha Convention and Visitors Bureau has helped promote that growth. Its efforts have helped Omaha become a favorite regional year-round destination for meetings and vacations.

The bureau, a division of Douglas County government, is a full-service, one-stop agency that promotes lodging, the arts, attractions, and other hospitality vendors and venues in the community. It has three divisions:

• The Tourism Department is charged with marketing Omaha to travel agents, group tour operators, travel writers, and individual travelers. Tourism personnel promote Omaha at major travel/trade shows across the U.S. and Canada. They also conduct familiarization tours of Omaha for group-related planners.

• The Convention Department is the marketing arm that reaches national and regional meeting planners. The convention services manager coordinates registration personnel, housing, spouse activities, transportation, and on-site activities.

• The Omaha/Douglas County Film Commission solicits filmmakers to

use the resources available in the community in feature films, mini-series, made-for-TV movies, and commercials. It acts as the liaison between production companies and the local entities that can assist film professionals.

The Greater Omaha Convention and Visitors Bureau wants to make it easy and fun to visit Omaha or to schedule a meeting here. Its friendly, competent, and experienced staff members are experts on what the metropolitan area has to offer. They have a wealth of attractive materials to help you plan your visit to Omaha and make the most of your time here.

Unlike communities that are blasé about tourism and almost indifferent to small groups, the Greater Omaha Convention and Visitors Bureau warmly welcomes groups of all sizes. Its staff members know that groups and individual guests who have had a great time are the community's best public relations agents.

All bureau departments offer visitors and meeting planners assistance with public relations, contacts with government agencies, site selection, and various data-based marketing projects. Staff members keep current with national trends by participating in all major U.S. travel-related associations.

The bureau has been recognized locally, regionally, and nationally for its outstanding marketing and service programs. It is committed to excellence in service.

So, when you think travel, think Omaha.

Make our city your next destination for a personal stop or your organization's convention. When you plan to visit, remember the Greater Omaha Convention and Visitors Bureau.

Hospitality is their job. It's also their pleasure.

At the University of Nebraska at Omaha (UNO), faculty members can't just sit in an ivory tower aloof from the concerns of the city where they work.

As a metropolitan university with a strong urban thrust, UNO embraces its community. Its mission sets it apart as a pacesetting, comprehensive institution dedicated to superior teaching, vital public service, and relevant research in an urban environment.

UNO was founded as a private college in 1908. Later it became Omaha University, and it finally merged with the University of Nebraska in 1968. Today, with an annual enrollment of about 15,000, it is the second-largest member of the Nebraska University System.

The university was a pioneer in meeting the needs of working students. About half the students pursue their degrees on a full-time basis. Others work full time and take their courses at night on the main campus or at more than a dozen locations throughout the metropolitan area.

UNO's Peter Kiewit Conference Center in downtown Omaha is home to the College of Continuing Studies (CCS). Each year the center serves more than 65,000 clients who use the facilities for training seminars, meetings, conferences, credit and noncredit courses, and teleconferences. Distance education technology enables CCS to bring UNO programs to students outside the Omaha area via satellite.

If it weren't for UNO, a college education would be out of reach for many highly motivated students with families to support.

UNO offers nearly 90 baccalaureate degree programs and 65 advanced degrees. The latter includes doctoral programs in public administration and criminal justice, a joint doctoral program in educational administration, and cooperative doctoral programs in industrial psychology, experimental child psychology, and psychobiology.

The joint and cooperative programs are with the University of Nebraska-Lincoln (UNL). In addition, students can enroll in degree programs through the Institute of Agricultural and Natural Resources and the Colleges of Human Services and Family Sciences and of Engineering and Technology, all administered by UNL.

UNO also has affiliations with sister universities in Europe, China, Japan, and the Philippines that provide study abroad and exchange opportunities. Numerous foreign students are attracted to UNO by its Intensive Language Program.

UNO's international reach continues to grow. In 1996, for example, faculty and students were involved in a major archaeological dig in Bethsaida, business revitalization in Rumania and Moldova, and techtonics research in the Himalayas.

UNO is widely recognized for its excellence in business education. Its Executive Master of Business Administration, a special two-year weekend program, is designed to give experienced managers the knowledge and skills to assume broader responsibilities within a compact schedule.

Many Nebraskans who have never set foot on UNO's campus are familiar with it because of its excellent outreach and service programs, including:

• The Nebraska Business Development Center, a cooperative program with the U.S. Small Business Administration. It offers guidance to new businesses through its regional centers in Omaha, Lincoln, Kearney, Wayne, Chadron, Peru, Scottsbluff, and North Platte.
• The UNO Aviation Institute, which co-publishes a national rating of airline quality.
• The Midlands Institute for Non-Profit Management.
• The Metropolitan Omaha Educational Consortium.
• The Center for Public Affairs Research.
• Omaha Free-Net, an on-line link to information providers and services throughout Douglas County, developed in cooperation with several community partners.

The UNO campus is attractive and modern. Most campus buildings are less than 30 years old. UNO was the first institution in the NU System to develop multimedia classrooms. Twelve such classrooms are located throughout campus. Faculty have limitless possibilities to integrate text, graphics, audio, video, and computers into their teaching.

Every building in UNO is wired with fiber-optics. Five major computer labs, including a 24-hour lab, serve most students, while an additional 18 computer labs across campus are dedicated to specific instructional and research requirements.

UNO's strategic plan calls for assisting business and government agencies with information technology needs, developing appropriate graduate programs in information technology, and establishing a new applied research program focusing on information technology.

UNO's goal is to become one of the best metropolitan universities in the nation. With more graduates in the Omaha metropolitan area than any other university in the state, UNO increasingly is becoming an institution of choice . . . a university of the community, not just in it.

ACKNOWLEDGMENTS

Each of the following businesses and educational, health care, and religious institutions made a valuable contribution to this project. Longstreet Press gratefully acknowledges their participation.

AAA Nebraska
Abrahams, Kaslow & Cassman
Accent Service Company, Inc.
Acceptance Insurance Companies Inc.
Ag Processing Inc.
Alegent Health
All Makes Office Equipment Company
Archdiocese of Omaha
Baird Holm
Borsheim's
Campbell Soup Company
Campos Construction Co.
Childrens Hospital
Clarkson College
Clarkson Hospital
Clubhouse Inn
Commercial Federal Bank
ConAgra, Inc.
Cox Communications
Creighton Saint Joseph Regional
   HealthCare System
Dan Witt Builders, Inc.
Dana Larson Roubal and Associates
Data Documents
Empire Insurance Group
First Data Corporation
First National Bank of Omaha
First Nebraska Credit Union
Garden Cafe
Greater Omaha Chamber of Commerce
Greater Omaha Convention and
   Visitors Bureau
Guarantee Life Insurance Company
HDR, Inc.
1/2 Price Stores
Holiday Inn
HunTel Systems
Hyatt Reservation Center
Inacom
ITI Marketing Services

Kirkpatrick Pettis
KMTV
Leo A Daly
Lovgren Advertising
Lozier Corporation
Lucent Technologies
MEGA Corporation
Methodist Health System
Metropolitan Community College
Midwest Express Airlines
Modern Equipment Company
Mutual of Omaha Companies
Norwest Bank
Oriental Trading Company
Omaha Printing Company
Omaha Public Power District
Packers Bank
Pamida Incorporated
Physicians Mutual and Physicians Life
PKS Information Services, Inc.
Rainbow Video Productions
Redfield & Co., Inc.
SITEL Corporation
Sterling Software
Streck Laboratories, Inc.
Travel and Transport
Union Pacific
University of Nebraska Medical Center
University of Nebraska at Omaha
U S WEST
Valmont Industries, Inc.
West Telemarketing Corporation
Woodmen of the World Life Insurance
   Society

This book was published in cooperation with the Greater Omaha Chamber of Commerce and would not have been possible without the support of its members. Longstreet Press is especially grateful to the following individuals and businesses for their commitment and assistance:

C. R. Bell
Barbara Haggart
Vicki Krecek
Sue Eledge
Leo Smith
Tess Fogarty
Susan Elliott
Lenore Honke
Rainbow Video Productions
Linda Lovgren
Mayor Hal Daub
Jay Baum

INDEX

Abrahams, Milton, 132
Acceptance Insurance Companies, 51
Ag Processing, 26
Ak-Sar-Ben Coliseum, 97
Alegent Health, 56
Alexander, Jane, 94–95
All Makes Office Equipment Company, 25
American Business Information, 26
American Gramaphone Company, 92
American Laboratories, 29
Applied Communications, 26, 28
Applied Information Management
    Institute (AIM), 28
Aschenbrener, Carol, 55
Azriel, Aryeh, 119

Bates, Robert D., 47, 70
Bay, Mogens C., 29, 33
Beard, Dick, 29
Bell, Terrel, 128
Bellevue University, 130
Bemis Center for the Contemporary
    Arts, 8, 94–95
Benson neighborhood, 124
Berkshire Hathaway, 20, 31, 102. See also
    Buffett, Warren
Blankenau, Richard, 56
Blue Barn, 95
Blumkin, Rose, 22–23, 96
Bohemian Cafe, 102
Borsheim's Fine Jewelry and Gifts, 102
Boys Town, 131
Boys Town National Research Hospital, 56
Brownell Talbott school, 129
Buffett, Warren: as businessman, 20, 23,
    26, 31; and civic participation, 96, 97,
    130, 131

Cain, Herman, 26, 131
California Energy, 30
Campos Construction Company, 25
Campos, Robert, 25
Candlewood neighborhood, 125
Cathedral Arts Project, 123
Center for Human Nutrition, 56
Central Park Mall, 109
Chavez, Ignacio, 91
Childrens Hospital, 56
Clarkson College, 53
College of Saint Mary, 130
Commuting, 70–71

ConAgra, 4, 26, 29, 42, 57
Cornett, Mary Galligan, 67
Corporate Cup Race, 57
Council Bluffs, Ia., 4, 97, 125
Cox Communications, 27
Creighton University, 28, 130
Creighton University Dental College, 56, 63
Creighton University Medical School, 49,
    53, 56, 61, 63
Criss, C. C., 48
Crook, George, 124–25
Cunningham Lake, 125

Dana College, 130
Dana Larson Roubal and Associates, 26
Davis, Chip, 92. See also Mannheim
    Steamroller
DeSoto National Wildlife Refuge, 99
Dodge Park, 98
Dominguez, Eli, 131

Edmonson, Joe, 131
Elmwood Park, 8, 15, 98
Eppley Airfield, 70, 71
Eppley Institute for Research in Cancer
    and Allied Disease, 53
Eugene Leahy Mall, 4, 20, 122

First Data Resources, 26, 28
First National Bank, 26
Fletcher, Phil, 42
Florence neighborhood, 124
Fonda, Henry, 95
Fontenelle Forest Nature Center, 8, 13,
    99, 125
Fort Omaha, 124
Foster, Norman, 94
Fries, Bill, 92

Gamble Hill Hounds, 13
Garden Cafe, 102–3
Gibson, Bob, 98, 124
Godfather's Pizza, 26. See also Cain,
    Herman
Gold Coast neighborhood, 123
Goss, Ernest, 22, 28
Grace University, 130
Grandmother's restaurant, 103
Great Plains Black Museum, 124
Greater Omaha Chamber of Commerce,
    28, 120, 128

Greek Islands restaurant, 102
Guarantee Life Insurance Company, 26, 51
Gupta, Vinod, 25–26

Habitat for Humanity, 133
Haggart, Barbara, 120
1/2 Price Stores, 102
Happy Hollow Country Club, 5
Harper, Mike, 57
Harriman Dispatch Center, 4, 38, 68
Harriman, E. H., 68
Hartung, Jim, 97
Harvey, Thomas, 127
Hawks, Howard, 26
Hayes, Frank, 19
HDR, 26, 94
Health care industry, 52–65
Heartland of America Park, 2, 4, 122
Henry Doorly Zoo, 98, 99, 101, 108, 112
Holy Name Housing, 132
Hyatt Hotels, 28

Idelman, Steve, 27
Insurance industry, 46–51
Iowa West, 97
Iowa Western Community College, 130
ITI Marketing, 27, 28

Jacobs, Morris, 132–33
Jeffries, Richard, 81
Johns, Judy, 136
Johnson, Richard, 71
Jones, Charles, 95
Joslyn Art Museum, 33, 93, 94, 105
Josyln Castle, 123

Kaneko, Jun, 95
Kavich family, 25
Kavich, Larry, 25
Kerrey, Bob, 103
Kiewit Plaza, 20
Kimball, Thomas, 14
Kirkpatrick Pettis, 51
Kizer, William M., 57
Klutznick, Philip, 132
Kyle, Adam, 120

LaHood, Tom, 132
Lauritzen, John, 26
Lawlor, Kevin, 95
Leahy, Eugene A., 75

Leo A Daly, 26, 29
Lied Foundation, 131
Livestock Exchange Building, 124
Lo, Lormong, 77
Louisville State Recreation Area, 99
Lozier Corporation, 23, 132
Lozier, Allan, 23–25

Mad Dads, 131
Magic Theater, 95
Mahoney State Park, 99
Mannheim Steamroller, 8, 92
Marriott Hotels, 28
Matthews family, 96
Matthews, Amy, 96
Matthews, Hope, 96
Matthews, Sandy, 95
MCI Corporation, 27
Memorial Park, 141
Menolascino, Frank, 131
Mercer family, 146
Messiah Lutheran Church, 77
Methodist Health System, 53
Metropolitan Community College,
    124, 130
Metropolitan Utilities District (MUD),
    73, 84
Millard Public Schools, 129
Missouri River, 4, 70, 71, 121, 122
Modern Equipment Company, 71
Mormon Cemetery, 124
Mutual of Omaha Dome, 50
Mutual of Omaha: and civic participation,
    127; and Omaha business community,
    22, 26, 48–50, 57

NCAA College World Series,
    8, 97, 116
Neale Woods, 125
Nebraska Furniture Mart, 22–23, 102
Nebraska State Historical Society, 123
Nebraska Theater Caravan, 95
Nelson, Ben, 34
Nogg Paper Company, 39
Norris, George, 73
North High School, 125, 129
North Omaha, 124–25
Northwestern Bell, 27

Offutt Air Force Base, 27, 78, 79
Old Market: and downtown development,

122, 146; as entertainment/shopping site,
    8, 16, 30, 94, 105, 114
Omaha Children's Museum, 108
Omaha Community Playhouse, 94, 95
Omaha Housing Authority, 132
Omaha Lancers, 97
Omaha Public Power District (OPPD), 73
Omaha Public Schools, 127, 128–29, 130
Omaha Racers, 97
Omaha Riverfront Marathon, 8
Omaha Royals, 8, 97
Omaha Symphony, 94, 95–96
Omaha Theater Company for Young
    People, 96
Omaha World-Herald, 128
Omaha, Neb.: and business environ-
    ment, 7, 18–45; and cultural diversity,
    77, 124, 133; and cultural life, 94–96,
    107–17; and education, 22, 30, 34,
    127–30; and health industry, 53–65;
    history of, 4; and festivals, 8; and
    insurance industry, 46–51; and local
    government, 74–75; neighborhoods
    of, 122–26, 138; and philanthropy,
    131–32; and quality of life, 34, 56–57,
    92, 105, 118–51; and religious life,
    132–33; and retail market, 102–3;
    and sports and recreation, 97–99,
    107–17; and transportation, 68–72;
    and utilities, 73
Omni Hotels, 28
One Pacific Place, 35
Opera Omaha, 96
Oriental Trading Company, 22, 30
Orpheum Theater, 93, 96, 115

Pamida stores, 102
Parks, 98, 99. See also under specific names
Partners of London, 94
Paxson, James, 34
Peoples Natural Gas, 73
Peter Kiewit Foundation, 131
Peter Kiewit Sons, 20
Peterson, Paul, 74
Physicians Mutual, 26, 50–51
Platte River Park, 99
Poley, Jeff, 34
Popp, Ron, 102–3
Prairie Systems, 26
Psota, Ron, 30
Purtilo, Ruth, 56, 58

Radisson Hotels, 28
Raven Biological Laboratories, 29
Regency complex, 35, 102
Reinert, Carl, 132–33
River City Roundup, 8, 109, 112
Riverfront Industrial Park, 39
Rose Theater, 96, 115
Rosenblatt Stadium, 97

SAC. See Strategic Air Command
Sacred Heart School, 132
Salem Baptist Church, 124
Sarpy County, Neb., 125
Sayers, Gale, 124
Schonlau, Ree, 107
Scott, Walter, 20, 97
Shakespeare on the Green, 8
Shamrock Computer Resources, Ltd., 131
Shaw, Byers, 53
Siekmann, Tom, 125
Simmons, Lee, 99
SITEL Corporation, 28
Skutt, V. J., 48
Sokolof, Phil, 57
Sorensen, A. V., 75
South Omaha, 123–24
Spaghetti Works, 102
St. Cecilia's Roman Catholic Cathedral,
    13, 123
St. John's AME Church, 124
St. Joseph Regional Health Center, 49,
    56, 57, 62
Standing Bear Lake, 125
Standing Bear, 124
Staton, Eddie, 131
Strategic Air Command (SAC),
    27, 79, 98
Suthar, Jitu, 131
Sweeney, Bob, 28

Telecommunications industry,
    27–28
Temple Israel, 132
Tenaska, 26
Terry, Megan, 95
13th Street retail district, 122
38th Street, 123
Tomlinson Woods neighborhood, 98
Trinity Episcopal Church, 132
24th Street business district, 124
Two Rivers State Recreation Area, 99

U. S. Army Corps of Engineers, 79
Union Pacific Railroad: and civic participation, 97, 101, 127; and Omaha business community, 30, 38, 57; and Omaha history, 3, 4
University of Nebraska at Omaha, 15, 28, 30, 130
University of Nebraska Cornhuskers, 97
University of Nebraska Medical Center, 53, 60, 61, 64, 130
U.S. Strategic Command, 78, 79
U S West, 27

Valmont Industries, 26, 30

Wellness Councils of America (WELCOA), 57
Welsh, Bill, 37
West Omaha, 125
West Telemarketing, 28
Western Electric, 27
Western Exchange Fire and Marine Insurance Company, 50
Western Heritage Museum, 104
Westin Aquila Hotel, 38

Westin Hotels, 28
Westroads shopping mall, 39
Westside Community Schools, 129
Woodmen of the World Life Insurance Society, 26, 50
Woodmen of the World Tower, 50

Zoo. *See* Henry Doorly Zoo
Zorinsky Lake, 125

INDEX FOR ENTERPRISE PROFILES

AAA Nebraska, 174
Abrahams, Kaslow & Cassman, 246-47
Accent Service Company, Inc., 164
Acceptance Insurance Companies Inc., 165
Ag Processing Inc., 212-13
Alegent Health, 182-83
All Makes Office Equipment Company, 194-95
Archdiocese of Omaha, 255

Baird Holm, 244
Borsheim's, 190

Campbell Soup Company, 203
Campos Construction Co., 208
Childrens Hospital, 186-87
Clarkson College, 252-53
Clarkson Hospital, 178-79
Clubhouse Inn, 189
Commercial Federal Bank, 162-63
ConAgra, Inc., 202
Cox Communications, 242-43
Creighton Saint Joseph Regional HealthCare System, 180-81

Dan Witt Builders, Inc., 215
Dana Larson Roubal and Associates, 245
Data Documents, 228

Empire Insurance Group, 175

First Data Corporation, 234-35
First National Bank of Omaha, 160-61

First Nebraska Credit Union, 158

Garden Cafe, 192
Greater Omaha Chamber of Commerce, 154-57
Greater Omaha Convention and Visitors Bureau, 256-57
Guarantee Life Insurance Company, 172-73

HDR, Inc., 250
1/2 Price Stores, 197
Holiday Inn, 198-99
HunTel Systems, 227
Hyatt Reservation Center, 229

Inacom, 238-39
ITI Marketing Services, 230-31

Kirkpatrick Pettis, 167
KMTV, 223

Leo A Daly, 248-49
Lovgren Advertising, 251
Lozier Corporation, 210-11
Lucent Technologies, 216-19

MEGA Corporation, 193
Methodist Health System, 176-77
Metropolitan Community College, 254
Midwest Express Airlines, 222
Modern Equipment Company, 206-7
Mutual of Omaha Companies, 166

Norwest Bank, 159

Omaha Printing Company, 200
Omaha Public Power District, 220-21
Oriental Trading Company, 209

Packers Bank, 168-69
Pamida Incorporated, 201
Physicians Mutual and Physicians Life, 170
PKS Information Services, Inc., 232-33

Rainbow Video Productions, 237
Redfield & Co., Inc., 191

SITEL Corporation, 224-25
Sterling Software, 226
Streck Laboratories, Inc., 214

Travel and Transport, 196

Union Pacific, 240-41
University of Nebraska Medical Center, 184-85
University of Nebraska at Omaha, 258
U S WEST, 236

Valmont Industries, Inc., 204-5

West Telemarketing Corporation, 188
Woodmen of the World Life Insurance Society, 171